T5-ANT-848

DEFLATION

DEFLATION

How to Survive and Thrive in the Coming Wave of Deflation

A. GARY SHILLING

McGraw-Hill

New York San Francisco Washington, D.C. Auckland Bogotá
Caracas Lisbon London Madrid Mexico City Milan
Montreal New Delhi San Juan Singapore
Sydney Tokyo Toronto

Library of Congress Cataloging-in-Publication Data

Shilling, A. Gary.
Deflation : how to survive and thrive in the coming wave of deflation / by
    A. Gary Shilling.
New York : McGraw-Hill, 1999.
p. cm.
HG540.S487   1999
0071351817
Deflation (Finance)—United States.
99021969

McGraw-Hill

*A Division of The **McGraw·Hill** Companies*

Copyright © 1999 by The McGraw-Hill Companies, Inc. All rights reserved.
Printed in the United States of America. Except as permitted under the United
States Copyright Act of 1976, no part of this publication may be reproduced or
distributed in any form or by any means, or stored in a data base or retrieval
system, without the prior written permission of the publisher.

5 6 7 8 9 0   DOC/DOC   0 9 8 7 6 5 4 3

ISBN 0-07-138251-8

Printed and bound by R. R. Donnelley & Sons Company.

McGraw-Hill books are available at special quantity discounts to use as
premiums and sales promotions, or for use in corporate training programs. For
more information, please write to the Director of Special Sales, McGraw-Hill,
Professional Publishing, Two Penn Plaza, New York, NY 10121-2298. Or contact
your local bookstore.

This publication is designed to provide accurate and authoritative information in
regard to the subject matter covered. It is sold with the understanding that neither the author nor the publisher is engaged in rendering legal, accounting, or
other professional service. If legal advice or other expert assistance is required,
the services of a competent professional person should be sought.
                    —from a declaration of principles jointly adopted by a committee
                        of the American Bar Association and a committee of publishers

 This book is printed on recycled, acid-free paper containing a minimum
of 50% recycled, de-inked fiber.

CONTENTS

Acknowledgments   ix

Introduction   xi

PART ONE

MAJOR DEFLATIONARY FORCES

Chapter 1
Government Spending Is Shrinking   3

Chapter 2
The Role of Central Banks   11

Chapter 3
Restructuring in the United States Continues   19

Chapter 4
Mergers at Home and Restructuring Abroad   30

Chapter 5
High Tech Is Deflationary   38

Chapter 6
The Internet and Mass Distribution   48

Chapter 7
Global Deregulation   57

Chapter 8
Global Sourcing and New Market Economies   63

Chapter 9

The Strengthening Dollar   69

Chapter 10

The Asian Contagion   77

Chapter 11

Slow Recovery in Asia   88

Chapter 12

American Consumers Will Save More   100

Chapter 13

U.S. Saving Spree, Triggered by a Bear Market, Ensures Deflation   110

PART TWO

THE WORLD ECONOMY UNDER DEFLATION

Chapter 14

Deflation Is Self-Feeding   129

Chapter 15

Deflation and the Kondratieff Wave   137

Chapter 16

The Two Faces of Deflation   144

Chapter 17

The Looming Threat of Protectionism   157

Chapter 18

Western Central Banks and Governments
Can't Stop Deflation   169

Chapter 19

The Coming Era of Good Deflation   182

Chapter 20

Interest Rates and Profits   192

PART THREE

INVESTMENT STRATEGY FOR DEFLATION

Chapter 21

Bond-Based Investment Strategy for Deflation   209

Chapter 22

Utilities and Stocks as Deflationary Investments   221

Chapter 23

The Myth of Global Diversification   230

Chapter 24

New Technologies Win in Deflation   239

Chapter 25

Consumer Spending Winners   253

Chapter 26

Avoid Commodities and Real Estate   262

Chapter 27

How to Invest in Deflation   279

Chapter 28

Market Timing, Stock Exposure, and Leverage   290

PART FOUR

BUSINESS AND PERSONAL STRATEGIES FOR DEFLATION

Chapter 29

Twenty-Five Business Strategies for Deflation   303

Chapter 30

Six Personal Strategies for Deflation   320

Index   333

ACKNOWLEDGMENTS

In some ways, writing this book was easy. After all, it is a sequel to *Deflation: Why It's Coming, Whether It's Good or Bad, and How It Will Affect Your Investments, Business, and Personal Affairs* (Lakeview Publishing Co., 1998), which I completed a little over a year ago. The basic reasons for expecting deflation, what it will be like, and many of the strategies for dealing with deflation in your investment, business, and personal activities haven't changed. Also, updating that earlier book was relatively easy, since much of what's happened in the intervening 12 months was predicted in it.

At the same time, writing this book was a major effort, because the orientation is much more toward the strategies for succeeding in deflationary times. This required a great deal more research and consideration. Earlier, I figured that I'd thought about as much as anyone about the implications of deflation, but was amazed at how many more strategies we were able to develop. I guess it goes to prove that after 60 years of inflation, almost no one knows a great deal about its opposite. I'm sure that by the time subsequent editions of this book are published, we will have come up with many more ideas for living in deflation—and that the actual arrival of widespread and chronic price declines will still contain many surprises.

In any event, my task in preparing this book was lightened by the wealth of excellent research and clear thinking of many good friends and professional colleagues. Special thanks go to Ed Hyman of the ISI Group, the nation's absolute best at preparing and interpreting graphs of almost everything in the economic and financial spheres; to Marc Faber, whose *Gloom, Boom, & Doom Reports* provide some of the most insightful analyses of economic, financial, and political conditions, past and present; and to Kiril Sokoloff of 13D Research, co-author of my first book and another long-range and serious thinker about major trends. I am also deeply indebted to Jim Bianco of Bianco Research for his excellent long-term data and analysis of U.S. stock and bond markets; to Steve Leuthold of The Leuthold Group, who always impresses me with his ability to prove with hard numbers many of the ideas I can only conceptualize; to Dennis Gartman of *The Gartman Letter*, who has an uncanny ability to see through the facade of political maneuvers and financial markets and who is one of the few conservatives I know who reads the *Chinese People's Daily* regularly; and to Ed Moos, whose memory and records of past fixed-income prices and Federal Reserve actions never cease to amaze me.

With the brains and expertise of these gentlemen and my shameless willingness to borrow their ideas and data, this book is a far better work than it would be otherwise. Nevertheless, the blame for misinterpreting and otherwise screwing up their concepts is mine alone.

Furthermore, I thank my colleagues at A. Gary Shilling & Co., past and present, for their considerable help in preparing this book. Kelly Hinkle put together many of the basic charts at night and on weekends while holding down a full-time job in New York City. Among our current staff, Kristin Lucas, although relatively new in economic research, was very helpful with data sources and charts. Sean Martin was extremely effective at gathering and analyzing security market data. Mike Webb also pitched in to provide special research and analysis.

I also thank our new editor, Fred Rossi, and my personal assistant, Janice Gramm. Both volunteered to get involved, even before they formally joined our firm, to help meet our deadlines. Finally, my very special thanks go to Jeannie Diamandas. Jeannie did a masterful job of not only deciphering my nearly illegible handwriting and turning it into passable prose, but also in pointing out my many inconsistencies. Furthermore, she was essential in setting deadlines and pointing out to all of us the consequences of not sticking to them.

A. Gary Shilling

INTRODUCTION

WHY YOU SHOULD READ THE BOOK

Since I finished writing *Deflation: Why It's Coming, Whether It's Good or Bad, and How It Will Affect Your Investments, Business, and Personal Affairs* in March 1998, events have been unfolding very much in line with that book's forecasts. Asia's woes have spread to Russia and Brazil, both of which have stopped supporting their currencies and allowed them to collapse. Japan has returned to recession and remains mired in deflation despite interest rates close to zero. Junk bonds have been junked. Investors who thought Asia was on the mend in early 1998 and rushed into stocks and bonds there have been pulverized. The Asian Contagion has spread to Europe, contrary to the previous majority view that those countries were immune. Financial derivatives are dangerous, as proved by the problem of Long Term Capital Management.

Commodity prices were low in early 1998, but as we forecast then, they've moved sharply lower. Raw sugar prices recently reached a 12½-year low, and copper sold at its lowest price in 11½ years in late 1998. Crude oil prices reached levels not seen since the 1986 collapse, and in real or inflation-adjusted terms, U.S. gasoline prices are the cheapest since record keeping began in 1919. Soybean futures prices hit an 11-year low. French farmers complain that with the nose-dive in European pork prices to $0.40 per pound, they're losing money. But they're lucky. U.S. prices for lean hogs plummeted to 7 cents a pound at one point. The Bridge/Commodity Research Bureau index of 17 spot commodity prices (Figure I–1) is lower than it has been since 1975, and overall producer prices have risen 133 percent since then. Boy, are commodities cheap!

DEFLATION SIGNS

Furthermore, few beside ourselves were bold enough to utter the "d" word in early 1998. Now "deflation" is widely used and for good reason. The signs of excess supply and its inevitable result, falling prices, are multiplying. The Canadian dollar, reflecting the heavy dependence of our northern neighbor on commodity exports, fell to new lows before its rebound. U.S. manufacturing prices are

FIGURE I–1

Bridge/Commodity Research Bureau Index, tracking 17 commodity prices
1975–1999

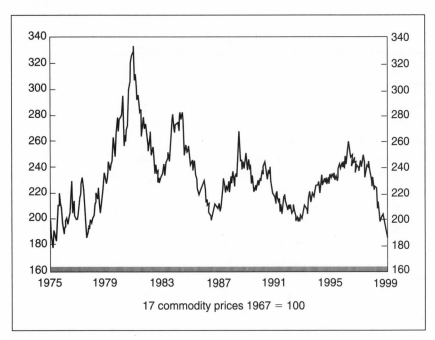

Source: Haver Analytics

collapsing, according to recent National Association of Purchasing
Managers surveys. In December 1998, the National Federation of
Independent Business, a small-business group, revealed the biggest
deflationary gap ever reported between firms and companies raising prices. In October 1998, the Business Council, 300 active and retired CEOs of the country's largest firms, said that 62 percent of its
members have lost pricing power and half think that their ability to
maintain prices will drop in the next six to nine months. A recent
survey finds that chief financial officers expect their firms to be able
to raise prices only 0.8 percent in 1999, even though they foresee 4.2
percent higher wage costs and 6.6 percent rises in health-care costs.
The National Association of Manufacturers recently surveyed 2,500
of its members and found that 44.2 percent have falling prices for
their products compared to only 28 percent a year ago.

Wholesale prices are falling in the United States, Italy, Germany, France, Argentina, South Korea, Japan, and Taiwan while consumer prices are declining in Japan, Switzerland, China, Sweden, Denmark, the Czech Republic, Hong Kong, Thailand, Singapore, New Zealand, and also beleaguered Brazil, with its first deflation in 60 years.

Excess supplies of almost everything are developing—on a global basis, and rapidly. Joining traditional excess supply industries like autos, semiconductors, and steel are everything from silver jewelry, cashmere, aluminum cans, and blue jeans piled high at Levi-Strauss and The Gap. Thailand has excess golf courses and Hawaii suffers from unused beaches and hotels as the Asian collapse slashes recreation and travel. Chinese apparel factories continue to produce even though inventories are already far too big. South Africa is mining more gold and diamonds than her markets can absorb. In the United States, more than 100 cities are moving rapidly from two cell phone systems to six or more competing wireless providers.

As discussed in *Deflation: Why It's Coming, Whether It's Good or Bad, and How It Will Affect Your Investments, Business, and Personal Affairs*, in the last decade eager lenders with scads of cheap money fueled massive investments that built huge capacity in Japan, developing Asian countries, and elsewhere, even in the United States—all under the assumption that explosive growth, especially in Asia, would last forever. The collapse in Japan at the beginning of the decade and then in the rest of Asia slashed demand at the very time that production was soaring. This has left the world with not only far too many factories, but also surplus office buildings, ships, airplanes, and other vehicles of production, as well as redundant people to operate them. Even electric generating capacity, normally in short supply in developing countries, is in excess in Indonesia and Russia due to nosedives in their economies and, therefore, in demand for power.

SO, WHY WRITE MORE ABOUT DEFLATION?

With these many examples of deflation all around us, why should I write a sequel to *Deflation: Why It's Coming, Whether It's Good or Bad, and How It Will Affect Your Investments, Business, and Personal Affairs*? For many reasons.

First of all, after 60 years of inflation, most Americans don't believe that deflation is possible. Most economists think that price declines are transitory, largely confined to internationally traded commodities, and are highly unlikely to pervade the entire economy, especially the dominant service sector, which they see as immune to foreign competition. Consumers are even more convinced that deflation is out of the question. In fact, polls show that the vast majority think that current inflation is much higher than the consumer price index (CPI) indicates (1.6 percent in 1998), despite the belief by most economists that the CPI increases are overstated by more than one percentage point. The fact that the prices of many goods and services fell last year hasn't convinced many (see Table I–1 for a partial list).

TABLE   I–1

U.S. Consumer Price Declines

	Dec. '97–Dec. '98
Information processing equipment	−26.6%
Gasoline	−15.4%
Fuel oil	−15.2%
Computer & software accessories	−10.0%
Lettuce	−8.8%
Coffee	−8.8%
Cellular telephone service	−8.3%
Audio equipment	−7.4%
Pork chops	−7.4%
Rentals of video tapes and discs	−7.1%
Toys	−6.1%
Ham	−6.0%
Eggs	−5.4%
Photographic equipment	−5.2%
Televisions	−4.8%
Bacon	−4.5%
Video cassettes & discs	−4.1%
Utility natural gas service	−3.5%
Girls apparel	−3.4%
Electricity	−3.2%
Sports equipment	−3.2%
Frankfurters	−3.2%
Intra-city transportation	−2.7%
Tools, hardware & supplies	−2.6%
Laundry equipment	−2.5%

Source: U.S. Bureau of Labor Statistics

TABLE I–2

Deflationary Forces

---

1. End of Cold War led to global cuts in defense spending.
2. Major-country government spending and deficits are shrinking.
3. Central banks continue to fight the last war—inflation.
4. G-7 retirements lead to reduced benefits and slower growth in incomes and spending.
5. Restructuring continues in English-speaking lands and will spread.
6. Technology cuts costs and promotes productivity.
7. The Internet increases competition and slashes prices.
8. Mass distribution to consumers reduces costs and prices.
9. Ongoing deregulation cuts prices.
10. Global sourcing of goods and services curtails costs.
11. The spreading of market economies increases global supply.
12. The dollar will continue to strengthen.
13. The Asian Contagion will intensify global glut and reduce worldwide prices.
14. U.S. consumers will switch from borrowing and spending to saving.

Source: A. Gary Shilling & Co., Inc.

Nevertheless, 13 of the 14 deflationary forces listed in Table I–2 are hard at work and the first 12 were in place before the Asia collapse started in mid-1997. The last, the conversion of U.S. consumers from three decades of borrowing and spending to many years of saving, will be initiated by a major bear market in U.S. stocks that destroys a considerable part of the portfolio appreciation that many Americans have been using as a substitute for saving. This stock sell-off will be touched off by disappointing U.S. corporate profits, especially if the Asian melt-down proves as significant as I believe, or by a Federal Reserve-induced recession if the American economy continues to boom and to tighten labor markets. Either way, global and chronic deflation will follow. Chapters 1 through 13 explore briefly these reasons for global and long-lasting deflation, but if you want further detail, please refer to my recent book, *Deflation: Why It's Coming, Whether It's Good or Bad, and How It Will Affect Your Investments, Business, and Personal Affairs.*

DEFLATION IS DIFFERENT

There are other reasons to write this book. Some see no difference between deflation— prices falling on a widespread and chronic basis—and the disinflation of the last 17 years, in which U.S. inflation has fallen from double-digit rates to essentially zero. But there is a big difference, as you'll learn in Chapter 14. People anticipate lower prices by waiting to buy. Piled up inventories and excess capacity result, so producers will cut prices to unload them. Suspicions are confirmed, so buyers wait even further, forcing prices lower in a reinforcing cycle. As noted in Chapter 20, real interest rates will be much higher in deflation than inflation.

To many, the mere word "deflation" conjures up the financial collapse of the 1930s. Deflation, however, is the norm at this point in the 50- to 60-year Kondratieff wave (see Chapter 15), and usually occurs without a 1930s-style financial collapse, which severely depressed incomes and demand. Indeed, we expect the coming deflation to resemble much more that of the late 1800s and of the 1920s, when declining prices in both eras resulted from technological advances and vast increases in supply (Chapter 16). Furthermore, with technology and capital now free to move around the globe in search of the most cost-effective locations, the West is exporting the Industrial Revolution to developing countries and is importing the resulting low-cost output. It also looks like good deflation, not bad deflation, because the financial crisis will probably remain confined to Asia (Chapter 17).

Deflation also differs from inflation of any magnitude because, in deflation, declining interest rates do not stimulate demand and precede good times and a bull stock market. Capacity is so ample that lower interest rates can do little to induce investment in more of it, and consumers are more influenced by expectations of lower prices than lower borrowing rates, as you will learn in Chapter 18.

WHAT DO YOU DO ABOUT DEFLATION?

Still others are convinced deflation is likely, but don't know what to do about it. You may well fit into this category. In an interview that preceded her Sunday, November 22, 1998, *New York Times* Business Section cover story, "If Deflation Hits, It's a Whole New Game," reporter Reed Abelson told me that many professional money managers were in exactly that position. That's why this book concentrates on the implications of deflation and strategies for dealing with what promises to be the dominant condition for decades, only interrupted briefly by wars.

Chapters 21 through 28 outline my 18-point investment strategy for a deflationary era and the transition to it. High-quality bonds will be winners. U.S. stocks overall will do reasonably well once deflation sets in, but will probably be beaten up in the transition to it. Real estate and commodities will have rough times. You'll also learn in Chapter 24 how deflation separates the technological sheep from the goats. With people saving more and waiting for lower prices to buy the goods and services that don't change their form or function much over time, many consumer discretionary spending sectors will be losers. In sharp contrast, buyers will continue to rush to new tech areas where rapid innovation leads to significant new products, dramatically lower prices, and technological advances that make old models obsolete, and replace old tech goods and services.

Chapter 29 explores my 25-point strategy for businesses that want to survive, indeed thrive, in deflation. The elements range from ruthless cost-cutting to emphasizing proprietary products to sharing company risks with employees. Finally, Chapter 30 provides a six-item list of dos and don'ts for consumers in deflation. (Hint: save more and make sure you're worth more to your boss than he's paying you.) These last 10 chapters also provide summary tables of investment, business, and personal winners and losers. Even Federal Reserve Chairman Alan Greenspan has become a convert. In testimony to Congress last September, he said that "deflationary forces are continuing to emerge around the world," and that "there's evidence of which I am aware which suggests that the process . . . has stabilized."

Finally, deflation must certainly be approaching when the IRS gets into the act. The 1999 deduction for business use of cars drops to 31 cents per mile from 32.5 cents, the first decline ever, reflecting lower auto operating costs. Not the kind of deflation we all want, however.

Move on to Chapter 1 to learn why the end of the Cold War and falling government spending and deficits are removing inflation's most significant support and promoting deflation.

PART ONE

MAJOR DEFLATIONARY FORCES

1 CHAPTER

Government Spending Is Shrinking

In late 1975, as the U.S. economy began to recover from the worst recession since the 1930s, I first forecast that inflation was on the way out, even though prices were still accelerating. Our analysis showed that in this country, the history of serious inflation is the history of big government spending—usually in shooting wars but in the Cold War and the War on Poverty as well. We noted that in the 1949–1974 period, wholesale prices rose 1.4 percent per year on average; but about 12 percent in the war years, while declining 1.3 percent per year in peacetime.

Why this linkage between wars and inflation and peace and deflation? It's simply a question of supply and demand. Most economists like to make complex errors out of simple truth, and talk about demand pull, cost push, and other complicated forms of inflation. At root, however, inflation is caused by more demand than supply. When there is more purchasing power than available goods and services, prices go up. Similarly, an excess of supply over demand is deflationary. Prices fall.

Any sector of the economy could, theoretically, create excess demand by spending more than its revenues plus normal borrowing from sectors. Real estate, for example, has periodical booms, with oversized borrowing to finance them. But no sector except the federal government can borrow excessively for long without the loss of credibility that leads to collapse. Think about real estate booms that eventually turn to busts. Consider New York City's huge boosts in welfare payments and city employee compensation, which led to the default on city bonds in the mid-1970s.

The U.S. federal government and the governments of most other developed countries enjoy the credibility that allows them to spend and borrow excessively almost indefinitely. And periods of oversized outlay tend to be periods of war, when governments do not want to levy taxes to offset their spending. Conversely, tax systems, especially progressive income tax systems, absorb such a chunk of economic growth that in peacetime, when government spending is muted, surpluses mount rapidly. With government spending less than revenues, economy-wide supply tends to exceed demand and deflation results.

DEFICITS AND INFLATION

Spending leaps and large deficits almost always go together. Unless the economy is in a deep recession, with excessive numbers of unemployed but employable people and idle equipment, demand rises at a time when supply is constrained by capacity, and inflation results. Inflation also works to government's benefit in a reinforcing cycle by inflating taxable incomes. Wages rise to offset inflation, and that moves individuals into higher tax brackets and creates more payroll taxes. Inflation also creates taxable but artificial profits through increases in the value of inventories and under-depreciation of corporate assets and also capital gains that only keep assets abreast of overall prices but are still taxable. Figure 1–1 shows the clear correlation between the federal deficit and inflation.

Government spending on defense creates inflation in yet another way. It's because you and I don't drive tanks. People are paid to build them, but civilians can't buy them—although defensive driving advocates might wish they could replace their banged-up cars with M-1 tanks. Unless taxes are raised enough to offset the government spending on those tanks—seldom the case in times of heavy military spending—income is created without a comparable new supply of consumer goods and services. So, overall demand exceeds overall supply, and prices rise.

The Cold War ended in the late 1980s and, as a result, U.S. defense spending is falling in real dollar terms and even more rapidly

FIGURE 1–1

U.S. inflation rate and the federal deficit as percentage of Gross Domestic Product (GDP), 1900–1995

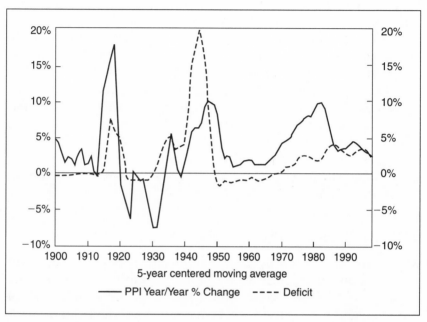

Source: U.S. Commerce Department

as a percentage of gross domestic product (GDP). Furthermore, this is a global phenomenon. In effect, one of the prime causes, if not the cause, of inflation—military spending—is being removed.

GOVERNMENT EFFICIENCY?

Non-defense spending is also inflationary, especially when it produces things that nobody wants or uses, like many "pork barrel" projects. Building public housing satisfies political patronage demands, but provides little value if located in areas of such high crime that it is soon abandoned. Furthermore, there is no bottom line incentive for efficiency in any government spending. Quite the opposite, there is every incentive for inefficiency so that more resources can be employed and bigger empires built by government managers. Indeed, the term, "government efficiency," ranks with airline food, congressional ethics, military intelligence, postal service, tax simplification, vegetarian vampires, beloved mothers-in-law, clairvoyant economists, and other oxymorons. If you don't agree, just take a trip to your local post office. It's a technological excursion into the nineteenth century. Obviously, the less of the economy that is mired in the inefficient government sector, the less inflationary and more deflationary it becomes.

Furthermore, the bigger the government and the more its involvement in the economy, the more likely that there will be inflation by fiat, a term we coined in 1977. This refers to all the ways in which, with the stroke of a pen, Congress, the Administration, and the regulators can push up prices. Obvious examples include dairy price supports, sugar tariffs and import quotas, the minimum wage, and Social Security taxes.

WHY IS BIG GOVERNMENT TOLERATED?

Most Americans detest inflation, and the link between government spending and rising prices isn't all that complicated. Why, then, have voters tolerated the rise in the federal government's share of the economy from a few percentage points until the 1930s (excluding shooting wars) to more than 17 percent today? To a great extent, it's probably inertia carried over from the days when voters saw government as a positive force in their lives, starting with the New Deal in the 1930s.

Whether the New Deal, which touched off this stratospheric climb in government involvement in the economy, can be credited with getting the nation out of the Depression is highly debatable. The return to full employment was probably caused by the rise in military spending in Europe, the rebuilding of the military structure in this country, and finally, World War II. Nevertheless, the inclination then was to give credit to the New Deal for the economic revival because recovery and government programs moved in parallel.

Then the United States entered World War II, a popular war from which she clearly emerged as the leader of the Free World. This nation was the only major country not in ashes after the war, and was the last bastion against communism in the Cold War period. After the war, the nation entered decades of substantial economic growth. It was also a period of growing government involvement, and prosperity and federal spending continued to be associated with each other in the eyes of many.

Almost any trend that humans create tends to get overdone, however, and confidence in government was no exception. As usual, it was followed by an era when everything seemed to go wrong: frustration over Vietnam and the disappointment in Great-Society programs that failed to live up to expectations, and the tremendous excess demand created by spending on both issues. The Vietnam War and social welfare programs sired serious inflation here and abroad and, eventually, the massive global inventory-building spree that resulted in the 1973–1975 recession—the most severe in this country since the 1930s and the first of global significance since World War II.

CHANGED ATTITUDES ABOUT UNEMPLOYMENT AND GOVERNMENT PROGRAMS

Voters also turned on the government because their attitudes about unemployment and inflation changed markedly, beginning in the late 1960s. Earlier, a majority of the population had vivid memories of the Depression and its peak 25 percent unemployment rate; few people, however, had seen significant inflation. Consequently, unemployment was consistently ranked as the country's number one economic problem in the polls. By the late 1960s, however, the Depression-scarred constituted a much smaller percentage of the population, and everyone had begun to witness inflation of frightening proportions. Not surprisingly, the polls began to show inflation as the top-rated national economic concern. Furthermore, people started to relate inflation to government spending and deficits.

But then came Proposition 13 in California in June 1978, the first big voter revolt against big government and taxes, which put a ceiling on property taxes at 1 percent of market value. The final proof, of course, was the election of Ronald Reagan as President in 1980. And, in 1994, Republicans gained control of both Houses of Congress, a body that came very close to passing a balanced budget amendment to the Constitution. The proof in the pudding was the phasing out of farm subsidies and the welfare reform movement in the mid-1990s, as well as the constraints on government medical care spending.

It seems clear, then, that the long liberal swing that began in 1932 in reaction to the Great Depression has ended. Even President Clinton, with all of his liberal instincts, says that the era of big government is over. He endorsed the end of farm subsidies and the forcing of welfare recipients to work. In April 1999, he crowed that welfare caseloads had fallen 38 percent since he signed the welfare reform bill, and almost 50 percent since he became President. Furthermore, despite the record wave of corporate merger announcements, his Justice Department's Antitrust Division has been relatively inactive. My liberal friends no longer call themselves liberals, but moderates. If history is any guide, this shift in attitude toward more reliance on markets and the private sector to allocate the nation's resources and away from inflationary government will last for many years.

WASHINGTON RESPONDS

On balance, then, it's not surprising that Washington has become zealous about curtailing government spending, and the result has been a mounting federal surplus—much to the amazement of many. This really isn't amazing, however. It simply demonstrates the tremendous revenue-generating power of the federal government. All that has ever been needed to eliminate the budget deficit in the postwar era is to restrain federal spending while letting revenues run.

AMERICA IS NOT ALONE

At the same time that America's attitude toward government was changing in the 1980s, Great Britain, under Prime Minister Margaret Thatcher, made an even more radical shift from near socialism to capitalism. The labor unions were brought under control, many government programs dismantled, and scores of state-owned companies were sold. These actions led to a substantial fall in nominal government spending growth in the 1990s. Recognizing the change in voter attitudes, the British Labor Party, under Tony Blair, realized that it had to shift to the right to get elected. And the new Labor government is out-conservativing the conservatives in privatizations and tax cuts and in measures to encourage the unemployed to leave welfare and enter the workforce.

Canada considers herself a kinder and gentler United States—a combination of Anglo-Saxon capitalism and Continental European social concern. Yet Canada has joined the parade recently as fiscal responsibility spreads from the western provinces east to Ontario, where the "People's Republic of Ontario" government was replaced by the free enterprise, privatization-oriented Harris provincial administration. Federal budget outlays are falling and the government projects a balanced budget or even surpluses in future years. New Zealand and Australia, too far away and too small economically to receive proper attention, have done bang-up jobs in eliminating government subsidies and spending.

THOSE CONTINENTALS AND JAPANESE

While English-speaking countries are rushing to cut government involvement in the economy, the more socialist Continental Europeans have moved in the same direction, but primarily for a different reason. Despite double-digit unemployment, European governments have squeezed their deficits in order to meet the Maastricht Agreement maximum, 3 percent of GDP, that was required for the initiation of the common currency, the euro. Even with her new, leftist government, Germany's budget is little changed from that of the old conservative administration.

Japan has been mired under a deflationary depression for eight years. To get out of it, consumer spending could certainly use a boost to offset their legendary zeal for saving. Yet, the government is so unhappy with its soaring budget deficit that it continues to resist tax cuts big enough to reinvigorate consumer spending. Indeed, the increase in consumer taxes of April 1997 remains on the books.

Without question, wars provide the easiest opportunity for governments to expand their influence and their share of the economic pies. In the last 60 years, we've seen lots of wars, but now they're all over, assuming that the problems in the Balkans have no more lasting consequences on government spending than the Gulf

War, and deficits have turned to surpluses. This is the first of a one-two government deflationary punch. As you'll see in Chapter 2, central banks are also encouraging deflation by fighting the last war—against inflation.

2

The Role of Central Banks

I argued in Chapter 1 that government spending is the root of all, or at least most, inflation. But what about money?

Money has something to do with the levels of economic activity, at least in nominal terms, and a lot to do with inflation (Figure 2–1). The monetarists, of course, believe that inflation is a purely monetary phenomenon. If more money is introduced into the economy, they argue, it will get spent and the prices of goods and services will be bid up to accommodate it. Similarly, if money is withdrawn, prices fall. It's also argued that more money stimulates production of goods and services by pushing interest rates down. Less money does the reverse by increasing interest rates and, in the case of deflation, by destroying productive capacity by spawning bankruptcies.

MONETARY POLICY AND POLITICAL REALITY

Even if the money supply is the immediate cause of inflation or deflation, however, it isn't the prime mover, as monetarists believe. Technically, the Federal Reserve and, increasingly, other central banks as well are politically independent. Nevertheless, the Fed pays close attention to the political leanings of Congress and the Administration. After all, a bill could be passed tomorrow that would transfer all the monetary policymaking functions to the Treasury, leaving the Fed to simply count coins and bills.

If you don't focus on government spending as the prime mover, you might reach the incredulous conclusion that the inflationary bulge in the money supply in the early 1940s (Figure 2–2) was the result of irresponsible credit managers. Of course, World War II was then in progress and the federal government didn't increase taxes enough to pay for its increased spending. That left it up to the Fed, along with Treasury borrowing, to fill the gap. If the Fed had stuck to slow growth in credit, the jump in interest rates needed to get consumers and business to save the additional required amount would probably have pushed rates to politically unacceptable levels.

If you still don't believe that central banks and money supplies are the handmaidens of government spending and deficits, compare the federal deficit on Figure 1–1 with money supply (M2) growth on Figure 2–1. They look a lot alike.

FIGURE 2–1

U.S. inflation and money supply (M2) growth, 1900–1996

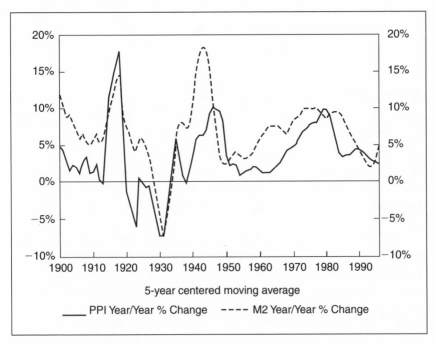

5-year centered moving average

_____ PPI Year/Year % Change   - - - - M2 Year/Year % Change

Source: U.S. Commerce Department

FIGURE 2-2

U.S. money supply (M2) quarterly levels, 1913–1950

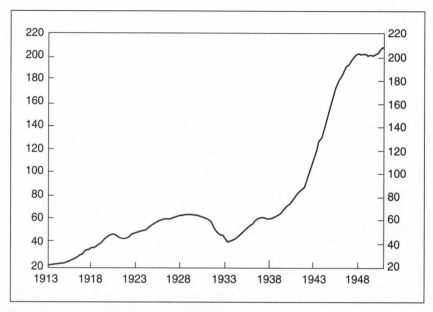

Source: National Bureau of Economic Research, A. Gary Shilling & Co., Inc.

MONETARY POLICY HAS CHANGED

From World War II through the 1970s, the nation's orientation was to accommodate government expansion and promote low unemployment, with little concern about inflation. Small wonder, then, that the Fed not only supplied ample credit to help finance federal deficits and increased private transaction demand, but also didn't hesitate to stimulate the economy whenever it showed signs of slipping.

As the political mood of the country changed, however, so did the policy orientation of the Fed. Since the late 1970s, the Fed has been determined to eliminate inflation—with considerable backing from Congress, successive Republican and Democratic administrations, and the public. The only problem now, however, is that the credit authorities are still fighting the last war, inflation, and not the next, deflation.

This was certainly the case in early 1994 when the Fed mounted a pre-emptive strike against inflation, ultimately raising the federal funds rate that it controls from 3 to 6 percent. At the time, we thought the Fed was sitting with us in the audience watching the disinflation play unfold on stage. As it turned out, the credit authority was center stage as one of the principal actors to ensure not only the end of inflation, but possibly the beginning of deflation.

Note that after backing off somewhat in 1995, the Fed raised interest rates again in early 1997, even though inflation rates were falling. It's clear that the only thing that staved off further tightening in late 1997, and prompted cuts in interest rates in 1998, was the collapse in Asia. Even as late as October 29, 1997, Fed Chairman Alan Greenspan said, according to *The Wall Street Journal*, "It is inflation, not deflation . . . which serves as the major threat to this expansion."

THEY'RE ALL IN THE SAME BOAT

Developed countries' central banks comprise what is probably the world's most exclusive club. And like good club members, they all essentially think and act alike—all are more worried about inflation than deflation. The Bank of England, made independent by the Labor government in 1997, lost no time in raising interest rates repeatedly, despite no evidence of a surge in inflation, and only recently cut rates as the U.K.'s economy softened. The German Bundesbank also raised rates late that year even though the unemployment rate continued to push further into double digits and inflation stayed below 2 percent. It also continued to harp on the need to control inflation right up to the day it lost its power to the new European Central Bank. And Wim Duisenberg, the president of that new institution, strongly resisted calls by leftist Continental governments for much easier credit. He said last year that even though it is "normal" for politicians to express their views on monetary policy, "it would be abnormal if these suggestions were listened to," according to the February 3, 1999, edition of *The Wall Street Journal*. The Bank of Japan is only moderately active in spurring money supply growth amid Japan's ongoing deflationary depression and leaping unemployment.

Also note that even though the money supplies in the United States and abroad appear to be growing rapidly, the short-term interest rates controlled by central banks are very high in real terms (see Figure 18–1 and Table 18–1 in Chapter 18, Western Central Banks and Governments Can't Stop Deflation). The disappearance of inflation has not been matched by declines in nominal rates. So, borrowers, on average, are suffering very high interest costs in relation to their static selling prices, and those with deflating prices are really hurting.

AN OLDER WORLD

Central bankers tend to be old men, but the world's population is getting older. And the process will accelerate, noticeably in developed countries (Figure 2–3). The U.S. postwar baby boom is well-

FIGURE 2-3

World population; percentage of people over 65 years of age

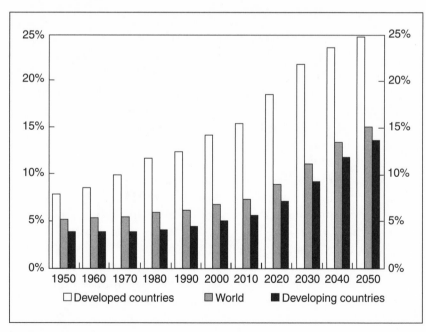

Source: United Nations

known, but its importance is magnified by the low birth rates that followed. The aging phenomenon is even bigger in Europe and Japan than in the United States. Japan is producing so few people that if current trends continue, her population will actually shrink in time. Similarly, in the European Union, women now give birth to 1.4 babies in their lifetimes, on average, far short of the 2.1 needed to maintain the current population. At this rate, the E.U. population will decline more than 50 percent in two generations.

Older people, of course, have largely raised and educated their families, bought and furnished their houses, and accumulated most of the goods they will ever own. They tend to spend more on medical and some other services than younger folks do, but in general, they are modest consumers. With relatively more of them, and fewer of the younger big spenders who are forming households and raising families, consumer outlays will moderate throughout the developed world, which today buys over 80 percent of global output. This is clearly deflationary, but there is even more long-run deflation in this age shift.

TOO MANY RETIREES

In future years, there will be fewer people working for every retiree (Table 2–1). In the United States, the number drops from 5.3 in 1990 to 3.1 in 2040, but in Canada it plummets from 5.9 to 2.6 and in Japan from 5.8 to 2.6. This means trouble ahead because America and most other developed countries' government retirement plans are not savings accounts, but pay-as-you-go schemes. They amount to income transfer mechanisms with money moved from those still working to retirees. This worked just great for the U.S. Social Security system from its inception in the late 1930s (the Supreme Court upheld it the day before I was born on May 25, 1937) up until today. Employment expanded rapidly, more and more workers became covered by Social Security and were paying into the trust fund, and wages taxed by the system leaped. At the same time, retirees drawing Social Security benefits have been relatively few.

But economic activity and wages will grow more slowly in the years ahead as restructuring continues in the United States and intensifies in other developed countries, as deflation slows spending while people wait for lower prices, and as U.S. consumers switch from big borrowing and spending to big saving.

TABLE 2–1

The Ratio of Working-Age to Retirement-Age Populations

Year	Canada	France	Germany	Italy	Japan	U.K.	U.S.
1960	7.7	5.3	6.3	7.5	10.5	5.6	6.5
1990	5.9	4.7	4.5	4.7	5.8	4.3	5.3
2010	4.7	4.1	2.8	3.9	3.4	4.5	5.3
2030	3.5	3.3	3.0	3.4	3.0	3.9	4.9
2040	2.6	2.6	2.1	2.4	2.6	3.0	3.1

Source: The Federal Reserve Bank of St. Louis and Organisation for Economic Co-operation and Development

More important, the burden that retiree benefits under present policies would put on those still working in future years is simply not politically acceptable. By 2020, 25 million more Americans will be getting Social Security checks as the postwar babies retire, at an additional cost of $232 billion in real terms. If they also receive today's level of Medicare benefits, the annual deficit of both programs will run $1.7 trillion. And bear in mind that deflation will increase the real cost of these benefits even more.

To cover these costs, the current payroll tax of 15 percent would have to roughly triple by 2040. Add in federal, state, and local taxes, and the majority of American personal incomes would be paid to governments. Unfunded pension liabilities are even bigger abroad, notably in Italy, Germany, Japan, and especially in France, where they run 100 percent of current GDP. It stands to reason that those working in coming decades will not be willing to see major chunks of their income transferred to the old folks, even if those retirees include their own parents. In the solutions to this problem lie many deflationary forces.

NO EASY SOLUTION

In the United States, most observers want the nation to embark on a massive saving campaign. President Clinton wants federal surpluses devoted to the Social Security system. Many others want to encourage saving by taxing only consumption, and to enact mandatory individual savings accounts, much as in Chile and Singapore. More saving means less spending, which is deflationary, as would be larger federal surpluses that are earmarked for Social Security.

Other proposals include raising the retirement age—and it probably will be increased eventually because people now live much longer than when the standard was set at 65 years of age. Of course, as people work longer, the resulting increase in the labor supply would be deflationary. Another is to force retirees into HMOs to contain Medicare costs, and this, too, is likely and deflationary. A partial solution would be to open the borders to young, productive immigrants, whose income could be taxed to support the postwar babies in retirement. Attitudes that have surfaced in California—a bellwether for trends—suggest, however, that concerns about foreigners stealing natives' jobs and swelling the welfare roles will intervene. If that saving is invested in new technology and equipment and education, those still working when the postwar babies retire will be able to produce more for themselves and the retirees. This will help curtail supply constraints.

BOTH SIDES GIVE IN

To keep supply and demand in balance when the postwar babies retire, they will need to receive less than current Social Security programs provide, while those then working will have to be taxed more to transfer a bigger part of what they produce to the retirees. The net effect will be less spending on both sides. Similarly, retirement bulges in other developed countries will require deflation-enhancing restraints on the purchasing power of those still working as well as retirees, who will also be required to work longer before drawing benefits. The exception is Japan, because she can draw on her immense foreign assets to pay for imports to supply retirees' needs. At the same time, muted spending by both retirees and those still working will curtail demand for imports, another deflationary force.

Admittedly, these demographic issues in developed countries and their deflationary effects will take decades to play out, but we're entering a long deflationary era. Restructuring, however, is a here-and-now force for deflation, as you'll learn in Chapter 3.

3

CHAPTER

Restructuring in the United States Continues

After World War II, America faced no meaningful foreign competition. The other major countries were in ashes. Indeed, the U.S. economy grew in part by helping Europe and Japan to rebuild. At home, expansion was strong due to pent-up demand. Consumer spending had been curtailed in the 1930s Depression years by lack of income and during World War II, when everything went to the military. Ditto for residential and non-residential construction. All this catch-up spending was financed by the gigantic liquidity accumulated during World War II, when civilian goods were unavailable and people and businesses were essentially forced to save. In this environment, economic activity and real wages and salaries rose rapidly and with few competitive constraints, either domestic or foreign.

EUROPE AND JAPAN CATCH UP

By the mid-1960s, Europe and Japan had caught up with the United States, but this went largely unnoticed, because the nation's attention and economic activity were diverted by the Vietnam War and Great Society programs, both of which precipitated the high inflation of the late 1960s and 1970s, which disrupted the U.S. economy even further. It transferred corporate profits to foreign producers of commodities, like oil, that were soaring in price. It also transferred earnings to government, which taxed what were purely inflationary gains—inventory profits and under-depreciation, as noted in Chapter 1.

The inflation of that era also hid the growing global competition from American businessmen, many of whom looked at their corporate earnings in nominal terms and overlooked the pounding they were taking during that decade in terms of real dollars. Most felt duty-bound to keep their employees at least abreast of inflation with no idea that their profits were falling far behind.

At the same time, the productivity growth needed to offset inflation and remain globally competitive was low in the 1970s. Postwar babies and older women were entering the workforce as untrained raw recruits. Work ethic declined, along with a general collapse in respect for authority and traditional values. Rampant inflation diverted attention as well. Why bother with productive work and investments when there were fortunes to be made speculating in soaring real estate?

THE RUDE AWAKENING

The fading of inflation in the early 1980s, however, left American business naked as the proverbial jaybird (are jaybirds really featherless?). In any event, it exposed the United States not only to strong competition from Europe and Japan, but also to the fierce onslaught of newly industrialized countries like Taiwan, South Korea, Hong Kong, and Singapore. Imports surged and many segments of American manufacturing faced virtual extinction.

Fortunately, the response of U.S. producers was to restructure, cut costs, and promote productivity, but the process took time to develop. I recall that in the midst of the double-dip recession of the early 1980s, many of the industrial companies we work with initially did what they always had done in reaction to recessions. They cut travel, entertainment, and advertising—temporary cost cuts that could be reversed rapidly. Several division managers told me that if they did any more substantial and permanent retrenching in a recession, they would have barely signed the last severance checks before the downturn was over and it was time to rehire.

SUBSTANTIAL ACTION

It's noteworthy that as fierce international competition persisted into economic recovery, however, it became apparent that much more restructuring was needed. Layers of management were eliminated and then, to make sure they didn't reappear, organization charts were redrawn without all those boxes that have a tendency to get refilled. Employees were given more responsibility—and more respect. I recall vividly being told by a client's senior officers that they provided $500 in paint to the employees so they could repaint their rather drab lunchroom on a Saturday, and how amazed those managers were at the resulting improvement in morale.

The restructuring process has only gained momentum in the last 15 years. Part-time and temporary workers are now routinely used to improve efficiency, because they often work only during peak demand periods and usually don't receive fringe benefits. Less and less of labor compensation is fixed as more and more is in the form of bonuses, pay for performance, stock options, etc. A recent survey by William M. Mercer Inc. reveals that of 1,800 employers, 51 percent compensate non-management, non-sales employees with pay tied to group or individual performance.

It's noteworthy that increasing portions of retirement funds are 401(k) plans, which I'll address further in Chapter 28. These have largely replaced defined benefit plans, which obligate employers to fixed pension payments regardless of profitability. Instead, it's largely up to employees to satisfactorily invest the 401(k) contributions that they and their employer make year by year. The other big fringe outlay, medical insurance, has been attacked ruthlessly.

AND EVEN MORE

Outsourcing is another major component of restructuring, with production moving not only to foreign locations, like Mexican border plants or *maquiladoras* (see Chapter 8), but also to lower-cost U.S. locations, and from unionized to non-unionized shops. The power of unions has been steadily eroding for 40 years (Figure 3–1). Their appeal has dropped as non-union compensation today often equals or exceeds that paid under union contracts. Also the growth in the economy in recent years has been largely in industries like finance, retail trade, and services that are not susceptible to unionization, while employment in heavily unionized sectors such as mining, manufacturing, construction, and transportation

FIGURE 3–1

Percent of U.S. labor force in unions, 1930–1998

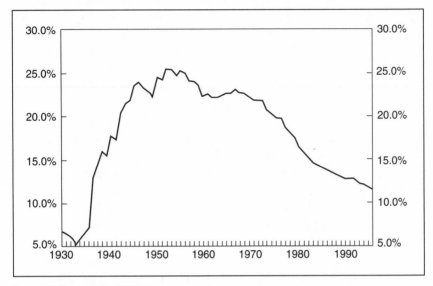

Source: U.S. Bureau of Labor Statistics

has dropped. In fact, without public employee unionization in recent decades, the percentage of the labor force in unions would be
much lower. Weak unions make it easier to move work to non-
union shops and this, in turn, reduces the number of union members and their power.

Outsourcing also allows firms to concentrate on the businesses they know best and excel in, another technique for improving productivity and competitiveness. In February 1999, Electronic
Data Systems and MCI WorldCom announced a series of transfers
worth about $17 billion that will swap assets and 13,000 employ-
ees. The guts of the deal shift software development and computer
operations from MCI to EDS and transfer networking operations
from EDS to MCI.

Another technique for cutting labor compensation, which for
American corporations in aggregate is about two-thirds of total
costs, is to encourage the retirement of older workers whose pay
has crept up over time to levels that exceed their value. They are re-
warded for taking early retirement or otherwise bought out and re-

placed with younger, cheaper employees—or even themselves, hired back on a lower paid part-time basis.

MANUFACTURING, THEN SERVICES

Service industries ranging from health care to retail trade to banking were largely oblivious to the productivity zeal of manufacturers in the 1980s because many faced little direct foreign competition. But pressed in part by customers who were confronted with the onslaught from abroad, this huge sector, where three-quarters of us work, joined the ongoing parade. Restructuring and layoffs in the service industries are only starting. The undershooting of service productivity growth relative to the trend shown in Figure 3–2 means that 15 million more people were hired cumulatively in the 1970s and 1980s to do the work than would have been the case, had

F I G U R E   3–2

U.S. service sector productivity with 1948–1973 trend

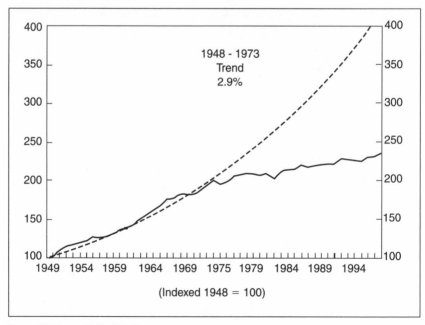

(Indexed 1948 = 100)

Source: U.S. Bureau of Labor Statistics

the trend prevailed. The process of shedding them is underway, but will take many more years.

As in manufacturing jobs, many service jobs are now being exported. American companies employ Indian and even Bulgarian software engineers who work via satellite at a fraction of the salaries of their U.S. counterparts (see Chapter 8). Visa Card does its credit card processing in Ireland, where skilled labor is cheaper and where—because of time zone differences—the finished processing work is back here by the next U.S. business day.

A PERMANENT APPROACH

Restructuring has come a long way since the temporary measures I saw implemented in the early 1980s. It has even moved beyond the next phase, which was, in effect, a huge but ad hoc project in the eyes of corporate management. We Americans love well-defined projects that we rally to take on and complete, and then move on. Unlike the Japanese and other Asians, we don't enjoy never-ending battles. (Maybe that's why we're so unsuccessful at controlling our weight. It's the battle you never win, at least as long as you're breathing. It's also probably why World War II was a hugely popular war. The bad guys were clearly identified, we geared up and beat them, and then demobilized—much too soon, as we learned when the Soviets took over Eastern Europe. The Vietnam war, of course, was the reverse, and we hated it. No clearly defined bad guy. No well defined goals. No end in sight.)

When American business got serious about restructuring in the mid-1980s, many of our consulting clients assumed they'd finish the project in a few years. "After we reorganize and cut out excess management, outsource, and install just-in-time inventory control, we'll be down to the bits and pieces," they thought. But by the late 1980s, they began to realize two things. First, they'd barely scratched the surface of what could be done. Second, the process would never end. Foreign and domestic competition, as well as technological change, would keep their business climates in constant turmoil. The need for major cost-cutting and productivity enhancement would continue indefinitely.

Not surprisingly, restructuring has been institutionalized in the management training process, both informal and formal, and in business school curricula. And, it can only intensify in deflation. As an example, in recent years, overpaid employees' compensation has been reduced to correct size in real terms by holding pay flat and letting inflation take its course. Not so in deflation when even flat nominal compensation rates produce real cost increases. The result will be more layoffs and more careful compensation administration.

LAYOFFS RESURGE

In the last several years, however, many thought that the big restructuring-related layoffs were over, as the booming economy seemed to shift business attention from cost-cutting to sales growth. Then, layoffs again began to increase (Figure 3–3). This trend is strong, with layoffs in 1998 second only to 1993's peak of 615,000, and it is likely to intensify.

FIGURE 3–3

Total U.S. employee layoffs, 12-month average, 1994–1999

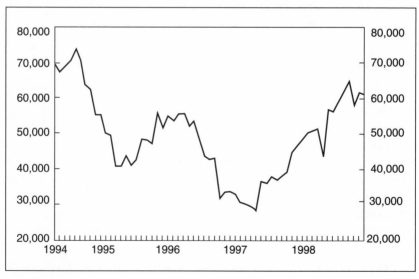

Source: ISI Group

Most of the new layoffs are driven by pressure on profits spawned by excess capacity. This in turn is often, but not always, the result of the Asian Contagion, which is slashing U.S. exports and corporate sales abroad. At the same time, it is flooding the country with lower-priced imports, which are pressuring domestic competitors to follow suit. The negative effects on earnings are greater for companies that face increased foreign competition, which is often the case as producers abroad—with collapsed domestic markets and more-than-ample capacity—view the United States as their market of first and last resort.

Corporate managements that have not been vigorously promoting productivity in the past have even more need for cost-cutting and layoffs. According to Bureau of Labor Statistics data for output per hour for 169 Standard Industrial Classification (SIC) 3-digit industries, in 1987–1996, 44 percent had productivity growth of over 2 percent annually. But another 40 percent saw minimal gains of zero to 2 percent, and 16 percent actually suffered productivity declines. To be sure, some of the losers have not had to face the bracing winds of foreign competition and, hence, are under less profit pressure. This group includes bakery products, logging, millwork and plywood, wood buildings, newspapers, periodicals, business forms, greeting cards, ordinance, musical instruments, cable TV, food stores, restaurants, fuel dealers, and funeral services and crematories. Importing a funeral can be difficult.

THE TRIPLE WHAMMY

Some industries, however, are confronted with the lethal combination of all three profit squeezers—declining or low productivity growth, excess capacity, and blistering foreign competition. Despite all the restructuring hullabaloo from Detroit, the motor vehicle industry had trivial productivity growth of 0.4 percent per year over the nine years from 1987–1996. Furthermore, producers suffer worldwide excess capacity of 18 million units, more than U.S. annual sales of about 15 million. And more is on the way as developing countries expand capacity to promote national prestige and to increase exports to earn desperately needed foreign exchange. DaimlerChrysler and BMW suffer from sales plunges in Asia, but to add insult to injury, in Europe, their home turf, Korean car sales are soaring, in part due to the weak won. No wonder that Volvo sacked 6,000 of its employees worldwide.

Aircraft productivity gains haven't been much better. When Boeing finally realized that Asian airlines with empty planes won't buy more aircraft, the firm announced staff cuts from 231,000 at the end of 1998 to the 185,000–195,000 range in 2000. Ditto for grain companies; Cargill rolled heads and ConAgra, with falling sales and disappointing earnings, seems destined to follow. The paper and nonferrous industries are also in this category, with International Paper laying off a bunch, and Phelps Dodge planning to close two mines and terminate 700.

RAPID PRODUCTIVITY GROWTH IS NO SHIELD

Even rapid productivity growth in recent years is no shield against weak demand, too much capacity, and robust global competition. The oil industry has enjoyed sizable productivity gains thanks to improvements like larger tankers, 3-D imaging, and horizontal drilling. In the North Sea, production costs have fallen from over $16 a barrel to $4. But when the resulting increase in supply and collapsing Asian demand submerged oil prices, Texaco, Chevron, Conoco, Shell, Phillips, and Atlantic Richfield had no choice but to slash staffs. Just as a drop in airline travel has an even greater negative effect on the demand for new aircraft, the weakness in oil prices and demand is killing the petroleum service and drilling business, and the number of working oil rigs has collapsed. Halliburton is responding to planned spending cuts by energy company customers by dropping 2,750 employees. This comes on top of 7,350 job losses earlier following the firm's merger with Dresser Industries and 2,700 terminations by both firms in the month before the merger was completed.

The steel industry is getting mugged with cheap imports, especially from Russia, Japan, and Brazil, despite huge productivity gains of 4.9 percent per annum in 1987–1996. Laclede Steel and Acme Metals went bankrupt, and even highly efficient Nucor had to slash productivity and drop prices 7 percent. Strong productivity advances in photographic equipment and supplies didn't protect 10,000 employees at Kodak, with 10,000 more scheduled to go.

Telephone communications have enjoyed large productivity gains, 5.5 percent per year. Yet the pressures of domestic and foreign competition forced AT&T to cut 18,000 employees, and the firm completed the terminations a year ahead of schedule.

NO OTHER PLACE TO HIDE

Furthermore, those businesses with rapid productivity gains and limited foreign competition can still be forced to cut costs and staff if faced with excess capacity. Farm equipment productivity rose substantially, 3.5 percent per year between 1987 and 1996, and the industry has limited import competition. Yet the nose-dive in grain prices and demand from Asia, which takes 40 percent of U.S. grain exports, slashed farmers' profits. The Agriculture Department expects a 16 percent decline in 1999 net farm income. Lower grain prices are usually good news for livestock producers but animal prices are at record lows. Farmland prices are falling and farm equipment manufacturers expect a 20 percent decline in 1999 sales. So, Case recently announced its third round of layoffs since last September, a total of 3,400 cut from its work force of 18,000. Furthermore, agricultural equipment companies tried to recoup their losses by slashing their construction equipment prices in a bid to cut into Caterpillar's market share; consequently Cat was dragged in at home after suffering earlier sales collapses in Asia.

Innovative products and little competition didn't insulate Gillette when demand dropped in Asia, Latin America, and Eastern Europe. The firm closed 14 factories and cut 11 percent of its employees. Similarly, falling foreign sales overcame 3M's strong brands and high efficiency and cost 4,500 people their jobs.

The financial demise of Russia and the Long-Term Capital Management collapse convinced Wall Street that it has too much leverage and excess capacity. Hence the bloodletting at Merrill Lynch, where 3,400 met the guillotine, and at J. P. Morgan, among others.

Industries with poor productivity performance and no foreign competition can also be susceptible to layoffs if excess capacity reigns. Newspapers, with shrinking circulation, suffered a huge 2.8 percent annual productivity decline between 1987 and 1996, and the *Los Angeles Times* has eliminated 12 percent of its labor force, with further layoffs pending. Furniture and home furnishing stores had less than 2 percent annual productivity gains. Levitz Furniture, the country's largest furniture retailer until the mid-1990s, recently fired a further 25 percent of its staff, and has cut its number of stores in half since filing for Chapter 11 in 1997.

The ongoing rash of mergers only intensifies layoffs, as does restructuring as it spreads beyond the United States. To learn more, please turn to Chapter 4.

4
CHAPTER

Mergers at Home and Restructuring Abroad

The ongoing round of U.S. layoffs has been spawned primarily by excess capacity, as discussed in Chapter 3. Much of the recent merger wave is in reaction to the same conditions—and there have been a lot of them. The stock value of U.S. merger partners was $1.7 trillion in 1998, up 85 percent from the previous record in 1997, and $2.3 trillion worldwide. The CEOs involved usually stress the wonderful strategic fits. The driving force, however, is more often the oversized costs that management didn't face earlier and which now must be whacked, using mergers and the resulting staff overlap as scapegoats. In announcing the Citicorp–Travelers Group merger, top brass talked about the wonderful opportunities for cross-selling, with bankers hawking insurance policies while insurance agents flog credit cards and loans. Increased revenues would be the bulk of the expected $1 billion windfall from the deal, they proclaimed. Now it's clear that the $1 billion will come from cost-cutting and 10,400 job losses. Citigroup faces substantial bad loan write-offs and excess capacity, because automatic teller machines (ATM) and Internet banking and insurance transactions make many of their employees redundant.

Other U.S. banks are in a similar pattern. Bank One is cutting 4,700 jobs as it takes over First Chicago NBD, or 5 percent of the combined staff. After a series of acquisitions, First Union is eliminating 5,850 positions, or 7 percent of its total. Fleet Financial will probably slash staff after its purchase of BankBoston. Similarly, the possible merger of Mexican banks Grupo Financiero Banamex-Accival and Grupo Financiero Bancomer would lead to employment cuts. Ditto in Italy where UniCredito Italiano and Bianca Commerciale Italiana plan to merge as do San Paolo-IMI and Banca di Roma, and in France where Societe Generale hopes to merge with Paribas, and Banque Nationale de Paris wants to buy the other two banks.

MERGERS GALORE

Exxon and Mobil plan to save $2.5 billion by laying off duplicate staff when they merge. The total saving of $4 billion expected from the merger is about half of Exxon's earnings. Similarly, France's Total will combine with Belgium's Petrofina, and British Petroleum is buying Amoco, with $2 billion in projected cost cuts. Kerr-McGee plans to drop 19 percent of the combine's employment after acquiring Oryx Energy. Even big government-owned oil producers are joining the trend, with a proposed alliance among Petroleos de Venezuela, Petroleos Mexicano, Brazil's Petrobras, and Saudi Aramco.

Mired in an eight-year deflationary depression, Japan suffers from excess capacity in many industries, including financial services. That, plus deregulation, has led to a flood of domestic and international alliances. Excess capacity is also a problem in the global defense industry in the aftermath of the Cold War's end, despite productivity gains. So, British Aerospace is buying Britain's General Electric Co. PLC's Marconi defense unit.

Global excess supply and cost-cutting necessity also inspired the DaimlerChrysler merger, and the rest of the auto companies here and abroad are rushing to combine forces. Volvo, with only 1 percent of the global car market, is selling its auto business to Ford in order to concentrate on trucks. Nissan, with debts close to $30 billion, is essentially bankrupt; it plans to cut capacity in Japan from 2 million to 1.7 million, after losing money in five of the past six years. A takeover is likely. GM is increasing its stake in Suzuki Motor and Isuzu Motors and is talking to Toyota about expanding their cooperation in developing electric vehicles, fuel cells, and other technologies. After buying Rolls-Royce, Volkswagen is interested in BMW. Meanwhile, Fiat, now without generous government car purchase incentives at home and collapsing sales abroad, especially in Brazil, is looking for partners, as is Renault, which paid $5.44 billion for a third of Nissan. American auto parts maker TRW is buying Britain's Lucas-Varity. With the huge global excess vehicle capacity, current and future mergers can only result in massive cuts in costs and people.

Slowing global demand for drugs has spawned proposed mergers of the U.K.'s Zeneca Group with Sweden's Astra, Germany's Hoechst and France's Rhone-Poulenc, and the French firms Sanofi and Synthelabo. Some big blockbuster drugs are coming off patent in the next several years and are unlikely to be followed by similar successes. In the same vein, American Home Products will eliminate 3,000 pharmaceutical research jobs. Consequently, as managed care companies replace the expired patented drugs with generics, drug company profits will suffer. In addition, the possible extension of Medicare to pharmaceuticals would definitely set limits on drug prices.

Aetna recently announced its third large acquisition in health care in three years—the health-care business of Prudential Insurance Co.—as cost pressures consolidate that industry. At the same time, Cigna plans to sell its property and casualty insurance business to concentrate on health care and employee benefits.

The number and size of recent mergers show just how intense the pressure of excess capacity is, because most CEOs know that combining corporate cultures, computer systems, sales forces, etc. is difficult at best. A study by management consultant McKinsey & Co. of 115 mergers in the early 1990s involving U.S. and U.K. companies reveals that only 23 percent were successful in terms of subsequent returns on capital. It's often a case of two drunks leaning back-to-back to try to keep each other standing. A survey by Right Management Consultants found that of 179 merged companies, fewer than one-third believed they had successfully combined their cultures. Another study by Cerulli Associates found that most international joint ventures have only a three-year life span, and more than half formed between 1979 and 1995 have been dismembered.

OTHER REASONS TO MERGE

Some mergers aren't forced by excess capacity problems, but are specifically made to cut fat. WorldCom wasted no time in slashing the overhead at newly acquired MCI (an extraordinarily high 30 percent of revenues), and may drop 3,750 jobs. America Online will cut 20 percent of the payroll at newly acquired Netscape as it reorganizes the business. SPX Corp., a supplier of auto parts and industrial and electrical equipment, bought industrial manufacturer General Signal last year with the express idea of slashing costs. So far, it has announced the closing of 25 facilities and the elimination of 2,000 jobs.

Other mergers are inspired by the urge to enter rapidly growing markets, as with AT&T's forays into European telecommunications and its purchases of IBM's Global Network and Tele-Communications Inc.'s cable TV system. Bell Atlantic is merging with GTE to combine local and long distance phone services. With excess capacity, deregulated foreign utilities are concerned about losing market shares at home and are consequently invading the United States. Scottish Power's announced purchase of PacifiCorp is a case in point. At the same time, with deregulation in the United States, electric utility holding company GPU is buying an Argentine electricity distributor as it moves out of power generation and into global retailing of electricity.

With recent lofty stock prices, some mergers may be inspired by the urge to buy something with a company's overvalued equity. Last year, 67 percent of the payments in mergers were in stocks as opposed to cash. Nevertheless, most mergers are ultimately driven by the stark reality of excess capacity, and cost-cuts and big layoffs are the inevitable result. Some firms are even thinking ahead and anticipating disappointing profits with job cuts. Raytheon announced terminations of 8,700 in January 1998 and more recently boosted the total to 14,000, or 16 percent of its workforce, even though it foresees 10 percent to 12 percent earnings growth in the next four years—a decent range, but below Wall Street hopes. At the same time, managements preoccupied with making mergers work may be slow to respond to weakening Western economies in the future and deteriorating business climates. The ultimate result will be lower earnings and more layoffs.

WHO CARES?

With or without mergers, the renewed layoff wave is obviously unsettling to those affected. Especially because so many of them were middle-level managers and professionals who thought their jobs were secure, and even more so because one in five is forced to take a job with lower pay. Others worry, "will I be next?" Still, most easily get new jobs in today's drum-tight labor markets. Indeed, the unemployment rate for managers and professionals was a mere 1.8 percent in December 1998, the lowest in the 16 years in which the BLS has been measuring this jobless category.

Nevertheless, the low level of unemployment and rising labor costs, especially in real terms, are themselves putting pressure on corporate earnings over and above the constrictions originating overseas. This, in turn, is an added inducement for cost-cutting layoffs.

At the same time, many firms are also slashing capital spending budgets, as noted in the cases of airline and petroleum companies. Oil producers and refiners typically have big capital outlays, so multibillion dollar cuts wreak havoc on the sales and earnings of their suppliers, leading to still more layoffs; this is already true with Halliburton. But the oil industry is not alone by any stretch of the imagination.

RESTRUCTURING ABROAD

You learned in Chapters 1 and 2 that other major countries have pursued the same deflationary fiscal and monetary policies as the United States in recent years. This also can be said of restructuring, even though the United States and most other English-speaking countries have commanding leads. When former Prime Minister Thatcher tamed the British labor unions in the 1980s, the door opened for immense restructuring of business, given the near-socialist starting point at the time and the fact that many key industries were owned by the government. Voter-inspired changes in government policies also paved the way for privatization and business restructuring in New Zealand, Australia, and, more recently, Canada. Our northern neighbor is about to run a government surplus for the third year in a row, but still has a long way to go. The slide in the Canadian dollar from US$0.87 in 1991 to US$0.67 in February 1999 has kept Canada reasonably competitive against America, which takes more than 80 percent of her exports, and has blunted her zeal for restructuring and deregulation. Manufacturing productivity in

Canada has risen at less than half the U.S. rate since 1990 and is now only about 70 percent of the American level.

Restructuring has lagged on the Continent of Europe because of the long and cherished history of social safety nets. German worker welfare programs—enacted over a century ago by Bismarck as he sought to fend off socialists, and which insured workers against accidents, sickness, and old age—became the models throughout Europe.

France, Italy, and other Western European countries also deliberately put primary emphasis on splitting the economic pie more equally, even though many of their leaders realize that in so doing, they will not see the pie grow as rapidly as under the Anglo-Saxon approach. New leftist governments are committed to the approach. *The Wall Street Journal* quoted Gerhard Schroeder, the new German Chancellor, as declaring, "We will not throw the tested German model overboard only because of a few idealogues."

NO CHOICE

Still, the Continental countries know that they must restructure to compete globally. Table 4–1 reveals that productivity is much lower on the Continent than in the United States. In 1997, the value added per hour worked in Germany was only 81.4 percent of the U.S. level, and after accounting for longer vacations and other factors that reduce German working hours, it dropped to 63.1 percent. Of course, lower productivity can be offset with lower compensation to hold down unit labor costs (a ratio of the two), but in northern European countries, wages and especially benefits are much higher than in the United States.

Recently, however, Germany has begun to show serious interest in restructuring, as high costs have taken their toll on employment. In order to prevent further production shifts elsewhere, including across the Czech border, where labor costs are a fraction of those in Germany, labor unions have become much more accommodative. Real average hourly earnings are actually falling. The far-left Finance Minister, Oskar Lafontaine, has been dismissed. Italy lifted her ban on temporary help firms and American companies wasted no time in marching through the open door. The euro will further encourage restructuring by making it easier to

T A B L E 4–1

Relative Productivity Levels in Manufacturing (1997)

U.S. = 100	Value Added Per Hour Worked	Value Added Per Employee
U.S.	100.0	100.0
Japan	72.8	74.8
Germany	81.4	63.1
France	85.1	70.1
U.K.	69.7	59.9
Canada	69.6	68.4

Source: Organisation for Economic Co-operation and Development and U.S. Bureau of Labor Statistics

move production to the most cost-effective sites within Europe without worrying about currency risks.

EVEN IN JAPAN

Of developed lands, Japan has the biggest problem with restructuring, given the tradition of lifetime employment in large firms and her slow process of making decisions by consensus. As a result, she is even further behind the European Continent in the process. Nevertheless, some movement is starting, especially in financial services.

Lingering financial fallout from the bursting of the 1980s' bubble economy is being augmented by new economic and financial difficulties generated elsewhere in Asia and renewed domestic recession. Still, the Japanese government, aided and abetted by intense pressure from foreign investors and governments, seems committed to proceed with the "Big Bang" deregulation of financial markets. Stock brokerage commissions are being decontrolled. Accounting standards and capital requirements are scheduled to rise to Western standards. And not only are banks permitted to own brokerages and other financial services, but foreigners are as well—and they are buying Japanese financial firms.

By cutting costs and promoting productivity growth, restructuring is clearly deflationary, not only directly but also by pressuring foreign and domestic competitors to follow suit. Cost-cutting is manifest, but the productivity fruits of restructuring have not been apparent until recently in U.S. government statistics, which were probably understated.

5

CHAPTER

High Tech Is Deflationary

Without question, high tech spending is mushrooming, especially in the United States, where it has risen from 0.2 percent of GDP in the first quarter of 1959 to 8.1 percent in the fourth quarter of 1998. As a result, graphically (Figure 5–1), it looks like high tech spending has exploded while GDP has hardly grown. Moreover, this measure vastly understates the size of high tech, because it doesn't include such things as semiconductors in cars, watches, and washing machines, or gene-spliced seeds, and the tons of software that isn't, like hardware, counted as business investment. The Commerce Department estimates that computers and telecommunications alone have accounted for one-fourth of American economic growth in the past five years, and now equals one-third of capital spending.

With few businesses able to raise prices, many are hoping to increase or at least maintain profit margins with more technology. This often involves research and development spending, which is scheduled to rise 9.3 percent in 1999, much faster than corporate sales. As usual, high tech industries such as computers, semiconductors, drugs, and telecommunications will be the big R&D spenders. Microsoft normally spends 16 percent of revenue on R&D, and start-up Internet-related firms may spend 80 percent.

Despite its awe-inspiring accomplishments, high tech is nothing new. The industries involved today are, but the phenomenon isn't. It's the same play with a different cast of characters. Today's high tech is just the latest development in an evolutionary chain that

FIGURE 5–1

Real high-tech* GDP and real total GDP, 1959–1998

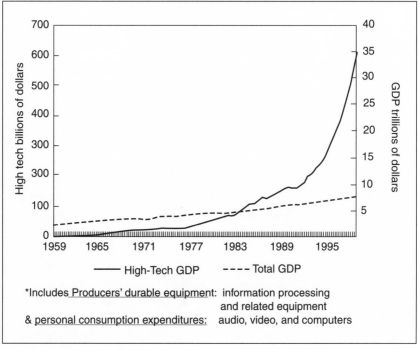

— High-Tech GDP   ---- Total GDP

*Includes Producers' durable equipment: information processing
and related equipment
& personal consumption expenditures: audio, video, and computers

Source: U.S. Bureau of Economic Analysis

goes back to the beginning of the American Industrial Revolution after the Civil War (see Chapters 15 and 16). A PC may keep your checkbooks and calendar straight, allow you to trade stocks on line, or even from a wireless phone, let you tap into the Internet, and help you keep in touch with the kids via e-mail, but think about the transformations that occurred over a hundred years ago in industries like steel, chemicals, paper, and textiles. Think about the glass blowers that you've seen in historical exhibits, taking 10 or 15 minutes to blow a bottle. And then think of the bottle machines that replaced them, spewing out glassware faster than they could be counted. And think about the productivity advances when horse-drawn reapers replaced men with scythes, or when tractors replaced horses, for that matter. In telecommunications, measure the recent dazzling developments against the revolution of the tele-graph, first developed by portrait painter Samuel F. B. Morse in 1838. Once they strung the wires across the continent, it wiped out the Pony Express, virtually overnight.

HIGH TECH ENHANCES PRODUCTIVITY

This historical perspective, however, doesn't detract from the con-tribution of today's high tech to cost-cutting and productivity en-hancement. Legions of executives now compose their own correspondence and many of their reports by themselves on com-puters. Add voice mail to that and you eliminate the cost of a lot of secretaries and receptionists. There are also those employees who, with computers and modems, can do their jobs at home, thus sav-ing themselves the cost of commuting and their employers the cost of office space. The International Telecommuting Association estimates that 11.1 million people were telecommuters in 1997, triple the 1990 number. And what about the entrepreneurs who want to start their own businesses? The computer lets them be their own accountants, inventory managers, marketing managers, researchers, and developers, all in one. For restructuring-oriented CEOs and efficiency-conscious self-employed businesspeople, computers are a boon to lowering costs and increasing productiv-ity. Similarly, telecommunication advances have eliminated the need for much business travel and have made it possible to man-age global operations much more efficiently. Cost-cutting and pro-ductivity-enhancing characteristics are also dominant in other high tech areas like semiconductors, biotechnology, and the Internet.

Semiconductor-laden pocket calculators are now so cheap and prevalent that some school systems don't even insist that stu-dents memorize multiplication tables. In contrast, when I was in high school and college in the Dark Ages of the 1950s, we not only memorized multiplication tables, but also took a lot of time to gain proficiency with a slide rule. This story of how tough we used to have it never impressed my kids; "What's a slide rule, Daddy?" was their usual reply.

LOWER HIGH TECH PRICES

Besides improving the productivity of its users, high tech hardware and software are doing so with rapidly falling prices. In 1997, Intel reduced prices on its 166-megahertz Pentium/MMX chips by two-thirds, and last year slashed the prices of two Celeron chips used in cheap home computers by 40 percent or more. Advanced Micro Devices recently developed a chip that can replace Intel's Pentium II chips in portable computers at one-third the price. DRAMs, low-end semiconductor chips that provide memory for computers, dropped in price from around $20 a megabyte in late 1995 to $2 in 1998. The prices of computers have also been dropping. Notice in Figure 5–2 that all the price changes are negative, and they range from 4 to over 25 percent annual declines. For Christmas 1998 sales, retail prices averaged about $1,000, down

F I G U R E 5–2

U.S. implicit price deflator of computers, year-to-year percentage change (1985–1998)

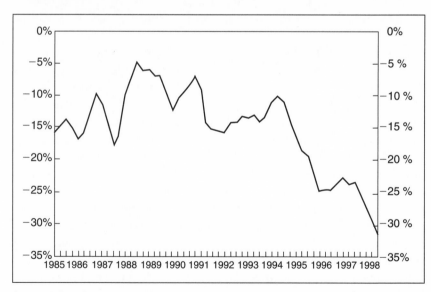

Source: U.S. Bureau of Economic Analysis

over 20 percent from a year earlier. With new chip technology, $400 machines are on the horizon, and the costs of related equipment is keeping pace. Hewlett-Packard is setting up a subsidiary to sell color ink-jet printers for less than $100. Dell recently announced a new workstation with two of the latest Intel microprocessors for about the same price as Hewlett-Packard and Compaq Computer models containing only one chip.

Consumers have taken to cheap PCs like my honeybees to their queen. At the end of last year, 50 percent of the nation's households owned a PC, a leap from 43 percent a year earlier. In their first year, sales of sub-$1,000 computers skyrocketed to account for about 40 percent of the market for retail PCs in the United States. Sub-$600 PCs now command nearly one-fifth of retail sales. In February 1999, the average retail price was $947. The next step will be a gradual expansion of these computers into the corporate market. Many feared that the sub-$1,000 PC would replace sales of higher-priced machines while not attracting new buyers, but surveys show that most cheap PCs were sold to first-time buyers. Total retail unit sales jumped 41 percent in December 1998 from December 1997 as prices fell 20 percent. Worldwide, PC shipments rose 18 percent in 1998's fourth quarter from the same period in 1997.

The ultimate low price for a PC, zero, may be close at hand. Free-PC.com, a new company, plans to give people free computers if they provide personal data about themselves and agree to be exposed to Internet advertising. The firm received 1.2 million requests for the first 10,000 free PCs. This would mimic cell phones that are given free or sold at nominal prices to those who sign up for cellular services. None of this is new, however; over a century ago, John D. Rockefeller's Standard Oil gave away kerosene lamps to encourage people to buy the fuel.

Today each of us carries a load of semiconductors around because the products they're embedded in are so cheap. Inexpensive quartz watches keep better time than the finest Swiss mechanical watch. Anyone who pays more than $50 for a watch today is paying for eyewash. I'm wearing an old mechanical Omega Seamaster that cost many times that, but only because my brother, Bruce, got it for me in Europe 40 years ago. Think of its price in today's dollars.

Twenty years ago, few cars had anything electronic in them, including clocks, which never worked anyway—at least none of mine did. Now vehicles overflow with chips that govern engine ignition, run clocks, automatically time head lights after you leave the car, adjust brakes, and more. The growth in auto electronics will mushroom. Soon you'll be able to replace your car radio with a PC, complete with voice recognition so you can retrieve e-mail and make cell phone calls with both hands on the wheel. Global positioning equipment for cars is in the trial stage. Microchips have gotten so cheap that they now are used to shift gears smoothly in the Zappy, Stealth, Zip, and other battery-powered scooters that allow people to zip through traffic jams with ease. And some brave souls foresee computer-regulated highways that will eliminate traffic jams.

EVEN FASTER DEVELOPMENT AHEAD

The Semiconductor Industry Association reports that, since 1994, new chip generation development time has dropped from two to three years. By 2012, the SIA panel of experts expects producers to put 1.4 billion transistors on a chip the size of your thumb, operating at a speed of 2,700 megahertz. Do those numbers mean anything to you? Not to this college physics major, but comparisons do. Intel's current Pentium II chip has a mere 7.5 million transistors and runs at only 300 megahertz. Also, memory chips in 2012 are slated to hold 275 billion bits of data compared with 16 million today. Let's hope that the quality of the data stored increases proportionately. The investment to produce these advanced chips will be huge, but if history is any guide, so too will be the returns.

Semiconductors and PCs will be far from alone in seeing technological leaps cut prices and open new markets in the deflationary years ahead. Biotechnology is speeding up the development of new pharmaceuticals to the point that some see half of all new FDA-approved drugs coming from biotech firms in five years. I love pork, and we'll probably eat a lot more when genetically altered pigs fed genetically altered corn produce nearly fat-free meat. Cotton production promises to expand as costs are cut by genetically rearranged plants that are far less succulent to boll weevils.

Monsanto made a double contribution to expanding soybean production. First, the firm developed Roundup, a highly effective herbicide, and then developed Roundup Ready soybeans that are genetically changed to tolerate the weed killer. Monsanto is also touting Roundup Ready corn, as well as corn and cotton that are genetically altered to resist insects. Furthermore, the firm is beginning to combine herbicide and insect resistance in the same corn plant. As a gardener, I don't feel one bit sorry for the weeds or insects—as long as they aren't my honeybees.

Despite the fears of the ignorant, genetic engineering doesn't create creatures from the black lagoon. It simply speeds and significantly lowers the cost of what's been done since time immemorial—selective breeding. For example, new cloning techniques for calves will drastically cut the costs of certain human medicines by slashing two years off the time it takes to create a herd of cattle that produces them.

THE TRIPLE WHAMMY

Anything that increases the productivity of its buyer as its own prices fall dramatically is bound to expand its sales volume like crazy as it increases its usage in existing markets and opens new ones. The combined effect is to depress prices economy-wide, as the high tech sector, with its rapidly declining prices, becomes a sharply rising share of total economy activity, and as high tech products' productivity-enhancing applications reduce prices elsewhere.

High tech has another deflationary effect by forcing down prices of competing older technologies and replacing those that lack strong productivity growth potential. Recently, long distance telephone companies have been trumpeting household rates of 10 cents or even 5 cents per minute for calls anywhere in the country at any time. Sure, deregulation has something to do with this (see Chapter 7), but so too does competition from new wireless services. Last year, AT&T offered a service that eliminated expensive roaming charges for cell phones and charges 11 to 15 cents for calls anywhere in the country with no extra charge for long distance. Bell Atlantic countered with a $39.99 monthly package for 60 minutes of cell phone time, including long distance, anywhere in its area, which extends from New England to the Carolinas. Teligent is introducing a wireless service for smaller businesses aimed at replacing Baby Bell local networks. The firm expects their wireless service to slash as much as 30 percent from local, long distance, and Internet bills. Among the losers are those that own those banks of pay phones in airports. Wireless phones may be an important development for the rest of the world as well. Indeed, some emerging countries that lack significant hard-wired phone services may jump directly to wireless systems.

At the same time, high tech is threatening futures exchanges like the Chicago Mercantile Exchange, where my son Steve works in the euro-dollar area. These rely on the "open-outcry" system, which, to the untrained eye and ear, seems chaotic, with huge numbers of brokers and clerks screaming and frantically waving their arms in the process of executing trades. In early 1998, the computer-based German-Swiss exchange managed to steal the important German government bond futures contract from the open-outcry pit in London. Since then, all-electronic trading has just about eliminated open-outcry systems in Europe and is threatening American exchanges. The latter are automating some of their functions to combat the lower-cost alternatives, but the declining prices of open-outcry exchange seats suggest that their days may be limited. I wonder what they'll do with those football-field–sized trading rooms and all the colorful jackets now worn by commodity brokers? At the same time, the new International Securities Exchange plans to be the first electronic options exchange in the United States and challenge the dominant Chicago Board Options Exchange by cutting trading fees by 50 percent.

Once more, this is nothing new. In the late 1800s, railroads, which could be built almost anywhere, replaced riverboats and canals, which obviously have geographic confines. Power looms sent Silas Marner and other hand weavers looking for new occupations. In the 1920s, cars and trucks supplanted horses and wagons. Sure, better breeding and advanced medical care can improve the productivity of horses somewhat, but the animals still eat the same amount and can only move so fast.

HIGH TECH ISN'T ALWAYS THE ANSWER

When I started in economic forecasting in the early 1960s, it was routine for each economist to have two research assistants who looked up data in books and government releases and then drew charts by hand. Then it was off to the art department to get the charts prepared for presentations. Each economist also needed a secretary to type reports and retype each draft. At today's prices, two research assistants and a secretary would cost about $120,000, including fringes. Add in about $20,000 for art work and you've got $140,000 in total back-up costs.

Today, one research assistant with a PC and a modem suffices to download data and draw graphs, and the economist and research assistant can prepare the reports without a secretary. With some help from a desktop publisher, they can turn out finished reports that could only have been done by a professional printer 35 years ago—and at a back-up cost of less than $70,000.

I've witnessed, then, tremendous productivity improvements in the business-economist business in the last three and a half decades. But how about the quality of the economic forecasts we turn out? I honestly don't believe that we're able to make better forecasts now than 35 years ago. Much more data is available, but we're drowning in it. The more data you have and the easier it is to manipulate, the less valuable it becomes. Sifting through it and analyzing it can absorb so much time that if you're not careful, you have no time left to sit back, reflect, and come up with the significant insights that turn information into knowledge. As Francis Bacon wisely said, "knowledge is power."

When you're consumed with number crunching, it's also hard to make time to pursue soft data, the anecdotes that can be much more valuable because they're not yet fully understood and exploited. And don't forget that in the process of adjusting to rapid technological change, there is a lot of churning and inefficiency as people learn how to use technology that will soon be out of date, and then have to learn its successor and its successor's successor.

While I'm on the subject of how high tech may cut costs but not necessarily improve the quality of output, think about voice mail. How much of the cost savings are really just being pushed back on the caller, who spends five minutes and several disconnected attempts before getting a real live person on the line? Is it cost effective for a CEO to type a thank you note on his PC rather than tell a crackerjack secretary to compose a letter thanking Bill and his wife for a lovely evening? And are the savings you get by buying things by phone worth the telemarketing calls that always come when you're about to sit down for a nice dinner with your family?

Furthermore, high tech may not deliver the precision it suggests. With the old analog bathroom scales, you had to estimate where the needle came to rest. Our new digital model gives a precise number. The only problem is, the number can vary 2 or 3 pounds in successive steps on the scale. I always assume the lowest number is correct, of course.

And here's another example. I drive a 10-year-old Lincoln Town Car that our kids call "the barge" and whose advanced age embarrasses my wife. Anyway, it has an electronic message center, state-of-the-art when it was built. It records the average speed, miles to a preset destination, elapsed miles, fuel economy, and miles to empty, but in the last case, inaccurately. Ever notice that your gas gauge drops toward empty with the speed of light once it reaches one-quarter full, even faster when there's no gas station for miles? That's because it's attached to a float that drops as the tank empties, and the tank's walls taper in toward the bottom. Once the gas drops below one-quarter, the float drops much faster per gallon used. Well, despite the deceiving accuracy of my digital miles-to-empty readout, it's run by the same old float. I've coasted into more than one gas station, running on fumes, and sweating profusely.

Some high technologies have developed faster than users' ability to put them into perspective. Still, high tech is a substantial promoter of deflation. So, too, is the Internet, as you'll see in Chapter 6.

6

CHAPTER

The Internet and Mass Distribution

Since I finished writing *Deflation* a little over a year ago, the Internet has simply exploded. Few other words describe its phenomenal growth and its ability to promote productivity, slash costs, and compress sellers' margins—all deflationary processes.

Compaq is now bypassing dealers and selling personal computers directly to smaller businesses using the Internet and telephone sales. This strategy angers dealers, but is necessary to compete with direct seller Dell and that firm's 10 to 15 percent cost advantage and plans to sell 30,000 other electronic products on the Web. Intel now books $1 billion per month, about half its revenues, on the Internet, where Cisco Systems does 64 percent of its orders for computer networking gear. Hewlett-Packard also sells directly to consumers via the Internet.

Internet auctioneers sell computer parts, jewelry, Beanie Babies, and movie memorabilia. Almost anyone can offer goods through eBay, which lists over 1.8 million items for sale daily. Bookseller Amazon.com tripled its sales in the last quarter of 1998 from a year earlier, to $250 million, and added one million new customers in the holiday season. Amazon.com became the nation's fifth largest bookseller in four years. Overall holiday season online sales tripled, totaling about $13 billion for all of 1998. This is still tiny compared to $2.7 trillion in retail sales last year, but it won't remain so if recent growth rates continue. Not just booksellers but also books are being affected by electronics. The Encyclopaedia Britannica tried an on-line edition for $120 but it bombed. Then it turned to an $89.95 CD-ROM with the same contents as its $1,600 multi-volume set.

Catalog retailers as well as stores are beginning to be squeezed. Victoria's Secret advertised heavily its live fashion show on the Web, in newspapers and on TV during the January 1999 Super Bowl. More than a million people, or five times the norm, visited the firm's web site, and sales of the retailer's racy lingerie were triple the usual daily level. Sears plans to sell 2,000 appliances online. There are even Web sites to locate police speed traps.

Like telephone sales, Internet retailing eliminates the need for stores, large inventories, and sales staff—and sales taxes. It's even more efficient than telemarketing, because phone salespeople are unnecessary, as is the marketing literature, when you can sell the merchandise on the screen.

AT HOME ON THE NET

Shopping for a new home on the Web is also accelerating. Real estate firms now feature pictures and descriptions of every room in houses on the market, so if the bathroom's too small or you don't like the arrangement of the kitchen, you never have to bother to actually see it. Some programs even allow you to redecorate your prospective new house by virtual images. The many online real estate directories that are springing up around the Web feature listings in most major U.S. cities, and, surprisingly, in a lot of small ones. The most comprehensive directory of the National Association of Realtors includes more than a million listings. Some listings include maps showing the house's proximity to schools, shopping, banks, and other services. A few provide calculators that let you compare mortgages, the cost of living, and salaries in different cities, as well as typical moving expenses and insurance premiums. With a little work, you could find the lowest-priced house and the lowest mortgage rate in a city with the lowest cost of living. You can even bypass realtors and their fees completely by perusing lists of houses for sale by owners only.

Services as well as goods are being delivered more cheaply via the Internet. Online stock brokers now account for about a quarter of individuals' business and charge as little as $5 per trade. About 1 percent of all U.S. airline tickets, or more than 4 million a year, are sold through the Internet, cutting out travel agents as well as airline employees. The Commerce Department sees Internet bookings in the travel industry rising to $8 billion in 2000, up eight-fold from 1997. Complicated life insurance policies require a skilled agent, but straightforward term life insurance is readily available at low cost online. Berkshire Hathaway Insurance Co. will offer annuities via the Internet. Political candidates are also available online. To symbolize the power of the Internet, Steve Forbes chose that medium to announce and run his 2000 Presidential campaign.

Investment banking is going online, with costly functions like presentations to prospective investors and distribution of research reports delivered via the Web. This may threaten the traditional 7 percent fee of the money raised in initial public offerings of stocks, because new firms like W.R. Hambrecht & Co. charge 3 to 5 percent, and that company recently brought Ravenswood Winery public via the Internet. Just as electronic commodities exchanges are competing with open-outcry pits (see Chapter 5), online exchanges may challenge both. Already, low-cost electronic communications networks (ECNs), which function as quasi-stock exchanges and broker-dealers, are taking 20 percent of the business away from NASDAQ. They are also invading the New York Stock Exchange, which may join forces or set up its own electronic trading system. Similarly, mortgage banking expenses are being slashed through use of the Internet. New services allow home buyers to close mortgages online (over $4 billion in mortgages were closed online in 1998); by speeding up the evaluation of a borrower's creditworthiness, this forces the industry to compete on prices and services. The Mortgage Bankers Association of America estimates that automated underwriting will save borrowers $2 billion a year in closing costs and cut annual interest payments $100 million by moving some borrowers up from sub-prime status.

BRICKLESS BANKING

The banking industry is also jumping into the Internet with both feet and finding the cost savings invigorating. It typically costs $0.90 to $2 every time a customer does a transaction with a bank teller, about $0.40 at an ATM, but only around a nickel on the Internet. Bill paying on the Internet obviously saves time and costs, and electronic check processing is estimated to cost $0.50 (at most) compared to $3 per paper check. Major banks plan to quadruple their investment in the Internet. The industry predicts that 39 percent of corporate customers will use some form of Internet banking by 2000, and no wonder. The current average expense-to-revenue ratio for major U.S. banks is 60 percent. Direct banking produces ratios in the 35 to 40 percent range. Projections are that Internet banking could achieve something in the 15 to 20 percent range.

Low costs allow Net banks to pay attractive interest rates of 3 percent on checking accounts. Business savvy TV preacher Pat Robertson has noticed the opportunity and is helping the Bank of Scotland to set up a U.S. bank that will only operate by phone on the Internet.

Retailers like Nordstrom are taking advantage of a 1996 liberalization of S&L requirements to set up Internet facilities to offer credit cards, home equity loans, and money market checking accounts. Hillenbrand Industries established an S&L to set up bank trusts to pay for its burial caskets. (I love the name of the firm's thrift unit: Forethought.) Obviously, these businesses are competing with conventional banks and S&Ls at a fraction of their costs.

Other services are going to the Internet, including privately-owned University of Phoenix with 6,000 of its 43,000 students online, and a planned law school. Another institution, Concord University School of Law, projects tuition for its four-year online program at $17,000 compared with $23,900 for a single year plus $12,000 for room and board at Harvard Law School. Jones International University sells courses for profit and has become the first online-only school to be accredited to grant college degrees. It uses professors from such prestigious institutions as Stanford and Columbia to design the courses, but its faculty is adjunct professors who lead e-mail discussions and grade exams.

Plans are also afoot to use the Internet for missions ranging from monitoring appliances and calling for repair help to signaling when vending machines need refilling. Furthermore, the Internet cuts recruiting costs to less than $1,000 per hire, down from several thousand dollars, according to the Unisys Corp., which uses its Web site extensively to post jobs. And a recent survey indicates that two-thirds of executives believe that e-mail has cut back on face-to-face business meetings. At the same time, freelancers are using the

Internet to find assignments; job seekers not only look for new jobs but also see if they're adequately compensated. In addition, the Internet is responsible for much of the growth in telecommuting. In 1997, 3.6 million were employed at home, up from 1.9 million in 1991.

COMPARISON SHOPPING

Internet comparison shopping requires much less time and gasoline than physical shopping, and is decimating dealer markups. In the auto arena, Chrysler was the first auto maker to launch its own Web site in 1995 and, since then, just about every automaker has joined it. General Motors' online service, GMBuyPower, lets consumers compare prices on GM and rival vehicles, search dealer inventories, and get a dealer's best price. If you don't want to take the time to hit the manufacturers' sites, you can one-stop shop at independent services, such as Autobytel.com or Microsoft's CarPoint, that charge dealers a fee to represent them, market their products and prices, and refer the potential customer directly to the dealer. The customer is charged nothing extra for the service, and the only time he goes to the dealership is to pick up the car and pay for it. The car buying services also offer vehicle financing and insurance and even e-mail notices of manufacturers' recalls and when it's time for an oil change. The pressure on conventional dealers has gotten so great that 25 of them in the Northwest threatened to boycott Chrysler cars because an Internet dealer in Kellogg, Idaho, was underselling them. He eliminates not only sales commissions but advertising costs as well. Another dealer noted that a full-page ad in a Sunday newspaper costs $3,000, more than his monthly Internet outlay.

Internet competition is threatening many established forms of distribution on Wall Street and elsewhere. Traditional firms are reacting nervously. They don't want to antagonize existing sales forces, but they know that selling online can cut costs up to 15 percent by slashing sales commissions and paperwork and that, if they don't participate, online competitors will eat their lunch. Consequently, many are sticking a toe, but only a toe, in the water. Consumer products powerhouse Procter & Gamble is pushing retailers to establish Web sites that will extol P&G products and link to retailers' stores. Merrill Lynch is making its stock research available free online, at least temporarily, and finally has allowed its biggest customer to trade stocks on the Internet. My old firm doesn't want to alienate its high-paid but productive sales force by emulating discount and Internet broker Charles Schwab, but realizes that the new technology is transforming the investment scene. Morgan Stanley Dean Witter has put its research on the Web, and also is running a deep-discount Internet trading system side-by-side with its "full service" business that uses commissioned brokers. Note that the Internet has virtually eliminated the financial barriers to entry in the brokerage business by allowing anyone with a computer network to set up shop.

Business on the Internet is moving abroad. Online U.S. brokers are moving into Japan, Hong Kong, and the United Kingdom, but Americans at home still account for 80 percent of global electronic commerce. In Europe, phone calls are still expensive, language barriers exist, and e-commerce's close relative, the mail-order business, is only half as large per capita as in the United States. Still, the Organization for Economic Cooperation and Development estimates that electronic commerce will leap from $26 billion in 1997 to $1 trillion in 2005, and recent growth rates suggest that number is low.

E-MAIL AND CHEAP DATA

And don't forget what the Internet and e-mail can do to cut costs by transmitting data quicker and cheaper. In terms of communicating with his parents, our son Geoff, a product manager at Microsoft, doesn't know what a postage stamp looks like, but he's always available by e-mail and even sent us a picture of his new boat—paid for by exercising a few Microsoft stock options. For taxpayers with relatively simple tax returns, e-filing is quick and easy, and speeds up refunds.

Then there is the global use of the Internet, which, along with fax machines, has spread information that challenges the authority of government and business leaders. The Starr report on Clinton's sexual escapades got huge distribution via the Internet. But he's not alone. Stockholders can keep tabs on corporate CEOs by tracing their executive jet flight plans on the Web. The Internet also may be speeding economic reforms and deflation-enhancing market liberalization by letting people in closed economies know what's happening in other parts of the world. The Chinese government is concerned enough about the resulting challenges to its control that it has tried to limit Internet access.

Back in the States, the Internet arms patients with information about their diseases that allows them to talk shop with their physicians—and eliminates the MD's omniscience. Television long ago slashed the power of newspaper editors to shape public opinion; the Internet has virtually eliminated it, since users can browse through tens of thousands of pages to read the information they themselves choose. Some historians believe that press lord William Randolph Hearst had such control of American opinion in the late 1800s that he single-handedly turned the explosion of the Maine (from still unknown causes) into the Spanish-American War. With the Internet widely available, no one could do that today. Hopefully.

MASS DISTRIBUTION

At the same time that the Internet is promoting deflation by slashing costs and sellers' margins while promoting productivity, mass distribution to consumers is doing the same. Ever since the Great Atlantic & Pacific Tea Company introduced the idea of chain stores in 1859, the principles of mass marketing have been employed by enterprising U.S. retailers to cut costs and underprice their competitors. The best ideas were adapted and enhanced by the first department stores—Macy's, John Wanamaker, and Marshall Field; the first mail-order houses—Montgomery Ward and Sears & Roebuck; and the most successful early chain store—F.W. Woolworth's.

Today, the advantages of volume buying are being exploited to the hilt by such booming mega-retailers as Wal-Mart; Office Depot in office supplies; Bed, Bath and Beyond in home furnishings and equipment; Revco and CVS in drugs and sundries; Borders and Barnes & Noble in books; and Home Depot and Lowe's in the home improvement area. If you doubt the ability of these giants to sell at lower prices than their smaller competitors, ask the proprietor of any locally-owned drug or bookstore—if you can find one. Most have already fallen by the competitive wayside. And, unlike their immediate predecessor, the discounters, the new mass merchandisers aren't selling off-brands or cheaper models from known manufacturers. They stock top-of-the-line, name-brand merchandise. They are genuinely improving efficiency. Wal-Mart, for example, has a hub-and-spoke distribution system that puts distribution centers less than a day's truck drive away from stores.

EXHIBIT 1—THE AUTO INDUSTRY

One of the best examples of the deflationary effects of expanding mass distribution is the U.S. auto industry. It has a host of complex and deep-rooted problems, especially gigantic excess global capacity, as noted in Chapter 3. On top of all these woes, Detroit also faces a huge blow from the "Wal-Mart syndrome," the growing loss of control of its distribution system. About 25 percent of a vehicle's costs are in distribution—sales, transportation, and advertising. In today's world of retailing efficiency, that is unsustainably large. And it's on its way to being slashed.

Big, no haggle, service-oriented used-car superstores, like those run by CarMax Group (controlled by Circuit City Stores) and the AutoNation USA unit of Republic Industries, are growing. They are also buying new car dealerships and putting together huge chains that sell a wide variety of cars. Republic Industries now has 400 new-car dealer operations in the nation's 50 best markets.

Put all this together and you end up selling cars like refrigerators. Armed with prices and model information supplied by the Internet, a customer walks in the door, views all the competing models side by side, listens to the salesperson explain the features, checks the no-haggle prices, and then picks the color and options, arranges the financing, and is out the door in an hour. No longer will the customer have to drive from one dealer to another and be accosted by fast-talking salesmen in shiny suits who never seem able to give straight and consistent stories on the cars' specs or prices. Buying may get even easier. Republic Industries expects to sell $500 million worth of cars through the Internet in 1999.

In the final analysis, new retailing methods will make cars much more like commodities as fewer distributors carry a wider variety of competing models. That will increase the power of the retailers and reduce the control of auto manufacturers. I wonder if Detroit knows the implications of its actions when it helps mega-dealers buy up franchises? Those dealers may come to control such huge volumes of product that they can dictate price, features, and quality—much as Wal-Mart and Home Depot do now. AutoNation is even considering a house-brand car. What does that do to manufacturers' margins? Ever talk to a Wal-Mart supplier? He'll give you an earful of his love-hate relationship.

Are automakers worried about the superstores? They seem to be. Ford is buying dealerships and then combining them to compete. Toyota, Nissan, and Honda sued Republic Industries to slow its purchase of their dealerships. If the manufacturers are worried, small dealerships are justifiably terrified. The National Automobile Dealer Association puts profit per car sale at $77. That doesn't leave the average dealer much leeway to afford a fight with Republic Industries and other superstores' economies of scale. Many are simply too inefficient to compete.

Another example of the growing power of mega-retailers can be found in magazine distribution. Several years ago, the major supermarket chain Safeway ended the cozy relationship between magazine wholesalers and retailers by putting its business up for competitive bidding. Other large supermarket and drug store chains followed, and the number of independent distributors dropped from 180 in 1995 to about 60. Before the consolidation, retailers paid wholesalers 80 percent of the magazine's cover price; after consolidation, the price dropped to the 70–75 percent range. Because wholesalers still pay publishers 60 percent, they are being forced to either cut costs, merge, or exit the magazine distribution business.

As the volume of Internet sales and the number of mass distributors goes up, prices come down. The same can be said for deregulation, as discussed in Chapter 7.

7
CHAPTER

Global Deregulation

Deregulation is deflationary. It opens to the bracing winds of competition areas where prices were previously fixed, and, consequently, where producers had limited incentives to cut costs and promote productivity. The electric power industry is a clear case in point. Australia, a pioneer in electricity deregulation, saw prices collapse by 40 percent and today is home to the lowest electricity prices in the world. Furthermore, deregulation is nothing new. It started decades ago in the U.S. Federal and state resale price-maintenance laws, a carryover from the 1930s and designed to prevent deflation, were among the first to go. They allowed manufacturers to set minimum retail prices on their wares, but were widely circumvented by discounters who sold off-brand as well as different models of well-known products.

FINANCIAL SERVICES DEREGULATION

Financial services deregulation started with U.S. stock commission rates in the early 1970s. Brokers zealously believed in free enterprise, of course—with one tiny exception: in setting their own fees, which were controlled by the NY Stock Exchange and blessed by the Securities and Exchange Commission. These fees were set to cover the costs of 100-share trades, typical for the individual investors who dominated the market until the 1960s. However, the same commission levels spawned unconscionable profits when pension and endowment funds and other institutional investors started buying 10,000-share blocks.

On May Day 1975, however, all restrictions on commissions were removed and competition began to blow the leaves off that famous buttonwood tree under which the New York Stock Exchange was formed in 1792. By 1978, the cumulative decline in commissions reached almost 40 percent. In one sense, financial institutions were telling brokers that they didn't want to pay for many of those brokers' costs and services.

These sorts of cuts, which occurred before the advent of today's discount brokers, led to the rapid consolidation of the industry and the disappearance of many fine, old firms. Gone are such stalwarts as Reynolds, Loeb Rhodes, DuPont, Hornblower, and White Weld (where I worked until Merrill Lynch bought it in 1978), and literally all of the research boutiques that were only viable with high fixed-commission rates.

Brokers, banks, and insurers, like many other deregulated industries, have high fixed fees and low marginal costs, along with the leverage of size—a guaranteed formula for keen competition and consolidation under deregulation, especially in times of weak demand. All are keen to invade each other's territory and have already begun to do so. With the allowed increase to 25 percent from 10 percent of revenues that banks can realize from securities business, Fleet Bank bought Quick & Reilly, and Bankers Trust acquired Alex Brown. The Travelers Group insurance company was already in the brokerage business with Salomon Smith Barney; they then merged with Citicorp (as noted in Chapter 4), thereby combining all three financial services. Brokers long ago entered cash management, and as the Glass-Steagall banking law continues to fade, more mergers and competition will follow among financial institutions. The winners will be the low-cost producers with deep pockets and those that add the most value to their services. Undoubtedly, that's deflationary.

BANKS ARE HOT

Banks are also benefiting from the Riegle-Neal Interstate Banking and Branching Efficiency Act of 1994 (that's a mouthful!). The final stage of a quarter-century–long effort to relax geographical limits on banks, Riegle-Neal enables them to establish branches and buy other banks across the country. In 1975, no state allowed out-of-state bank holding companies to buy in-state banks, and only 14 states permitted statewide branching. Since then, regulations have gradually eased, and those states that were most active in removing geographical limits learned that bank efficiency improved greatly once branching restrictions were lifted. At the same time, loan losses and operating costs fell sharply, and the reduction in bank costs was largely passed along to bank borrowers in the form of lower loan rates. Previously, branching restrictions acted as a ceiling on the size of well-managed banks, preventing their expansion and retarding the normal industry evolution that caused less efficient firms to routinely lose ground to more efficient ones.

Studies show that the expansion of efficient banks promotes growth of state economies as well, by routing savings to the most productive users. Efficient banks also tend to help customers by providing them with more information about the profit potential of different businesses. They also do a better job of monitoring their borrowers to ensure that bank funds are properly used.

FLYING HIGH—AIRLINE DEREGULATION

U.S. truckers were deregulated in 1978, and trucking rates collapsed overnight as the need for empty back-hauls disappeared and non-union carriers mushroomed. The airline industry is deep into ongoing deregulation, especially in the foreign arena, and this is depressing prices in the process. The United States led the way with the Airline Deregulation Act of 1978. Previously, the Civil Aeronautics Board regulated airlines, controlling the number of airlines, the fares they charged, the routes that each was allowed to fly, and even the food they could serve. This didn't stop competition entirely, however. At one point, only sandwiches were allowed on the New York-Chicago run, so airlines tried to outdo each other with the number of steaks, chops, and lobsters they could pile between two slices of bread. But with deregulation, that's all history and so is the food, except for an occasional bag of peanuts and a can of soda.

According to a 1996 General Accounting Office report, prices adjusted for inflation dropped by 9 percent at small community airports, 10 percent at medium-sized airports, and 5 percent at large airports between 1979 and 1988 as market forces took over. Furthermore, service increased. In 1995, according to the Department of Transportation, 55 percent of passengers traveled in city-pair markets served by three or more carriers, up from 28 percent in 1979. New carriers, such as Southwest Airlines, have concentrated on select routes and achieved lower costs than larger carriers, forcing bigger airlines to follow suit. Overall, the number of flights available from airports serving large communities increased by 68 percent between 1978 and 1995.

Europe and Japan Follow

Full deregulation for European airlines went into effect April 1, 1997. Prior to deregulation, airfares in Europe averaged about twice the cost of flights of a comparable distance in the United States; it can cost as much to fly between two European cities as it does to fly from the United States to either of those two cities. Expect new airlines such as Air UK and Ryanair, with their aggressive marketing and pricing, to assist in bringing airfares down much further.

Until 1996, the Ministry of Transportation had full control over Japanese airfares, routes, and the number of air carriers. Now Japan has followed the U.S. lead and allowed airlines to start setting their own ticket prices. Before deregulation, a one-way ticket for Japan's most traveled air corridor cost 23,000 yen. Now, if one books the flight in advance and accepts all the conditions, the price is only 11,200 yen. The Ministry of Transportation has finally allowed additional airlines into the domestic market this year, to challenge high-cost carriers like Japan Airlines with lower rates and lower fares.

The international skies are opening as well. U.S. officials have negotiated pacts with Europe and Japan to allow more airlines to fly to more cities abroad. Foreign governments have dragged their heels for fear of being swamped by U.S. airlines, but the trend is clear. To date, bilateral pacts between the United States and 12 European countries allow carriers to sell tickets on each other's flights.

U.S. ELECTRICITY DEREGULATED

Electricity deregulation bills have already passed in many states, and Congress and the Administration have made proposals that would require unrestricted selling of electricity to customers early in the next decade. Big price declines will result. Commercial users, such as manufacturing plants and office buildings, already receive discounts of 25 percent or more after threatening to build their own power plants or move factories to lower-cost areas. Enron Corporation, a veteran of natural gas deregulation in the 1980s, expects more than half the U.S. power market will open to competition within four years and estimates that full deregulation will reduce consumer electricity bills by 30 to 40 percent, or $70–$80 billion, a year. Citizens for a Sound Economy, a Republican think-tank, predicts that deregulation will lead to a drop of at least 43 percent in consumers' electricity bills. That's significant because the electricity industry accounts for roughly 4 percent of GDP. Also, note that electric power and natural gas are merging into one huge $315 billion industry in which suppliers will deliver to customers the most cost-effective energy mix.

DEREGULATION OF JAPANESE FINANCIAL SERVICES

Financial turmoil and deregulation of the financial services industry in Japan is opening opportunities there for efficient U.S. brokers, banks, and insurers, as noted in Chapter 4. This clearly pressures Japanese institutions to restructure and cut costs. Merrill Lynch entered the retail brokerage business in Japan by hiring former employees of Yamaichi Securities and buying attractive branch offices of the defunct firm. Although foreign firms used to be suspect, the Japanese Ministry of Finance now welcomes competition to help revive Japan's markets. Already, foreign investment banking firms have emerged as key players in resolving difficult problems such as disposing of bad loans and closing weak financial institutions smoothly. They are among the most active in buying up bank loans to resell as securities. Also, some U.S. banks have seen their retail banking business skyrocket as wealthy Japanese flock to open foreign-currency accounts and pull their deposits from ailing Japanese banks—all at lower costs than offered by clubby Japanese financial institutions.

TELECOMMUNICATION DEREGULATION IN GERMANY —A TALE OF TWO COMPANIES

Telecommunication deregulation in Europe is forcing former state monopolies to restructure or lose out to American firms. Germany's

Deutsche Telekom is a big loser. After only one year of deregulation, 51 new competitors have taken away a third of Telekom's long distance business, and prices have fallen nearly 90 percent from 1997 levels. This sounds like a lot, but I'm not surprised. Ever make a call from Germany to the United States in the old days and wonder if you'd bought the whole company, not just 10 minutes of phonetime? Telekom also faces local service competition.

In contrast, Germany's deregulated Deutsche Post has shaped up to the point that it is making life miserable for that paragon of efficiency, United Parcel Service. European governments have allowed their postal services to compete with the private sector, and compete they have. They've brought in private-sector leaders, sold stock to the public, invested in modernization equipment, and cut costs. Deutsche Post slashed 130,000 of 380,000 jobs, and increased the percentage of first class domestic letters that were delivered overnight from 60 percent to more than 95 percent. Like other deregulated European postal services, Deutsche Post has invested in other international courier, private mail, and parcel delivery businesses.

UPS has taken it on the chin in Germany from Deutsche Post; it's reported that revenue per package fell at least 30 percent between 1995 and 1998. Of course, the German postal service hasn't been hurt by the fact that it charges 66 cents for a first-class stamp, twice the United States level.

Deregulation goes hand-in-hand with two other deflationary forces, global sourcing and the conversion of command economies to market economies, as we explain in Chapter 8.

8

CHAPTER

Global Sourcing and New Market Economies

In today's world, technology and capital are relatively free to search the globe for the most cost-effective sites for the production of goods and services (see Chapter 19 for detailed discussion). So, as U.S. corporations restructure, they cut costs by moving production facilities out of the United States to take advantage of cheap labor, cheap expertise, cheap real estate, and cheap support services. What might once have been a difficult move is now easier because of the waning strength of U.S. labor unions (Figure 3–1). And not only are corporations manufacturing goods in other countries (particularly developing countries), they're also providing services there and exporting them back to the United States—everything from computer programming and airline revenue accounting to hospital record and insurance claim processing.

SOFTWARE IN INDIA

IBM, Texas Instruments, Apple, Microsoft, and John Deere are among more than 100 of America's top 500 firms that find India to be a great place to produce computer software. That's no accident or surprise, given the support from the Indian government and the low labor costs. Programmers there are paid less than a quarter of the American rate. Indian software exports are expected to grow from 3.4 percent of the worldwide software outsourcing business in 1995 to 6.1 percent in 1999.

NORTH AMERICA'S FASTEST GROWING REGION

Closer to home, the border territory of Northern Mexico has attracted many, many U.S. firms with its cheap labor pool, even after considering the area's much lower productivity levels. From deep in Mexico's heartland, hundreds of thousands of workers stream northward every year to seek work for wages that are attractive to them but low by U.S. standards. Foreign-owned assembly plants, or *maquiladoras*, number close to 1,500 in the border area, a 130-mile wide strip that may be North America's fastest growing region. Investment is not limited to U.S. companies: Sony, Samsung, Matsushita, and others have made Tijuana the TV manufacturing capital of the world, turning out 14 million units per year. Before the North American Free Trade Agreement among Mexico, the United States and Canada commenced in 1994, Mexico's auto parts business barely existed. Since then, auto companies have invested $4 billion and plan to spend another $10 billion in the next two years to make Mexico a major supplier of automotive glass, pistons, transmissions, axles, and engine blocks.

Maquiladora workers earn an average of $5 to $7 a day plus benefits (down from about $9 a day before the 1994 peso devaluation). Including rent and administrative expenses, it costs just $4 an hour per worker to run a plant in Tijuana, compared with $18 to $25 in San Diego. The number of maquiladoras, their employees, and their exports have been on the upswing since 1992, and more of the same is in prospect. Indeed, these facilities employed close to 1 million people last year. Volkswagen's new Beetle is made exclusively in Mexico, where production workers labor 42 hours a week at $13.50 per day. That's about the hourly wage of U.S. autoworkers. In Germany, they are paid even more than in the United States and work only 28 hours a week, so overhead costs are spread over many fewer hours. Elsewhere in Mexico, GM is investing heavily in auto component and subassembly facilities. This, in turn, is encouraging GM's suppliers to build parts-producing plants close by.

At the same time, U.S. services are increasingly being outsourced to Mexico. The Mexican side of the U.S. border has become a beehive of activity for credit card and check processing. In data processing, Mexico, where data workers earn less than $70 per week, is overtaking English-speaking competitors such as Ireland and India.

Among the traditional lands of low labor costs, those in Asia have become even cheaper sites of production in dollar terms because of the currency collapse in 1997–1998. Despite much lower levels of productivity in these countries, the gap between their unit costs and those in the United States has been great enough to attract U.S. industry, and the gap is obviously widening. By 2005, East Asia, including China, is predicted to command 20 percent of global manufacturing production, compared to 11 percent in 1995, while the manufacturing share of industrial countries continues to erode.

Even within the United States, corporations are moving manufacturing and service production out of the expensive Northeast to the South and Midwest, where labor and overhead costs are cheaper. Salomon Brothers, for example, moved its back office to Tampa, Florida, some years back, and Citicorp has its credit card operations in Sioux Falls, South Dakota. In high-cost New Jersey, where our firm is located, the manufacturing payroll employment index has dropped 39 percent since January 1981, whereas in the U.S. overall, the decline has been only about 8 percent (Figure 8–1). Construction payrolls are down 18 percent since their 1988 peak in the Garden State, while the national total has rebounded to new highs.

NEW MARKET ECONOMIES

Outsourcing has also increased among American companies because there are now many more countries from which to import goods and services. Political developments have created blossoming market economies, some in what might seem the most unlikely places. The break-up of the former Soviet Union in the late 1980s has had a huge impact on emerging markets, allowing many Eastern European countries to take off as exporters of a variety of products including textiles, petroleum, electronic equipment, and cars. India, haltingly to be sure, is moving toward free markets, pushed by global competition and the demise of her socialist idol, the Soviet Union.

China may still be communist politically, but the old command economy of Maoist days is giving way to unbridled, buccaneer capitalism. Recently, in a maneuver that only the Chinese can see as in sync with communism, Beijing announced that the number of government ministries will be slashed from 40 to 29. And—get this—

FIGURE 8-1

U.S. and New Jersey manufacturing payroll employment, 1981–1999

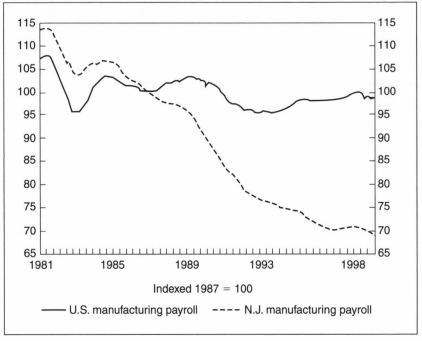

Indexed 1987 = 100

——— U.S. manufacturing payroll   ---- N.J. manufacturing payroll

Source: U.S. Bureau of Labor Statistics

some of the phased-out entities will be converted to free market enterprises that will borrow in capital markets and list their stocks on foreign exchanges. This category is likely to include petroleum and petrochemicals, fertilizer and chemicals, defense industries, textiles, telephones, and high tech industries. Furthermore, China is about to formally recognize family-owned businesses as an "important part of the socialist, market economy," according to *The Wall Street Journal*.

PRODUCTION DOWN, BUT EXPORTS UP

Already exports from these developing countries are leaping as they follow the trail blazed by Japan and the Asian Tigers. It works in a circle: a developing nation concentrates on the production of exports, which earn foreign exchange, which in turn is used to import the technology and capital equipment needed to increase exports. What's fascinating is that in many countries, industrial production is shrinking at the same time that exports are increasing. In the Czech Republic, industrial production fell by 24 percent from 1990 to 1996, but exports in dollar terms rose by 146 percent in 1991–1996 years. Russia suffered a 42 percent fall in industrial production between 1992 and 1996 while exports jumped 91 percent, if you can believe Russian numbers. Latvian output dropped 47 percent in the same years, but that didn't stop exports from exploding by 63 percent.

Furthermore, the aims of these new market economies fit hand-in-glove with foreign producers looking for cost-effective production sites, especially in Eastern Europe, where levels of education are much higher than in Asian and Latin American developing countries. Some, like Poland, are quite open to foreign capital—and former East Germany is the most open of all. Others, such as India, remain suspicious of foreign ownership.

Note that market economies are also being enlarged in countries that were never under communist domination. The privatization of Latin American mines, energy, telecommunications, and railroads are cases in point. So, too, are privatizations in Western Europe, Japan, and Canada. The results are more efficiency and more supply.

AUTOS AND OIL

Automobile industry production is predicted to almost double in Central and Eastern European countries in the next five years, a prime example of how the process of global sourcing will continue. The Economist Intelligence Unit forecasts car output in Central/Eastern Europe to rise from 1.89 million in 1996 to 3.67 million in 2001, almost a doubling. Exports will become increasingly important because local demand is expected to grow by only 40 percent in the same time period. Belarus, the Czech Republic, Hungary, Poland, Romania, Russia, Slovakia, Slovenia, Ukraine, and Yugoslavia are all involved in autos, and Poland, the powerhouse of the Central European vehicle manufacturing sector, is predicted to single-handedly increase output from 439,000 cars in 1996 to 1.09 million in 2001. All of this only enlarges the global glut in vehicle production.

Crude oil is another area that these new market economies are opening to foreign capital and expertise to promote growth. Oil-rich countries in the former Soviet empire, such as Turkmenistan, are bringing in companies from around the globe to help in prospecting, extracting, and pipeline building. Even Russia is opening a bit to foreign assistance in developing oil and gas, one of her few big foreign exchange earners.

As these countries continue to send their products out into the world, the question is, who's going to buy them? Without a net increase in demand, they'll simply add to the already deflationary global glut, and the U.S., the buyer of first and last resort, may be less likely to absorb the world's excess production of goods and services than in recent years (see Chapter 13). This is likely despite the flood of cheap U.S. imports that will be stimulated by a strong dollar, as you'll see in Chapter 9.

9

CHAPTER

The Strengthening Dollar

A strong dollar has distinctly deflationary effects on the U.S. As the buck rises, foreigners can reduce the prices of their exports to America in dollars and still receive the same number of yen, D-marks, or baht. This, in turn, encourages U.S. imports, to the detriment of domestic producers of competing goods and services. They are forced to cut prices or lose market shares. In either case, the response of domestic competitors to more imports at lower prices is deflationary.

A STRONG DOLLAR IS DEFLATIONARY

A robust greenback depresses domestic production of services as well as goods even though lots of U.S. services lack import competition. It's hard to import a haircut, and with my lack of thatch it's irrelevant, but many services do compete with imports. As discussed in Chapter 8, modern telecommunications have made it possible to import services ranging from financial back-office operations to computer software development. At the same time, some imported goods, such as certain consumer electronics, have few or no domestic competitors. Conversely, products like wall-to-wall carpeting, 25-cubic-foot refrigerators, and king-sized beds are not made outside North America.

Table 9–1 quantifies the penetration of 23 categories of import goods. Some, like tobacco and coal, have little import competition. Others, like industrial machinery, electronic equipment, and

T A B L E   9–1

Import Penetration in U.S. Markets (1996)

	U.S. Consumption ($ Billions)	Imports ($ Billions)	Imports % of U.S. Market
Lumber & wood products	46.2	12.2	26.4
Furniture & fixtures	26.7	9.3	34.8
Stone, clay & glass products	36.7	9.1	24.8
Primary metal products	63.9	34.6	54.1
Fabricated metal products	99.1	17.5	17.7
Industrial machinery	159.1	112.9	71.0
Electronic equipment	178.3	114.1	64.0
Motor vehicles & equipment	133.9	65.9	49.2
Food & kindred products	116.5	20.9	17.9
Tobacco products	13.1	0.2	1.5
Textile mill products	26.5	7.2	27.2
Apparel & other textile products	61.6	43.1	70.0
Paper & allied products	57.9	14.8	25.6
Printing & publishing	88.9	3.0	3.4
Chemicals & allied products	142.1	42.8	30.1
Petroleum & coal products	41.7	18.8	45.1
Rubber & misc. plastics	54.5	16.9	31.0
Leather & leather products	17.7	14.2	80.2
Agriculture, forestry & fishing	113.4	19.8	17.5
Metal ores & concentrates	7.1	1.4	19.7
Coal	8.8	0.2	2.3
Petroleum & natural gas	137.7	54.5	39.6
Nonmetallic minerals ex. fuels	9.9	1.0	10.1

Source: U.S. Bureau of Economic Analysis and Department of Commerce, Bureau of the Census

leather and leather products (shoes), are dominated by imports. Obviously these are broad categories and a finer breakdown (which isn't readily available) would show greater extremes. Still, most U.S.-produced goods do face foreign competition, in finalized form or in some of their components. All it takes to pressure domestic producers is for imports to have 1 percent of the U.S. market and the potential for much more. For most domestic producers, there are few places to hide from imports, certainly less than in the past. Note (Figure 9–1) that as a percentage of goods consumed in the United States, imports have risen from 5 percent in the early 1960s to 20 percent in the mid-1980s, and close to 30 percent today.

A booming buck also makes U.S. exports more expensive to our trading partners, in their currency, and discourages them from buying. This slows American production and increases price-depressing excess capacity. Again, deflationary.

THE DOLLAR'S SWINGS

Note two things about the trade-weighted dollar (Figure 9–2). First, the swings in the buck have been long-term affairs. It was weak from the mid-1960s until 1980, then strong for five years, fell for five years, and then was flat overall from 1990 to 1995. Second,

FIGURE 9–1

Ratio of U.S. goods imported to U.S. total goods consumed, 1947–1998

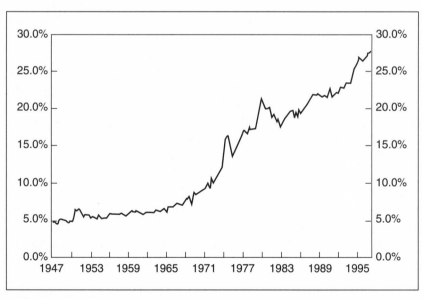

Source: U.S. Bureau of Economic Analysis

FIGURE 9-2

Federal Reserve's trade-weighted dollar

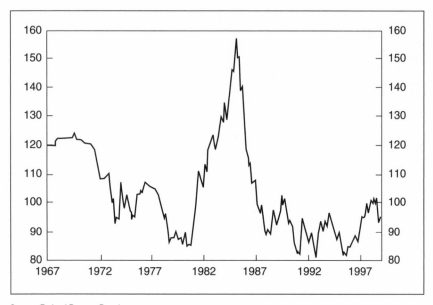

Source: Federal Reserve Board

since 1995, the buck's rise, on balance, is still small compared with its historic performance. Recently, however, the dollar has softened. Many reasons are offered, such as Clinton's personal troubles and the rising trade deficit, which results from foreign economic weakness coupled with U.S. strength. Long term, however, the greenback should continue to rally.

It seems highly likely that many developing countries' currencies will remain weak against the dollar for years to come. Some with fixed currencies, like China and Hong Kong, will probably devalue, forced by meager global demand for their exports and competitive pressures from those that have already devalued. Others may well let their currencies drift downward in deliberate competitive devaluation attempts to maintain or improve their export positions.

AMERICA'S COMPETITIVE ADVANTAGE IS HUGE

Against both developing and developed countries' currencies, the dollar will gain as U.S. consumers switch from borrowing and spending to saving, thereby reducing their demand for imports and shrinking the trade deficit—much to the dismay of the rest of the world, by the way! (See Chapter 13.) More important, through aggressive restructuring, America has gained a huge competitive advantage over other major economies, a force that almost always works to a country's currency's advantage. In Chapter 4, you saw the tremendous need for the Continent of Europe and for Japan to restructure, and the impediments to their doing so. The flip side is that the United States is way ahead of the pack (Table 4–1).

Furthermore, this nation has a commanding lead in semiconductors, computers, biotech, telecommunications, the Internet, and other new technologies, and will be unrivaled by Europe, Japan, or any other country for years. As noted earlier, these industries have grown rapidly since inception, but will soon be collectively large enough to drive the overall economy and productivity. As you'll learn in later chapters, deflation will create even bigger differences than now exist between the old technologies, like autos, and the new, like semiconductors, where America enjoys global leadership and explosive growth.

In contrast, Japanese orientation is toward perfection of old technologies, not the development of new. They are geniuses at taking a standard product and making constant improvements. They took the best features of two fine German cars, Mercedes and BMW, and made them even better in producing the Lexus. But the Japanese are not nearly as good as Americans at creative, new technologies. Hear anything lately about their plans, announced about a decade ago with great fanfare, to bury us with homegrown super computers? Other recent government-directed technological programs also have gone awry. Semiconductor memory chips have become commodities, while high-definition TV and artificial intelligence have sold poorly.

The annual world competitiveness ranking by Switzerland's International Institute for Management Development again ranked the United States first in 1997. The ranking of 46 countries weights

259 criteria ranging from liberal trade policies to economic strength, and emphasizes the attractiveness of a country for business. Japan dropped to 18th place from 9th in 1996 and 2nd in 1992. Germany wasn't much better, 14th, and France was worse, 21st.

THE IMPORTANCE OF PRODUCTIVITY GROWTH

History shows that the productivity leader enjoys a strong currency with reserve currency status. In the eighteenth century, Britain's productivity was below Holland's, the top dog, but growing faster. The United Kingdom overtook the Netherlands in productivity level about 1785. About the same time, the Industrial Revolution started in England and catapulted that country into a commanding lead in productivity—and in global power. In the nineteenth century, the U.K.'s per capita income was a third higher than that of France and twice the German level. Sterling became the world's reserve currency.

But as in Holland earlier, the British got too comfortable with success and let their productivity growth rate slip below that of two upstarts—Germany and especially the United States, in the late 1800s. As you'll learn in Chapter 16, the American Industrial Revolution was then at full blow, with railroad expansion exploding.

U.S. productivity growth averaged 2.1 percent per year from 1870–1890, far exceeding the U.K.'s 1.3 percent rate. As that 0.8 percent gap compounded, American productivity levels spurted beyond those of Britain (Table 9–2). Not surprisingly, by 1901, U.S. per capita GDP exceeded that of the United Kingdom. Many believe that it was the disaster of World War I that knocked the United Kingdom off the throne, but it actually occurred 13 years before the war started, and the seeds were sown about 45 years before that, when U.S. productivity growth leaped above that of Britain. Think about it! America, a mere colony in the eighteenth century, then a thorn in the side of mighty Britain in the late eighteenth and early nineteenth centuries, overtook the mother country at the beginning of the twentieth century and has been in the lead ever since.

It's not surprising then that the dollar replaced the pound sterling as the world's reserve currency. Nevertheless, currencies that other countries hold as part of their national treasuries die hard—they hate to desert old friends—so sterling did not begin to

T A B L E   9–2

U.S. Productivity Level

England = 100	
Year	
1870	88%
1880	90%
1890	96%
1900	106%
1913	124%

Source: *American Business, A Two*
Minute Warning,
C. Jackson Grayson, Jr.,
and Carlo O'Dell.
The Free Press. New York,
NY 1988.

fall against the dollar until World War I, and remained in some countries' official reserves until well beyond World War II.

THE EURO

Another reason for the soft dollar recently is anticipation that the euro, launched January 1, 1999, will have as bright a future as the 11 European countries involved in its development. Exports and imports within Euroland—Austria, Belgium, Finland, France, Germany, Ireland, Italy, Luxembourg, the Netherlands, Portugal, and Spain—will no longer have currency risks, so trade among these countries should increase. Euroland firms will also be encouraged to step up investments in facilities to service the common currency area. In addition, the euro may become a major reserve currency, to the detriment of the dollar, many believe.

Nevertheless, the recent shift to left-wing governments on the continent of Europe suggests that serious restructuring and attention to productivity growth remain on hold there. France is cutting its work week from 39 hours to 35 hours in 2000 with no cuts in pay. The new German government is considering a similar change and a lowering of the retirement age from 65 to 60 with no reduction in huge government-mandated benefits. And with layoffs so difficult and expensive on the Continent, it's no wonder that temporary employment is exploding by 10 percent a year, now that it's permitted in many European countries. In France, the Labor Minister stated that 86 percent of new hires are on short-term contracts. Indeed, in the Netherlands, 3.2 percent of workers are temps, a higher percentage than the 2.2 percent in the United States and 1.9 percent in the United Kingdom. The European Union spends a huge 42 percent of its budget on farm subsidies and pressures within the European Union and from the United States to cut them has been mounting. Yet at a recent E.U. summit meeting in Berlin, almost nothing was done. Clearly, these governments favor jobs over restructuring, even though the lack of restructuring keeps their countries less competitive in global markets.

This indicates that the euro will be weak against the dollar. Furthermore, the leftist European governments' zeal for more jobs suggests constant pressure on the new European Central Bank for monetary ease. Sure, the ECB is technically independent of the politicians, just like the Fed in the United States, but like the Fed, it will ultimately be swayed by political reality despite its basic central-bank bias toward tight money.

Many argue for reserve status for the euro because the Euroland economy will be close to America's in size, with a population of about 300 million and a GDP of about $7 billion (compared to 270 million and $8.5 billion in the United States). Again, it is not size but superior productivity growth that ultimately decides the issue. Productivity is what the United Kingdom, the first to industrialize, had in the 1800s, and that edge allowed the small island to dominate the previous century. In the productivity growth arena, Euroland has little chance of beating the United States.

A stronger buck will be deflationary for the United States. Another deflationary force can be found in Asia, as you'll see in Chapters 10 and 11.

10

CHAPTER

The Asian Contagion

Unless you've been on Mars since mid-1997, you're well aware of the financial and economic melt-down in Asia. Only when the depth of the Asian crisis began to be appreciated in mid-1998, however, did the word "deflation" start to become common. The Asian Contagion is an important deflationary force and has served to focus attention on the issue, but it's only one of 14 on my list (Table I–2). My earlier book, *Deflation*, discusses in detail the causes of the Asian crisis and the problems it has caused. Rather than rehash them here, I'll concentrate on what it has taught us and why it will intensify global glut and deflate worldwide prices.

PROBLEMS ARE SEVERE

We now know that when a developing country gets into financial trouble, it's severe trouble. This has been a huge shock to many. After all, the Asia work ethic, dedication to family, willingness to put the community above self, and huge savings rates were the envy of the world. This was the Asian miracle and we were about to enter the "Pacific Century." These were countries that had dutifully followed the successful—at least previously successful—Japanese model. According to *The Wall Street Journal*, the International Monetary Fund (IMF) in June 1997, just a month before the crisis started, praised Indonesia for "prudent macroeconomic policies, huge investment and savings rates, and reforms to liberalize markets." In May 1997, the IMF lauded Thailand as well as Indonesia as "exceptions to the boom-bust cycle," the same publication reported. Well, it's nice to know that I'm not alone in making some lousy forecasts.

Advances in the Asian Tigers had been so strong (Table 10–1) that even though those lands accounted for a small minority of global demand for raw materials, loans from developed-country banks, and sales by their companies, they were expected to provide a big majority of worldwide growth. Few recognized that this seemingly endless growth had attracted a gigantic burst of leveraged lending and investing, which resulted in far too much capacity.

Consequently, as the Asian bubbles broke one by one, starting July 2, 1997—when Thailand stopped supporting her currency, the *baht*—foreigners and locals pulled out whatever capital they could; $1 trillion in loans soured, $2 trillion in equity capital evaporated, and currencies collapsed (Figure 10–1). Overnight, rapid economic growth turned to economic decline, led by Indonesia with a 14 percent fall in GDP in 1998. The size of dollar-denominated bank loans in local currencies skyrocketed as those currencies fell and became impossible to service. No one could afford to buy much of anything, especially expensive imports. The value of real estate deals in Hong Kong, where property dominates the financial sphere, fell 61 per-

T A B L E   10–1

Asian Tigers Real GDP Annual Growth Rates

	1975–80	1980–85	1985–90	1990–97
China	8.4%	10.2%	7.9%	11.1%
Hong Kong	12.0%	5.6%	7.9%	5.3%
Indonesia	8.0%	4.7%	5.6%	7.4%
Malaysia	8.5%	5.1%	6.8%	8.5%
Philippines	4.6%	−1.4%	4.7%	3.1%
Singapore	8.5%	6.2%	8.0%	8.2%
Taiwan	10.6%	6.7%	9.1%	6.5%
Thailand	7.9%	5.4%	9.7%	6.7%
S. Korea	7.5%	8.4%	10.0%	7.1%

Source: Asian Development Bank

FIGURE 10–1

Devaluation in Asian currencies (U.S. dollars per foreign currency), January 1, 1997 to April 1, 1999

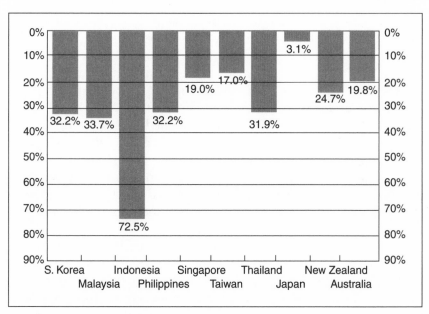

Source: Haver Analytics and A. Gary Shilling & Co., Inc.

cent in 1998, while the economy shrunk 5.1 percent in 1998 and unemployment hit an all-time high of 6 percent in early 1999. Housing prices in Singapore are 45 percent below their mid-1996 peak. In South Korea, the farm population rose 7 percent in the first quarters of 1998, as dismissed factory workers were forced to return to the land; this in a country where industrialization had slashed the farm population from 55 percent in 1965 to 10 percent in recent years.

THE ASIAN FLU IS CONTAGIOUS

When Asia's woes commenced, few saw them spreading beyond the immediate region: Thailand, Indonesia, and Malaysia. But then over-leveraged South Korea was infected, and even financially sound Taiwan and rock-solid Singapore were dragged in as their exports to other troubled Asian countries dried up. In 1998, Indonesia,

Thailand, Hong Kong, Malaysia, and South Korea suffered recessions while the Philippines and Singapore had flat economies. GDP
fell 5.8 percent in South Korea in 1998 from a 5 percent gain in 1997.

Russia, too, had plenty of domestic problems, but her currency collapse and default on government debt were touched off
by nervous investors wondering, "Who's next?" In the fall of 1997,
Brazil had fended off the first round of attacks on her dollar-
pegged currency, the *real*, with $10 billion in hard currency re-
serves, a leap in short-term interest rates to 46 percent, and plans
for draconian tax increases and spending cuts.

But Brazil's basic problem remained. Fiscal reforms that
would revamp the tax system, fire excess public employees, and
rein in the social security system that allows the majority of workers to retire in their 40s and receive pension raises thereafter were
not enacted. That left a federal budget deficit approaching 9 percent of GDP, the *real* overvalued in global markets, and the
Brazilian current account deficit soaring.

The only difference, compared to the earlier hyperinflation
days, was that with the advent of the *real* currency-pegging plan in
1994, the bloated government sector stopped using inflation to
shift purchasing power from other domestic sectors to it and
started relying on foreigners via the nation's mounting trade
deficit. Note that the *real* currency peg had slashed Brazil's inflation from 2,700 percent in 1993 to 1.5 percent in 1998.

Competitive devaluations in Asia heightened the problem as
Brazil maintained her currency peg rather than devalue and risk a
return to hyperinflation. Then the financial collapse in Russia pro-
moted capital flight that cut Brazil's reserves from $70 billion to
$40 billion in two months and pushed interest rates, which had
fallen since their earlier spike, back to 50 percent.

The high interest rates did not inhibit flight capital, leaving at
the rate of $1 billion or more on some days, but did push the
Brazilian economy into a serious recession. The unemployment
rate was over 8 percent in late 1998 and skyrocketing, while sales of
Brazilian-made vehicles fell 28 percent last year to a five-year low.
Industrial production in February 1999 fell 5.1 percent from a year
earlier, the ninth monthly decline in a row. Debt collection soon became a growth industry in Brazil. Still, a recession seemed preferable to devaluation and a possible return to hyperinflation.

Despite the $41.5 billion international bailout for Brazil, established in late 1998, her currency peg turned to sawdust in early 1999 as she threw in the towel and let the *real* collapse. Now the perennial "land of the future" just looks like one of her Asian predecessors in devaluation. Without excruciatingly high interest rates and fiscal reform, the currency will become worthless and hyperinflation will return, but with high rates and fiscal restraint, an even deeper recession is inevitable. How can the economy continue to function with debt-loaded consumers paying 200 percent interest rates? Brazil may get the worst of both worlds with high interest rates and a deep recession on the one hand and serious inflation on the other. Retailers, schooled in the old hyperinflation days, jacked up prices as soon as devaluation was announced.

To be sure, some fiscal reforms have been enacted by the fiercely unruly Brazilian Congress, but far from enough to make the government self-financing. Meanwhile, the government has turned to a third source to plug the gap—the sale of state enterprises. But what will Brazil do when they're all sold? Those sales, scheduled to reach $14 billion in 1999, and the remainder of the $41.5 billion international bailout are about the only sources of support for the government's excessive spending at present, and she faces foreign debt service of $31 billion in 1999.

SPREADING EFFECTS IN LATIN AMERICA

U.S. banks have $26 billion in exposure to Brazil and the collapse in the *real* makes repayment of many dollar-denominated loans doubtful. Similarly, many U.S. companies are heavily involved as exporters to Brazil or producers there. All of these problems will magnify if Brazil's problems spread to the rest of Latin America, as well they might. Note that Brazil is the largest country there, almost twice the economic size of Mexico (Table 10–2), and if she drags the rest down, 20 percent of U.S. exports will be affected. Devaluation in Brazil has killed the prices of two commodities, coffee and sugar, that not only Brazil but many other developing countries rely on for export earnings. The price of soybeans was knocked down as well. Furthermore, U.S. banks have twice as much in loans and leases in Latin America as they do in Asia.

T A B L E 10–2

Latin American GDP Levels and Percent of World
Total (1997)

	Level (in $ Billions)	% of World Total
Argentina	317	1.1
Brazil	804	2.7
Chile	79	0.3
Colombia	96	0.3
Ecuador	20	0.1
Mexico	402	1.4
Panama	8	0.0
Peru	51	0.2
Venezuela	87	0.3
Total	1,864	6.3
United States	8,110	27.5

Source: IMF, World Economic Outlook and IMF, International Financial Statistics

The rest of Latin America is shaky at best. Chile continues to be
buffeted by weak prices for copper, a major export, and by the collapse of Asian economies that take 30 percent of her foreign-bound
goods. The economy is slipping into recession. Venezuela is in recession—GDP fell 8.2 percent in the fourth quarter of 1998 versus a year
earlier—as weak oil prices, high interest rates of over 50 percent,
and government mismanagement and an unpredictable new president take their toll in an economy where oil accounts for a third of
GDP. Colombia is in recession, and recently devalued petroleum-de-
pendent Ecuador is so desperate to support her plunging currency
that her central bank raised interest rates seven times in one day during the Brazilian crisis (January 13, 1999), from 87 percent to 130 percent, touching-off a full blown financial, political and social crisis.

Argentina's economy was slipping even before Brazil's devaluation, which hurt Argentina's auto industry as well as other industries that are closely tied to those of her neighbors. The
currency vultures are circling even though Argentina keeps her
peso rigidly tied to the dollar. Of course, a similar tie of the Hong

Kong dollar to the buck didn't prevent speculators from having a run at that currency last year, and Argentina lacks Hong Kong's reserves as a defense. So, Argentina is considering eliminating the peso entirely and using the dollar as her currency. This is radical, but so too was enacting the currency link, or currency board, in 1991, to get rid of 2,300 percent annual inflation. Argentine President Menem described it as "surgery without anesthesia."

In Mexico, petroleum accounts for a third of government revenues, but only 10 percent of exports, due to the strong tie to the still-booming U.S. economy. Nevertheless, Mexico has slashed government spending and hiked taxes to close the budget gap caused by falling oil prices. This is squeezing average incomes that never fully recovered from the 1994 peso collapse. Meanwhile, purchasing power is under fire from the lifting of price controls on corn flour, the principal ingredient in the national diet staple, tortillas. The 1994 devaluation made Mexico very competitive, but subsequent currency drops in Asia and, more recently, in Brazil have destroyed that advantage. Mexico may face rough times, especially if U.S. economic activity softens.

Furthermore, Eastern Europe is not immune from the Asian flu, especially as Russia, a major trading partner, crumbles and Western Europe, an even bigger export market, slides. Czech industrial production, for example, collapsed in 1998.

IS CHINA NEXT?

With Brazil's devaluation, the "who's next?" question shifted to China. Chinese leaders continue to maintain the value of the tightly controlled *yuan* so far. They note that *yuan* devaluation would be followed by an offsetting round of competitive devaluations in Asia and elsewhere, given China's importance in the area (Table 10–3). They don't say so, but it is clear that devaluation would also take down the Hong Kong dollar, breaking its 16-year peg to the greenback with considerable loss of face in Beijing coming so close on the heels of the mid-1997 hand-over of Hong Kong from the British.

Furthermore, a weaker currency would push up the *yuan* cost of those considerable dollar-denominated debts owned by financially-troubled Chinese companies and wreck China's current efforts to

T A B L E   10–3

Asian Shares of World GDP and
Merchandise Exports (1997)

	GDP	Exports
China	3.0%	3.3%
S. Korea	1.5%	2.4%
Taiwan	1.0%	2.2%
Indonesia	0.7%	1.0%
Thailand	0.5%	1.1%
Hong Kong	0.6%	3.4%
Malaysia	0.3%	1.5%
Philippines	0.3%	0.5%
Singapore	0.3%	2.2%
Total	8.3%	17.7%
Japan	14.3%	7.7%
Total Asia	22.6%	25.3%

Source: IMF Direction of Trade Statistics and IMF International
Financial Statistics.

establish herself as a creditable borrower in international markets.
In addition, a devaluation would scare away foreign investment,
which is beginning to enter again, encouraged by the Chinese government's pledge to maintain the currency's value.

Nevertheless, China is at a considerable disadvantage against
her Asian competitors whose currencies have fallen (Figure 10–2).
And in the first quarter of 1999, exports fell 8 percent from a year
earlier. That nation desperately needs exports to promote economic
job growth, which is lagging badly. There are 200 million people in
coastal areas who are productively employed, about 1 billion in the
hinterland who would like to be, and 100 million more squatting in
coastal cities looking for work. This last group is potentially socially
disruptive. (The Tiananmen Square uprising was preceded by a
similar unemployment problem.) Furthermore, restructuring state-
owned enterprises will make about a third of their 100 million
workers surplus, as well as half of the 20 million civil ser-
vants—while 15 million people enter the workforce annually. Note

that purely private businesses only account for 11 percent of output in China. High growth is also needed to provide jobs for those who will be dismissed as bankrupt state enterprises restructure. Urban unemployment rates are headed for 8 to 9 percent in 1999, and close to 30 percent in China's depressed northeastern provinces, where debt-ridden state enterprises are concentrated.

HIGH GROWTH NEEDED IN CHINA

High growth is also needed to offset the numerous inefficiencies in China's still heavily controlled economy. Not only are many state enterprises essentially bankrupt, but so too are their lenders, including banks and big investment trusts. The military, and even the judiciary, own many businesses and are supposed to divest

FIGURE 10–2

Chinese yuan in Pacific Rim currencies: Hong Kong, South Korea, Indonesia, Malaysia, Philippines, Singapore, Taiwan, and Thailand. Equal weights (1996–1999)

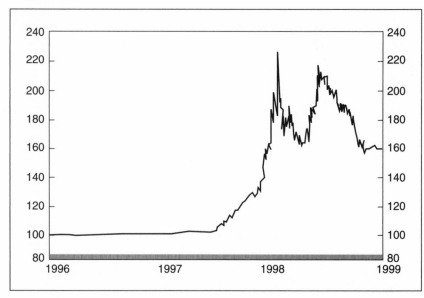

Source: ISI Group

themselves, but no one knows how or to whom they will be sold. Government spending, which rose over 20 percent in 1998 and accounted for half of China's overall growth, is the only current source of stimulus as retail sales shrink along with falling prices and exports. With retail prices falling 3.2% year-over-year in March 1999, consumers are saving more in anticipation of still lower prices. Potential borrowers are inactive and banks are too scared to lend. Official growth targets for 1999 are unrealistically high even after having been cut from 1998 rates, which are probably overstated, even though Beijing's budget deficit is scheduled to rise by 56 percent.

Her special economic zones are overbuilt and faltering. And much of government outlay goes to inefficient projects. Half of Shanghai's Class A commercial real estate is vacant, but lots more is being built. In Daqing, in northern China, laid-off oil field workers are paid as much as salaried people in coastal cities, and the government condones a red-light district to keep the men from getting bored and restless. Well, at least the money in Daqing gets circulated in classic Keynesian style!

With terrible timing, China recently infuriated the providers of much-needed foreign capital by not, as promised, bailing them out of the failed Guangdong International Trust and Investment Corp., or Gitic, the investment arm of that wealthy Chinese province. This was followed swiftly by the revelation of many other troubled and bankrupt financial institutions. Foreign lenders are recoiling, and foreign loans dropped 51 percent in the first three quarters of 1998 compared with the year-earlier period. Even though China is setting up a Resolution Trust Corp.-style institution to deal with these problems, foreign lenders are retreating and thereby squeezing credit supplies. Note that as of the middle of 1997, foreign banks had $59 billion in loans to China.

STEALTH DEVALUATION

The pressure for *yuan* devaluation is strong, and in effect, China is already engaged in stealth currency cuts. Tax rebates and loans for exporters have been increased. Meanwhile, new regulations make it very difficult for Chinese banks to sell even the small amounts of the foreign currency needed to pay for imports or other obligations, and the limited payments that are permitted for imports are being delayed. Prior approval is now required for importing equipment worth more than $100,000. Chinese companies are also being threatened with dire consequences if they don't repatriate their illegal foreign exchange holdings overseas, estimated at $80 billion. U.S. firms are being forced to withdraw from joint telecommunications ventures, and Beijing is pushing Chinese industries to buy domestic, not imported, materials. Furthermore, foreign companies can't run their own distribution networks, own their own retail stores, or warehouse their goods. With classic Chinese subtlety, exporters have been told to export more this year or lose their licenses and a campaign to curb smuggling of imports has been mounted, complete with numerous executions of the guilty. Note that smuggled imports, which often compete with overabundant domestic products, amounted to about $12 billion in 1997, a sizable sum in comparison with China's $42 billion balance of payments surplus.

What's the difference between these actions and out-and-out devaluation? The increase in export tax rebates alone is estimated to be the equivalent of a 7 percent devaluation of the *yuan*. Furthermore, the blow of a *yuan* devaluation to those with dollar debts has been softened by a market for so-called "non-deliverable forwards" that allow investors, for a premium, to buy an instrument that tracks the *yuan*, but is denominated in dollars.

At some point, China may well sweep away the facade of backdoor devaluation and formally reduce the *yuan's* value, perhaps in connection with broad-based financial reform, or during the next recession in the West, when her exports collapse. The likelihood that other competitive devaluations would follow a formal cut in the *yuan* against the dollar and offset its effects doesn't mean that it won't happen. Nations that start wars know that their opponents will retaliate, and may even win. Yet, wars are started all of the time. Rational behavior is not always—nor even often—the norm. One way or the other, China is striving to be more competitive with her Asian neighbors, and that puts additional pressure on them and their currencies.

Most emerging countries, then, are in deep trouble, and they will be slow to recover, even more so because Japan will not provide much help, as you'll learn in Chapter 11.

11

Slow Recovery in Asia

Besides knowing that problems with troubled emerging economies are major and will continue to spread to others, we now can see that Japan is unlikely to revive anytime soon and provide export markets for the desperate Asian Tigers.

JAPAN IS NO HELP

Despite continuing pressures from the United States and other Western countries for change, Japan continues to run a mercantilist system that would have made the eighteenth-century French green with envy. Tariff and, more recently, non-tariff barriers to trade are used consistently and effectively to limit imports of consumer goods and services and push up their prices. At the same time, the prices of competing domestic items are kept high by inefficient distribution systems with layers upon layers of wholesalers and mom-and-pop retailers as well as sanctioned cartels. As a result, the Japanese have about the same income as average Americans but only two-thirds of their spending power. Because goods and services are expensive, Japanese consumers are encouraged to save, and save they do— in legendary fashion—despite almost no interest return on their money. (See Figure 11–1.)

A cozy relationship exists among the Japanese government, bureaucracy, and big business. The whole system directs the investment of these low-cost savings away from foreign investments, through the banks, and into export industries where Japan can achieve global dominance. This satisfies their "export or die" men-

FIGURE 11–1

Japanese saving rate, 12-month average, 1968–1998

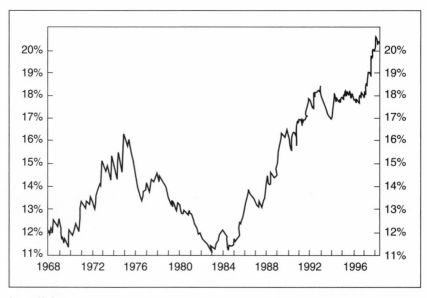

Source: ISI Group

tality—all for the greater glory of the Land of the Rising Sun, not the individual Japanese who make it possible.

One reason the Japanese are saving so much recently is to offset their huge losses in stock and real estate values since the nation entered her deflationary-depression at the beginning of the decade (Figure 11–2). Urban real estate prices are down about 80 percent from their late 1980s peak. So, for each yen of additional after-tax income, the average Japanese spends only 68 percent. A series of government fiscal stimulus packages have been insufficient, and from the third quarter of 1997 through the fourth quarter of 1998, real GDP fell 3.9 percent, the first five consecutive quarters of economic decline since modern record keeping started in 1955.

Busted Japanese Banks

Japanese banks are finally being cleaned up from the losses they suffered when the bubble economy of the 1980s broke, from further

F I G U R E 11–2

Japan's Nikkei Stock Market Index, 1981–1999

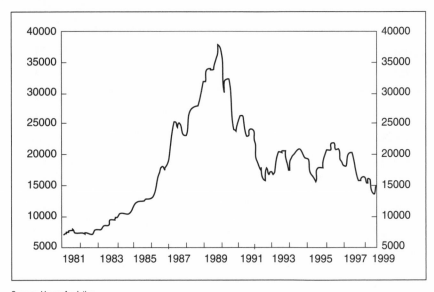

Source: Haver Analytics

setbacks caused by the collapse of the Asian Tigers, and from the renewed recession in Japan. Nevertheless, Japanese bank loans are falling at a frightening pace because lenders don't want to lend and borrowers are scared to borrow. Government spending is the only current source of economic strength. Japanese merchandise exports to Asia, 42 percent of the total before the Asian crisis, are obviously weak and fell to 35 percent in 1998. Bankruptcies rose 17 percent in 1998 and the busted left behind the highest debts of the postwar era. Unemployment, at 4.6 percent, is at its highest rate in 45 years of record keeping. Japan's 1999 spring labor offensive (Shunto) is likely to be more of a retreat with widespread pay cuts. Vehicle sales in December 1998 fell 24 percent from December 1997 and in all of 1998 were the lowest since 1986. On top of that is the ongoing deregulation of financial services, which allows banks, brokers, and insurers to invade each others' territories and foreigners to get into the act as well—a big shock for the clubby Japanese.

That great forecaster of economic and financial reality, the stock market, remains unimpressed with Japan's attempts to reinvigorate the economy and solve financial problems at least until recently. The Nikkei stock index recently hit a 12-year low in early 1999 and for good reason. Much of the new and recent tax cuts are temporary, so consumers may well save them in anticipation of higher taxes later. They're also encouraged to defer buying in anticipation of lower prices. Wholesale prices fell 4.4 percent in December 1998 versus a year earlier. Furthermore, for political purposes, much of Japan's public works spending is wasted in rural areas on paving river beds and the like, not invested in badly needed roads and airport runways in Tokyo. Bad public sector loans and investments equal perhaps a quarter of GDP. Cheap imports are still blocked by a labyrinth of rules and age-old customs. Instead of folding busted banks and writing off their loans while guaranteeing deposits, as the United States did with failed S&Ls, Japan is taking them over with no clear disposition plan while at the same time pumping money into questionable institutions.

Nevertheless, there are some encouraging signs in Japan. Although the disastrous consumption tax increase of 1997 is still on the books and the head of the Economic Planning Agency said in February that it will need to be increased in the future, recent legislation slashed income taxes by 20 percent commencing April 1, 1999, and other individual taxes were cut as well. Corporate taxes were also reduced to levels more in line with other industrial countries. It remains to be seen, however, whether lower taxes will encourage spending or, as in recent years, simply augment already high saving rates. Note that large Japanese businesses have little confidence since they plan to slash already weak capital spending by 9.4 percent in the fiscal year commencing April 1. Meanwhile, the Bank of Japan has reduced its overnight lending rates to almost zero—0.01 percent at one point. As discussed in Chapter 18, however, low interest rates in a deflationary climate are unlikely to encourage cautious potential borrowers to borrow and scared lenders to lend.

Elsewhere, there are indications of corporate restructuring in Japan. Mitsubishi Electric plans a 13 percent cut in its workforce, NEC Corp. announced a 10 percent job reduction over three years, and Sony said it would reduce its employment by 17,000 during the same period. Major banks plan to cut 20,000 jobs in three years. Overall, one third of Japanese companies with more than 5,000 employees plan to reduce the number of full-time staff in the next five years.

Most of these reductions will result from retirements and slower hiring, so the benefits to companies will be slow in coming. Still, the prospect of unemployment is terrifying to big company employees accustomed to guaranteed lifetime jobs. Furthermore, almost one million unemployed Japanese were forced out of previous jobs in February 1999, up one third from a year ago. Over the same period, lower-cost temporary workers were increased by 5.3 percent while full timers fell 2 percent. In effect, restructuring, brand new in Japan, will be beneficial in the long run but very disruptive to employment and worker confidence in the short run. This is especially true in a country that lacks the entrepreneurial spirit and labor mobility of the United States, where many of those restructured out of jobs have simply gone on to start new businesses.

On balance, then, Japan is sticking to her course of slow, incremental changes, an orientation toward exports for growth, and a mass manufacturing mentality. At a time that calls for bold action, this suggests that she will remain part of the Asian and, indeed, the global problem, not the solution.

NO QUICK RECOVERY

It is clear, at least to me, that the victims of the Asian Contagion will recover very slowly. Many foreign investors thought faltering Asian economies had recovered in early 1998 and rushed back into Asian stocks and bonds only to lose their proverbial shirts. They learned the hard way that emerging markets are those from which you cannot emerge in an emergency! More recently, with some Asian stock markets picking up, they're trying it again. A recent poll by Pegasus Fund Managers Ltd. of Hong Kong reveals that 70 percent of the area's fund managers are optimistic for 1999 about the Asian economies and financial markets, especially in Hong Kong, Singapore, Thailand, and South Korea.

Before you join them, consider several factors. To begin, no one has a clear idea of how to solve their basic problems. Sure, everyone applauds many of the International Monetary Fund's (IMF) demands—more transparent accounting; openness to foreign ownership of financial and non-financial firms; canceling wasteful government projects; giving the central bank full autonomy to raise interest rates; restructuring the banks; and an end to monopolies, trade restrictions, cronyism, government subsidies, and nepotism.

Nevertheless, the basic IMF approach is universally criticized—but that's expected if for no other reason than because it hasn't worked. It entails bailouts to developing countries in financial trouble, once they promise to raise taxes and cut government spending to balance their budgets and restore credibility, and to tighten credit and raise interest rates to prop up their currencies and re-attract foreign investment. These measures may work in developed countries that have temporarily strayed from fiscal and monetary prudence but retain basic international confidence. France or Italy in earlier decades are prime examples. But these techniques clearly don't work in developing countries where previously over-optimistic foreign investors stampede for the exits when disillusionment sets in, regardless of government actions. In fact, the IMF programs simply drive those economies deeper into the mud and spread the problems to others.

MEXICO IS NO MODEL

Don't be swayed by those who look at Mexico's quick recovery after the 1994 peso devaluation as a model for revival in Asia or even the rest of Latin America. Mexico's ultimate and not-so-secret weapon is her 2,000-mile border with the United States. Whenever she gets into financial difficulty, all she needs to do to get American aid, and promptly, is to point out that an economic collapse south of the border will result in another million illegals heading north of the border each year. Even in today's less stressful times, 835,000 make the trip each year. The advent of NAFTA in 1994 also aided Mexican recovery as did rising prices of petroleum in the 1994–96 years. Still, consumers' purchasing power is down 39 percent since the 1994 devaluation and since 1997, the number of Mexicans living in extreme poverty with less than $2 per day in income has grown twice as fast as the population.

No such long border exists between developing Asian countries and the island nation of Japan, the only close-by advanced country. Besides, the United States, despite recent concerns over illegal immigrants, is populated by outsiders and has always had a soft spot for immigrants. In contrast, the Japanese have been traditionally suspicious of outsiders and quick to repel them. The first Europeans to reach Japan, usually shipwrecked sailors, were often killed on the beaches. Even today there is no such thing as an immigration visa in Japan, although foreign work permits do exist. About 99 percent of the population are of pure Japanese ancestry, and professional baseball teams there are each only permitted to have three foreign players.

Also, Mexico's recent recovery came in the midst of a robust expansion in the United States, the major buyer of Mexican exports, as well as the trade liberalizations of NAFTA. When America grows, Mexico booms. Asian developing countries have no similar trade liberalization spur, and Japan, their biggest market, is back in recession. Furthermore, the deflationary atmosphere we foresee will be a big change from the previous postwar era. Almost every country will have excess capacity, and growth through exports will be tough.

In addition, the 1994–1995 "Tequila Crisis" was essentially isolated. Except for Argentina, no other country suffered any lasting effects. But Asia accounts for about a quarter of global output (Table 10–3) and the economics there are very interrelated, unlike Latin American countries until quite recently. And we've seen how those interrelationships lead to domino-like behavior.

Finally, a major reason for rapid recovery in Mexico was rapid reform. Banks, telecommunications, and other key industries (but not petroleum) were privatized. Foreign competition was allowed in, and foreign ownership became possible. President Zedillo recently proposed that private company involvement in the electric power industry be expanded greatly. It's far from clear that Asian countries, including Japan, really have similar plans.

DO THEY REALLY WANT TO REFORM?

Most of these countries, especially in Asia, are semi-dictatorships, and if they really wanted financial reforms, they'd have instituted them long ago. But why should they? For years, their growth prospects were so mouth-watering that foreigners showered them with money, while accepting opaque accounting, capricious or nonexistent financial regulation, severe limits on foreign ownership, nepotism, graft, corruption, and government guidance on investments and financing.

Still, change is being forced on them and they are responding, if slowly. Korea is forcing her family conglomerates, or *chaebols*, to dump many of their affiliates and reduce their vastly oversized debts. Korea's debt credit rating has been raised while the won has strengthened. Thailand's government has proposed measures to make it easier to foreclose on assets, a necessary step in cleaning up bad loans. And interest rates are falling back from earlier crisis peaks in Hong Kong, Singapore, South Korea, Thailand, and Malaysia. In real terms, however, rates remain excruciatingly high as excess capacity, collapsing real estate, and declining consumption generate considerable deflation.

We believe that, given the onset of global deflation, it will take at least a decade for meaningful recovery in Asia and maybe Latin America as well. It took that long in Latin America after the 1980s debt crisis, and that occurred in an inflationary world of excess demand, not the deflationary arena of worldwide excess supply that is now emerging. Indeed, the World Bank looks for growth of only 1.5 percent in the developed world this year, the lowest since 1982.

In many ways, the deflationary-depression in Japan since the beginning of the 1990s is similar to the 1930s Great Depression in the United States. Recall that it took Americans a decade to emerge from that slump and recovery probably only occurred then because of the big spending caused by World War II, not due to the New Deal programs. There's no such war or other large fiscal stimulus now in prospect to propel Japan. True, fiscal stimulus tools are now much better understood than in the 1930s and could be readily applied by Japan, but so far they haven't been on a sufficient scale. Perhaps offsetting this knowledge is Japan's very slow process of group decision making. Indeed, it is not yet clear that Japan has resolved to do what's necessary to revive the economy, other than rely on her traditional method—more exports, but in a world that already has too much of almost everything.

EXPORT-LED RECOVERIES

When recoveries do occur in Asia and other troubled lands, they will be export-led. Clearly, there is no other way for those depressed lands, with the exception of Japan, to get back on their feet except through massive export growth. The IMF, after huge bailouts in Asia, Russia, and elsewhere, is out of money, and Congress is in no mood to throw good money after bad by replenishing the IMF coffers. Foreign private investment has been largely scared off by excess capacity, economic and political uncertainty, and now Malaysian currency controls and Chinese defaults. The chances of internal growth are limited. The banks in many of those countries are in trouble, with dollar-denominated borrowing that has become much more expensive now that their currencies have fallen sharply. These problems are curtailing lending while high real interest rates are retarding borrowing. Similarly, governments with collapsed revenues and soaring deficits are in no condition to spend to revive their economies. In fact, they are doing the opposite and slashing budget outlays. Government borrowing costs in developing countries are often prohibitively high.

Without question, exports in Asia and other troubled developing countries are being emphasized in order to provide jobs and earn the foreign exchange needed to service huge foreign debts. So far, the results appear disappointing (Figure 11–3). For one reason, the export advantage of currency devaluation is partially offset if exports contain components imported from strong currency coun-

FIGURE 11–3

Developing Asian economies' monthly merchandise exports, 1992–1999

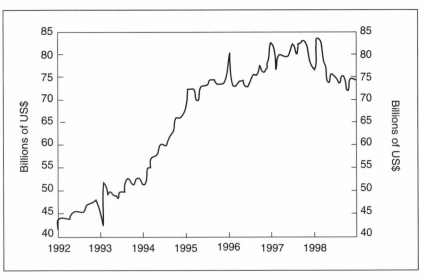

Source: Haver Analytics and A. Gary Shilling & Co., Inc.

tries. Nevertheless, the data is misleading. The collapse of Asian currencies means that, in dollar terms, it takes much more export volume to equal the same number of greenbacks. Indeed, physical exports in most Asian Tigers have continued to rise.

In any event, it takes time to reorient production from domestic to foreign markets, which often prefer different models or sizes. But this is happening. When Toyota's sales in Thailand fell more than 50 percent in one month after the crisis erupted, the firm closed its auto plants there for two months and retooled them for exports. But it also takes time to re-establish the financing needed for not only exports but also imported raw materials. The financial crisis has resulted in a severe tightening in lending by Asian banks as well as foreign banks, either directly or through their Asian correspondents. If a shirt manufacturer in Indonesia can't get the credit to finance either the cloth imports or the shirt exports, he can't make the garments to export to North America or Europe. This problem, too, is being gradually solved, in part by loans and guarantees from government institutions in developed countries (such as the U.S. Export-Import Bank) to ensure the sales of their country's raw materials.

Also, Asian exports have been retarded by the availability of ships. With the growing imbalance of U.S. imports and exports, vessels sailing from Asia to the United States are loaded, but are returning virtually empty. Shipping rates were not high enough to accommodate these empty trips, so ships sailing east across the Pacific are in short supply. Recently, however, a group of container-shipping companies announced plans to discontinue set rates and allow fares to rise enough to offset the imbalances. This added cost will offset a bit of the Asian deflation's downward pressure on U.S. import prices, but will make more ships available to transport more imports. The same is true of ocean shipping deregulation in the United States, which starts the same day: May 1, 1999. This will allow Asian exporters to pay whatever it takes to get their goods moved.

WHERE ARE THEIR EXPORTS HEADED?

Exports throughout Asia, Latin America, and from other troubled developing lands will accelerate over time as they get reoriented, but where will they wind up? Not in other weak developing countries that are importing little, or in recession-bound and import-

adverse Japan. Philippine exports to Japan, for example, were almost stagnant in 1998, but goods sent to the United States and
Europe leaped over 15 percent. And that's where exports from developing countries will increasingly go—to developed Western nations. It's clear that these emerging countries depend heavily on
developed nations, which already take over half of their exports.

The target, first and foremost, is the United States, the buyer of
first and last resort and the happy dumping ground for the world's
excess supply of goods and services. We have a merchandise trade
deficit of over $250 billion to prove it (Table 11–1). Nevertheless,

TABLE 11–1

Merchandise Trade Balances ($ billions)

	Trade Balance Latest 12 Months		Trade Balance Latest 12 Months
Australia	−5.5	Greece	−17.4
Austria	−6.1	Israel	−6.3
Belgium	13.9		
Britain	−37.5	S. Africa	0.6
Canada	14.2	Turkey	−19.0
Denmark	1.8	Czech Republic	−2.4
France	27.2	Hungary	−2.0
Germany	75.7	Poland	−13.1
Italy	26.9	Russia	16.3
Japan	126.7		
Netherlands	14.1	China	40.0
Spain	−23.9	Hong Kong	−8.5
Sweden	16.7	India	−8.8
Switzerland	−1.7	Indonesia	21.4
		Malaysia	15.6
United States	−254.4	Philippines	0.7
		Singapore	8.4
Argentina	−5.2	S. Korea	37.7
Brazil	−6.1	Taiwan	8.0
Chile	−1.8	Thailand	11.7
Colombia	−2.9		
Mexico	−7.4		
Venezuela	4.8		

Source: The Economist

Canada and Europe are not exempt from an import surge from Asian and other developing countries. In terms of imports and exports in relation to their economy sizes, they all have about the same exposure to the Asian Tigers as the United States. Indeed, the current economic slowing in Europe is a reflection of this exposure.

In effect, then, the recovery in distressed developing countries in Asia, Latin America, and elsewhere will be slow and will come largely at the expense of competing producers in Western developed countries as low-cost imports flood in. Even then, recovery in those troubled lands will be limited. It's one thing to again utilize existing capacity. It's another to finance the huge expansion of capacity and infrastructure needed to resume the Tigers' past rapid growth. That takes outside capital, and money returns slowly after being burnt. U.S. banks have only about a third the relative exposure in Latin America that they had in the mid-1980s before the debt crisis there fried them to crisps.

Any revival in Tigerland will be cut short if Western economies slump, especially that of the United States. Our analysis shows that even though low import prices increase import volume, the principal determinant of U.S. imports is American economic activity. If the economy is growing, people are buying more of everything, including imports. This is undoubtedly true of other developed countries as well. In recent years, the United States has been booming and growth in Canada and Europe has also been strong. But Europe is slowing, as noted earlier, and if our forecast is correct, the United States and Canadian economies will decelerate, perhaps entering recessions before long. Obviously, this would cut short any developing-country recoveries. They will be hurt even more if American consumers, who have been the engine of global growth in recent years, end their three decade borrowing and spending binge and curtail spending in a saving spree (discussed in detail in Chapters 12 and 13).

Before turning to Chapter 12, however, note that the net effect of the Asian Contagion is to reduce worldwide demand and increase global supply for many years to come. Both effects are deflationary.

12 CHAPTER

American Consumers Will Save More

In earlier chapters, you saw the large number of deflationary forces already at work in the world. The Asian crisis (Chapters 10 and 11) is important, but much more so because it comes on top of the many other downward pressures on prices, covered in Chapters 1 to 9. These 13 deflationary forces, listed in Table I–2, are probably enough to push the world into chronic deflation, but if one more falls into place—a switch by U.S. consumers from big borrowing and spending to big saving—deflation is assured.

THE SPENDING SPREE

Without question, U.S. consumers have been on a spending spree for about three decades. Not only have their outlays increased as a share of GDP, but they have also grown much faster than their personal disposable, or after tax, income. Why?

The purchasing power of the average American ended its rapid postwar growth in the early 1970s, despite the huge number of married women who entered the labor force in the years since then to try to keep alive the American Dream of ever-increasing purchasing power. Initially, growth was curtailed by commodity inflation, which transferred purchasing power abroad, and by very slow productivity growth. Then restructuring, starting in the 1980s, eliminated many high-paid but low-skilled jobs. Autoworkers, who even 15 years ago made close to $80,000 annually including fringes, found themselves retrained as computer programmers making half as much—if they were lucky and resourceful. Otherwise, they were flipping hamburgers at little more than the minimum wage.

Then in the 1980s, middle-class Americans resorted to heavy borrowing to continue to enjoy the American Dream they felt they deserved, but could no longer afford (Figure 12–1). The flip side of more borrowing is reduced saving, and the personal saving rate has declined to virtually zero (Figure 12–2).

INCENTIVES TO SAVE

Despite the lack of it in recent years, there is ample incentive for Americans to save. For one, high debts, which have propelled personal bankruptcies to record levels in recent years. Second, owner-occupied houses used to serve as wonderful piggy banks that

F I G U R E 12–1

U.S. total consumer and mortgage debt outstanding as a percentage of personal disposable income (1959–1998)

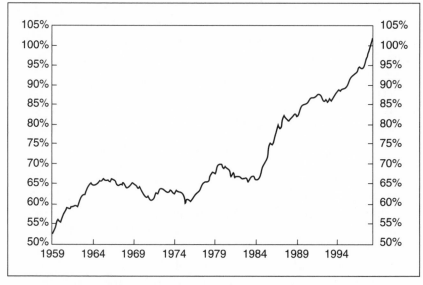

Source: Federal Reserve Board

F I G U R E 12–2

U.S. personal saving as a percentage of disposable income (1959–1998)

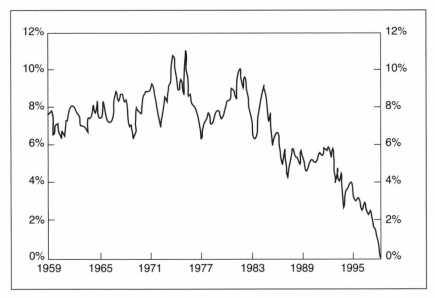

Source: U.S. Bureau of Economic Analysis

constantly refilled through capital appreciation and could be tapped for almost any need through refinancing or home equity loans. But no more. The unwinding of inflation has left house prices rising at no more than general inflation rates.

Third, while middle-class purchasing power has been shrinking, higher-end incomes have been the big winners, with the share of household income going to the top quintile—the only segment to rise in the 1980–1997 period. These are the people with the managerial and technical skills necessary to compete in today's global economy, and they are paid increasing amounts for their services. They are also the big savers, and as income continues to move into their hands, the overall saving rate should rise. For example, a KPMG Peat Marwick survey last year found that 90 percent of those earning more than $66,000 in 1996 contributed to their 401(k) plans compared with only 64 percent of all other workers. And the top earners contributed 6.8 percent of their incomes while the rest only put in 4.7 percent.

Fourth, the postwar baby phenomenon is really a double whammy—a bulge of people followed by a decline. Obviously, this means that, in the years ahead, there will be fewer people in their twenties and thirties who spend a lot and save little as they form households and raise families. At the same time, there will be lots of postwar babies in their peak earning years who don't need to spend as much. Their children will be leaving home, so they won't have big tuition bills and, if their kids are anything like mine, they won't have as many smashed-up cars to replace either.

They will, then, be able to save more, and they need to. Postwar babies are already beginning to look retirement in the teeth and few have saved enough to maintain themselves in the styles they desire. Two-thirds of Americans are saving little or nothing for retirement. Moreover, when people change jobs, 60 percent do not rollover their 401(k) and defined benefit funds into IRAs, but withdraw the money for current spending. The tendency to cash-out is strongest among low-income people with small retirement funds. With job changes now frequent, more saving is needed to offset this depletion of retirement money.

Fifth, polls consistently show that less than 10 percent of those below age 50 think they'll get a dime from Social Security benefits when they retire. The plight of Social Security has finally gotten Washington's attention, but the problem is far from solved, as discussed in Chapter 2. If Social Security won't be there in retirement, you'll not only have to save yourself, but save well before you retire. The ongoing threat of layoffs is a sixth reason for employees to build rainy-day funds by saving more while they still have jobs. Some thought earlier that restructuring layoffs were over, but as noted in Chapter 3 (see Figure 3–3), the recent upsurge in layoffs suggests that it will be an ongoing reality.

WHY AREN'T CONSUMERS SAVING?

U.S. consumers, then, have lots of incentives to save, but they haven't been saving. Why? Partly because they want to continue to enjoy the good life, regardless of their financial health. If a bank or other credit card issuer sends them more plastic, they'll use it, and some furniture and appliance dealers are even allowing customers to postpone interest and principal payments for as long as two years. Saving has also been deterred by rapidly appreciating stock holdings that have served as a substitute. This is the real-wealth effect. People don't have to sell their stocks to support current spending, but they are willing to save less and spend more of their current incomes because their appreciated equity portfolios make them feel wealthier. In government accounts, by the way, personal income includes wages and salaries; rent, interest, and dividends received; pension benefits, social security, welfare, and other transfer payments; but not appreciation in existing assets, including stocks and real estate. So, the saving rate (Figure 12–2) does not include capital gains.

This real-wealth concept makes sense when you note the close correlation between changes in stock prices and consumer confidence. Times of rising stock prices are times of prosperity, high employment, and plentiful job opportunities, as in recent years. These are times when people are especially willing to rely on their stock holdings to do their saving.

U.S. stocks, of course, have been in a 16-year bull market (Figure 12–3), and people have been pouring money into stocks and equity mutual funds. Ownership of stocks and mutual funds has leaped from 20 percent of households to over 50 percent. Including employee-controlled pension plans, variable life insurance holdings, and other indirect ownership of stocks, 43 percent of household assets are now in equities, according to a recent Federal Reserve study, up from 39 percent in the 1960s when stocks were at their previous red-hot peak.

Our statistical analysis indicates that this real-wealth effect has only become important in the last ten years, but boy, has it gotten important! Each 10 percent rise in stock prices has boosted consumer spending about one-half percent. With huge stock gains in the last four years, this appreciation has increased consumer outlays about 1.5 percent a year. That's almost 30 percent of the total growth (Table 12–1).

A TWO-WAY STREET

There's nothing wrong with relying on appreciating assets to replace saving. Why scrimp and save if you're a great investor? The real-wealth effect worked in the 1970s when the price of houses was

FIGURE 12–3

Standard & Poor's 500 composite index logarithms (1970–1999)

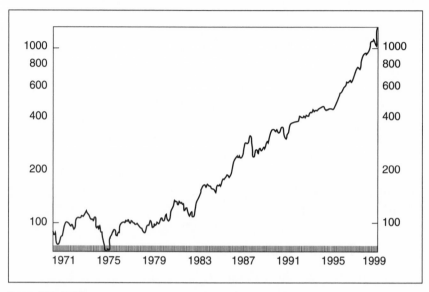

Source: Haver Analytics

TABLE 12–1

Stock Growth Effects on Consumption

	S&P 500 Total Year/Year Return	Change in Consumer Spending	Portion Due To S&P 500 Gains	Residual
1995	37.6%	5.0%	1.9%	3.1%
1996	23.0%	5.3%	1.1%	4.2%
1997	33.4%	5.3%	1.7%	3.6%
1998	28.6%	5.7%	1.4%	4.3%
Average Annual Change	30.5%	5.3%	1.5%	3.8%

Source: Haver Analytics and A. Gary Shilling & Co., Inc.

soaring with inflation, and in the last decade through stocks. There is no third major category of consumer assets, however. What can consumers do for an encore if stocks don't continue to jump or if inflation and heady real estate appreciation doesn't return?

This is an important consideration because stocks may not continue to surge forever. Since the early 1980s, when the personal saving rate was 10 percent, 9 percent of consumer spending growth and 8 percent of the gains in total economic activity came from the saving rate decline. The amount has been even greater when you figure the effects of robust consumer outlays in other areas, such as pushing up capacity utilization and, therefore stimulating capital spending. Obviously, a major bear market in U.S. stocks would have a profound impact on consumer confidence and spending, and would remove the shield that has been fending off all the big pressures to save.

THE TWO-TIER ECONOMY

In the meanwhile, the two-tier U.S. economy persists. The top tier—consumer spending, housing, and capital equipment spending—is floating on a sea of stock market appreciation. This stock appreciation has substituted for consumer saving to not only support robust current spending, but also to put the kids through college and finance early retirement. Robust consumer confidence as well as low interest rates aid housing, while increased sales and soaring stocks encourage businesses to borrow and float stocks to finance new equipment. This is all self-feeding, because strong demand justifies and encourages capital outlays and creates more jobs and income. Rapid job growth in turn pushes up wages, and real purchasing power has risen even faster as inflation rates fall.

But the Asian flu has infected the lower tier of the American economy, manufacturing and commodity producers. They are hurt by falling exports as economically troubled lands with collapsed currencies simply stop buying expensive imports. At the same time, rising imports at lower prices, which force domestic producers to also cut prices (Figure 12–4), hurt their domestic business. When you consider these two tiers of the U.S. economy, it's no wonder overall employment continues to soar while manufacturing jobs sink (Figure 12–5).

FIGURE 12–4

U.S. import price indices, 1993–1999

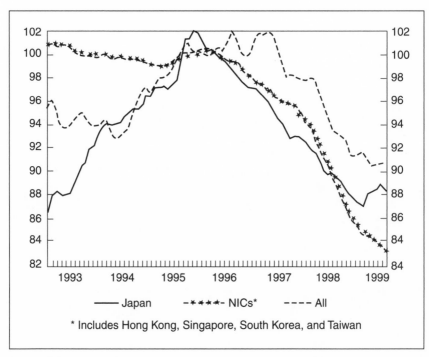

Source: U.S. Bureau of Labor Statistics

PROFITS UNDER FIRE

The gap between these two tiers is unsustainable. Something has to give, and I believe it will be the top falling to meet the bottom. Corporate earnings are the key. They are, of course, under considerable pressure in the bottom tier from sagging exports and rising imports at lower prices and collapsing commodity prices.

But top-tier companies are also being hurt. Firms like Coca-Cola, with a majority of their operations overseas, are being hit by weak sales in wounded developing lands, and their foreign earnings are even weaker when converted into dollars. The devaluation in Brazil and the spreading effects to the rest of Latin America, as well as slowing economic growth in Europe, only make matters

F I G U R E 12–5

Total employment versus manufacturing employment, 1997–1999

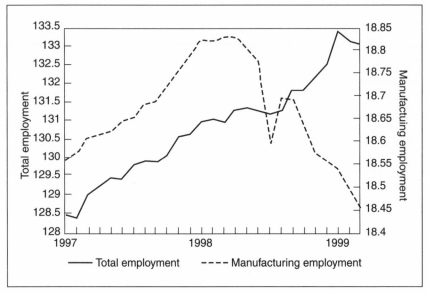

Source: U.S. Bureau of Labor Statistics

worse. These disappointments, especially in Asia, are particularly poignant. Many U.S. multinational firms may have only small current sales in the Far East, but they, along with their stockholders, counted heavily on those sales to mushroom. In any event, the total foreign sales of S&P 500 companies are now 35 percent of the total on average, up from 25 percent in 1985.

At the same time, there is no offsetting give in U.S. domestic costs, at least in the short run. American labor markets are drum-tight and wages are rising. Furthermore, ongoing heavy capital spending commitments will squeeze cash flow as operating earnings fall.

So far, foreign and domestic competition has kept labor cost increases from being passed on in higher prices. In fact, for many firms, the combination of productivity growth, and falling interest costs, corporate taxes, and depreciation, as well as other factors (discussed in Chapter 20) are propelling profits. But with the ef-

FIGURE 12–6

Pretax corporate profits, year-to-year percentage change, 1986–1998

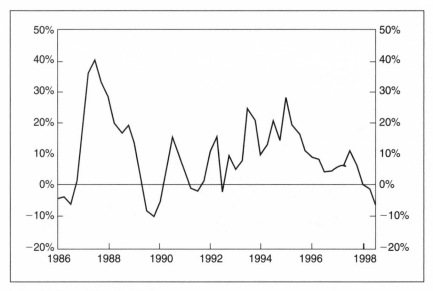

Source: U.S. Bureau of Economic Analysis

fects of the Asian crisis spreading and intensifying, earnings appear very vulnerable for many U.S. firms, and they are already showing weakness in aggregate (Figure 12–6). Indeed, earnings disappointments for U.S. companies are common. Driven fundamentally by global excess supply and growing deflationary forces, earnings declines are also leading to widespread layoffs and a huge merger wave (Chapters 3 and 4).

These profit shortfalls should sooner or later knock stocks off their lofty perch. If they don't precipitate a bear market, the Fed will, as discussed in Chapter 13. Either way, consumers will be converted from borrowers and spenders to savers, as you'll also learn in Chapter 13.

13

U.S. Saving Spree, Triggered by a Bear Market, Ensures Deflation

U.S. stocks are vulnerable to disappointing earnings because they are so over-valued. From the end of 1994 to the end of 1998, the S&P 500 index rose 161 percent, but only one-third of that came from higher earnings. Two-thirds resulted from leaping price/earning ratios (P/Es), which shoved stock prices to record levels (Figure 13–1), even though their supposed determinant, interest rates, are still above the levels of the 1950s and early 1960s (see Figure 21–1). Virtually every other measure of stock market value is also out of sight—price-to-book value, price-to-cash flow, stock market capitalization in relation to GDP, stock prices-to-sales ratios, the S&P 500 to hourly earnings, and stock prices-to-home values ratios. At the same time, dividend yields are at record lows (Figure 13–2).

From the bull market's start in August 1982 until the end of 1998, the S&P 500 index has had a compound annual total return (dividends plus appreciation) of 21.5 percent, about twice the historic norm. Sure, to a great extent, stocks have been celebrating the unwinding of inflation (see Chapter 22) and making up for the beating they suffered during the inflationary late 1960s and 1970s. Nevertheless, many investors believe that what has really been a catch-up will continue indefinitely.

F I G U R E 13–1

S&P 500 price/earning (P/E) ratio on trailing 12 months' earnings

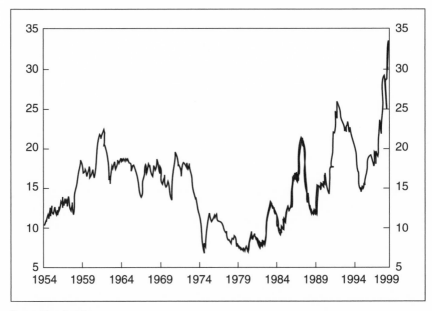

Source: Haver Analytics

Maybe the negative effects of the Asian Contagion on corporate earnings will suddenly cease. Maybe, if Asia proves to be a non-event, the Fed will never, ever again tighten credit and precipitate a recession that is preceded by a bear market in stocks. A number of self-reinforcing factors, common at major stock market tops, have convinced almost everyone that rising stock prices will continue forever. Those "foolproof reasons" for continued growth cry out that the end is near. In *Deflation*, I took 10 pages to list them. I don't need to repeat that list because in the months since I finished that book, many more signs of a top have emerged. I'll mention only a few.

In the old Wall Street saying, stocks are driven by greed, tempered with fear. In the scope of the 16-year bull market, (Figure 12–3), even the 1987 crash and the 1990 mini-crash were only temporary interruptions. They were so quickly retraced that they have trained, and I do mean trained, many to believe that sell-offs are wonderful opportunities to buy, not warnings to sell. That's cer-

FIGURE 13–2

S&P 500 dividend yield

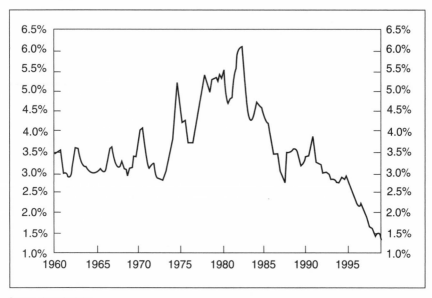

Source: Haver Analytics

tainly been investor reaction to the market declines at the beginning of the Asian meltdown in the summer of 1997, the Hong Kong
crisis in October 1998, the financial demise of Russia and crash of
Long-Term Capital Management starting in August 1998, and the
Brazilian devaluation in early 1999. Of course, these buying binges
were self-fulfilling as stocks promptly revived. Fear of anything
but temporary losses has been replaced by a conviction that the
strong upward trend will last indefinitely and by frustration if one
is not fully invested in stocks.

SIGNS OF A TOP

Confidence is rampant. A survey in November 1998, by Paine
Webber Inc. and the Gallup Organization, found that individual in-
vestors, on average, expect to make 13.5 percent in stocks in the
next six months and 14.7 percent in the following ten years.
Historically, stocks have only returned 7 percent to 10 percent.
Americans expect so much investment success that 40 percent plan

to be able to retire before age 62, when they become eligible for scaled-down Social Security benefits, according to a survey by the American Academy of Actuaries last fall. Another 31 percent think they can leave work after they reach 62, but before 65, when they can collect full benefits, although the retirement age will increase beyond 65 for people born after 1937.

Another sign of over-confidence is the popularity of mutual funds tied to the S&P 500 or other stock indexes, which have been consistently taking in more money than actively managed funds. In the first quarter of 1999, the low cost Vanguard 500 Index Fund took in $4.6 billion compared with an already large $3 billion the year before. Why pay an active portfolio manager when you can make about 30 percent each year in a low-fee indexed fund? True, Morningstar, Inc., a Chicago fund-research firm, found that in the past five years, 273 of 294 actively managed funds under-performed the average S&P 500 index fund. Still, this zeal indicates that investors believe they can't miss with stocks. It's even more true of the hordes who have abandoned mutual funds entirely in favor of buying and selling stocks on their own, often through discount brokers who offer no advice and research, or through Internet brokers. And shareholders seem to be oblivious to gigantic corporate executive pay packages, even for CEOs of companies that lose money. Apparently, they believe that as long as stocks are soaring, it doesn't really matter if corporate management's pay vastly exceeds their value added.

Faith in stock appreciation is so great that a group of senior executives at bookseller Borders Group exchanged their entire salaries and bonuses for stock options last year. Entrepreneurs, confident of future leaps in their stocks, are selling fewer shares as they go public, so that they can retain more control and enjoy more of the future appreciation of their stocks. In 1998, only 31 percent, on average, of new companies' total capitalization was sold in initial public offerings, the lowest in six years. High stock prices make it possible to raise needed money by selling fewer shares.

EVERYBODY'S ABOARD

Even non-profit organizations are offering key executives stock incentive plans tied to the performance of publicly traded stocks. Governments are in the same boat. Poland is joining Chile and

Singapore in investing workers retirement money in stocks; President Clinton has been bitten by the same bug and proposes that part of the Social Security fund be placed in equities instead of Treasury bonds, as in the past.

In contrast, one of the world's best pros, Warren Buffett, apparently thinks stocks are vastly overpriced. In the past year, he broke his long-term commitment to stocks with forays into Treasury bonds and silver. And his recent purchase of General Re reinforced his concern about the current level of stock prices in two ways. First, he forsook his long-standing practice and bought the company with shares of his own firm, Berkshire Hathaway, which rose 52 percent in 1998, rather than with cash. In effect, he used an over-inflated stock to buy an over-inflated stock. Second, with General Re, his overall portfolio is much more heavily weighted to ward bonds, because the acquired firm holds $19 billion in bonds and only $5 billion in stocks, which he has subsequently ordered the reinsurer to dispose of. He's also sitting on a mountain of cash.

Another indication that U.S. stocks may be near an important peak is the narrowness of the market's focus. In the first quarter of 1999, the S&P 500 rose 4.5 percent, with one-third of the advance coming from Microsoft and America Online. The top nine large-cap performers were all Internet, telecommunications or tech-related. Meanwhile, the Value Line index, which measures the average performance of 1,700 stocks, fell 6.4 percent. Similarly, in 1998, the S&P 500 index rose 26.7 percent, but the average stocks in that index gained just 10.5 percent. Using data since 1958, the Leuthold Group found that the spread had never been that large before. Quite the contrary, in the past, the average stock outperformed the index by three percentage points. Note that the S&P 500 index is weighted by the market capitalizations of its 500 components, so the performances of the index and its average stock can be quite different. Four stocks—Microsoft, Intel, Cisco, and Dell—account for about one-fifth of that index's gain last year.

This concentration on a few large growth stocks is reminiscent of the Nifty Fifty list that was the focus of investor's attention in the early 1970s, at the end of that long bull market. Those were the "one decision" stocks that had such promise that you only had to make one decision—to buy them—because they never would need to be sold. Nevertheless, disappointments began to multiply and the favored few shrank to the point that the only ones that continued to interest investors were amusement parks (Disney), gimmick cameras (Polaroid), motor homes (Winnebago), and hamburger stands (McDonald's). At the time, I pointed out that these represented the fluff of the economy, not its guts. If investors shunned the basic economy, they were anticipating big trouble, I reasoned. And they were right. The 1973–1975 recession followed, the deepest since the 1930s, and what was left of the Nifty Fifty collapsed. Panicked investors did make that second decision, and as they dumped Polaroid, its price fell from $150 to $14 per share.

BIG SPECULATIONS IN THE PAST . . .

This time, the object of investor endearment, of course, is Internet stocks. As with any speculation, there is an underlying grain of truth. When tulips were introduced to Northern Europe from Turkey in the sixteenth century, they were immensely popular. Think about all of those magnificent Dutch still life paintings that feature beautiful tulips. The tulip bulb mania took this reality to illogical extremes. Charles Mackay, in his well-known 1841 book, *Extraordinary Popular Delusions and the Madness of Crowds*, has a wonderful chapter on the 1636 Tulipomania, as it was called.

> The tulip-jobbers speculated in the rise and fall of the tulip stocks, and made large profits by buying when prices fell, and selling out when they rose. Many individuals grew suddenly rich. A golden bait hung temptingly out before the people, and one after the other, they rushed to the tulip-marts, like flies around a honey-pot. Every one imagined that the passion for tulips would last forever, and that the wealthy from every part of the world would send to Holland, and pay whatever prices were asked for them. The riches of Europe would be concentrated on the shores of the Zuyder Zee, and poverty banished from the favoured clime of Holland. Nobles, citizens, farmers, mechanics, seamen, footmen, maid-servants, even chimney-sweeps, and old clotheswomen, dabbled in tulips. People of all grades converted their property into cash, and invested it in flowers. Foreigners became smitten with the same frenzy, and money poured into Holland from all directions.
>
> The following list of the various articles, and their value, were delivered for one single root of the rare species called the Viceroy:

Two lasts of wheat	448 florins
Four lasts of rye	558 florins
Four fat oxen	480 florins
Eight fat swine	240 florins
Twelve fat sheep	120 florins
Two hogsheads of wine	70 florins
Four tuns of beer	32 florins
Two tuns of butter	192 florins
One thousand lbs. of cheese	120 florins
A complete bed	100 florins
A suit of clothes	80 florins
A silver drinking-cup	60 florins

. . . AND THE PRESENT

Similarly, the Internet stocks are based on a real phenomenon, as discussed in Chapter 6, and have reached the tulip bulb level of excesses. Most of these companies have no earnings and little prospect of making money for years, but that didn't stop buyers from pushing EarthWeb's stock up 379 percent in three days when it was offered to the public in November 1998, or theglobe.com, up 606 percent in its first day of public trading—a market capitalization on the firm that was 347 times its $1.74 million revenues. Compare that with five times the revenues for the average stock in the Russell 2000 index of small companies, and also note that the firm lost $5.8 billion in the first half of 1998. MarketWatch.com wasn't far behind, with a 474 percent gain on its opening day; that put a $1.15 billion value on a company that lost $8 million in the first three quarters of 1998. In order to make Internet stocks look more reasonable, many Wall Street analysts are replacing after-tax earnings per share numbers with cash flow earnings per share, which excludes such costs as interest, taxes and depreciation.

Furthermore, the new money isn't just flowing into stocks. A number of Internet companies are issuing convertible bonds with the expectations that their stocks will soar indefinitely. Amazon.com raised $1.2 billion in January this way with a 4.75 percent interest cost, just 0.1 percent above the 10-year Treasury bond yield. If

Internet stocks keep leaping, the bonds will be converted and stop the interest payments, but that will flood the market with additonal shares. If they don't, the issuers will be stuck with sizable interest costs. That happened to a lot of corporations that issued convertibles in 1969–70, and then the stock market nosedived.

Much of the zeal for Internet stocks comes from Internet users who trade through Internet brokers. With the ease of trading from the PC and the low commission costs of online brokers, they can hardly be called investors as they move in and out of their favorite Internet stocks many times per day. In fact, it's now apparent that many have become addicted to online trading and for good reason. To them, it's really just another form of gambling and, as in casinos, they'll soon be able to do it 24 hours a day as Internet stock exchanges become established.

Theglobe.com turned over each publicly held share more than five times on its first day of trading. This frantic pace has at times clogged Internet trading systems, especially on days of stock price declines. Nevertheless, the online zealots have created a self-reinforcing cycle. By using the Internet, especially through online brokers, they create the prospect of more growth and higher share prices for Internet companies, which encourages them to sink even more money into their darlings. As a result, late last year discount broker Schwab, with 61 percent of its trades online, was worth more in market capitalization than mighty Merrill Lynch.

To be sure, individual investors are not alone in the Internet frenzy. Managers of large mutual funds like Fidelity Magellan Fund have joined the fray. Companies with only a Web site or two and little Internet business are rushing to add '.com' to their names in hopes of attracting investor attention. Recall the jump in Sotheby's stock when the firm announced that it was tip-toeing into the online auction business. (My company isn't a public company, but we do have a Web site, www.agaryshilling.com. I'm thinking about changing the name of the firm to AGaryShilling&Co.com to be sure everyone knows we're up with the times.) Even normally cautious venture capitalists are aboard. Since mid-1966, as much as a third of their total outlays have been to new Internet firms and that figure soared recently to one-half.

My old friend Bob Farrell, Senior Investment Advisor at Merrill Lynch and the dean of Wall Street technical analysts, couldn't have put the Internet craze in better perspective. As quoted in *The Wall Street Journal*, he said, "If you were looking for something that was a fitting finale to the biggest bull market in history, it would be the biggest speculative mania in history—and that's what it does look like." Well, maybe, but John Law's Mississippi Scheme in France, which collapsed in 1720, and the South-Sea Bubble in England, which burst the same year, as well as Tulipomania may also be in the running for first place. In any event, previous recent American speculations pale by comparison to Internet mania, including the computer leasing craze in 1968, the banking stock binge in 1961, the personal computer stock mania of 1982–1983, and the biotech companies rage in 1991–1992. Even Polaroid, which sold at a peak P/E of 95 in 1972, looks like a widows-and-orphans stock compared to America Online's 418 P/E in early 1998.

WHEN THE BUBBLE BREAKS

There are already signs that the Internet bubble is fragile. Of 12 Internet-commerce stocks that went public in 1996, at the end of January 1999, seven were trading below their closing prices on their first trading days. This isn't really surprising since during the 1988–1993 era, the medium initial public offering under performed the market by 30 percent in its first three years, and 46 percent last value. To get some idea what the collapse of Internet mania will look like when it comes—and it will come—let's go back to Mackay.

> At last, however, the more prudent began to see that this folly could not last forever. It was seen that somebody must lose fearfully in the end. As this conviction spread, prices fell, and never rose again. Confidence was destroyed, and a universal panic seized upon the dealers . . . Defaulters were announced day after day in all the towns of Holland. Hundreds who, a few months previously, had begun to doubt that there was such a thing as poverty in the land suddenly found themselves the possessors of a few bulbs, which nobody would buy, even though they offered them at one quarter of the sums they had paid for them. The cry of distress resounded everywhere, and each man accused his neighbor. The few who had contrived to enrich themselves hid their wealth from the knowledge of their fellow-citizens, and invested it in the English or other funds. Many who, for a brief season, had emerged from the humbler walks of life, were cast

back into their original obscurity. Substantial merchants were reduced almost to beggary, and many a representative of a noble line saw the fortunes of his house ruined beyond redemption.

After World War II, aluminum appeared to have a great future, because it could be used for siding on houses, pots and pans, auto parts, wiring, and almost everything else. From 1949 to 1956, aluminum stocks on average leaped 11-fold compared to a mere triple for the S&P 500 index, and by the mid-1950s aluminum had fulfilled all of its promise. Yet, it soon became a commodity and it took until 1983 for the average aluminum stock to exceed its 1956 price.

A final sign of a significant top in stock prices is the arrogance now prevalent among Wall Street brokers. A full-page *Wall Street Journal* ad by Paine Webber late last year said in screaming letters beneath a picture of a bear cave, "A Thought To Ponder As You Watch For The Bear To Emerge. YOU MAY BE IN FOR A VERY LONG WAIT." Warburg Dillon Read recently brought in a hotshot investment banker from Citigroup with a pay package of $70 million over three-plus years. And brokers, especially those involved with online today, are on a hiring binge. Furthermore, in the face of electronic trading systems that are making physical trading floors anomalies, the New York Stock Exchange recently decided to move to new and vastly bigger facilities.

NOT THE EXPECTED END

Regardless of the lofty levels of stocks and the Internet madness, most individual and professional investors think they're safe in stocks as long as interest rates don't rise. After all, that's almost always been the case in the postwar era. In fact, they reason that falling interest rates will push up P/Es, as in the past. But the post-war era was one of inflation. History shows that in deflation, interest rates and stock prices can fall together. You can see this by looking at it from a different angle. Today we're in a global economy and interest rates have risen—not in the United States, but in Asia and Latin America—in the midst of financial crises. In any event, a major U.S. bear market is likely, driven by earnings disappointments.

Of course, most individual investors view themselves as long-term holders of equities, but if they were, major sell-offs would be impossible. History shows, however, that many of those who think they have millennium-long time horizons quickly become panicked sellers in major and prolonged bear markets. They dump the last of their holdings at market bottoms, swearing that they'll never buy another stock again. In my view, this history is relevant to today's stock investors because human nature changes very slowly, if at all, over time. Therefore, investors will react to similar circumstances in similar ways. As Sir John Templeton put it, the five most dangerous words in the English language are these: "this time it is different."

In fact, it is scared investors that make stock market bottoms, which occur when the last one who can be shaken out is shaken out. My great friend and colleague Dennis Gartman calls this the "puke point." By then the stock market is fresh out of sellers, faced with nothing but potential buyers, and therefore, ready for rebound. This is the exact reverse of a market top, which is formed when the last investor who can be sucked in has been sucked in. The market has run out of buyers and faces nothing but potential sellers. It's also true that a market pinnacle is reached when the last bear throws in the towel.

The problem is that those intending to be long-term investors panic on schedule at bottoms, and then fail to reinvest until the recovery is well underway. Consequently, they realize far less appreciation over the long haul than stock market indices suggest.

I've learned, repeatedly, that when a majority believe that a market will continue to move in one direction indefinitely, a reversal is at hand. Dennis Gartman has another wonderful statement: "When you're yellin', you should be sellin'; when you're cryin', you should be buyin'." Of course, convictions that any declines are magnificent buying opportunities are so ingrained that it will take big losses over a long period to disabuse investors of their bullishness. Furthermore, nature is perverse and will give investors what they least expect. Consequently, the next bear market will probably be a Chinese water torture affair, with sell-offs met with buying that spawn weak rallies, followed by more sell-offs—a long and frustrating saw-toothed pattern along a declining trend. As usual, even the true believers will ultimately dump their stocks, and thereby create the final bear market bottom.

A BIG SHOCK

How do you think consumers will take a major loss in the appreciation of stocks that have had big cumulative gains over many

TABLE 13-1

The Saver's Reward (1992–Present)—Summary Table

Market Decline	Cost	Value	Gain	Gain
Now	$72,500	$164,603	$92,103	127%
Down 10% Next 12 Months	$82,500	$155,626	$73,126	89%
Down 20% Next 12 Months	$82,500	$143,160	$60,660	74%
Down 25% Next 12 Months	$82,500	$136,974	$54,474	66%
Down 30% Next 12 Months	$82,500	$130,694	$48,194	58%
Down 35% Next 12 Months	$82,500	$124,414	$41,914	51%
Down 40% Next 12 Monts	$82,500	$118,228	$35,728	43%
Down 50% Next 12 Months	$82,500	$105,762	$23,262	28%
Down 60% Next 12 Months	$82,500	$93,295	$10,795	13%

Source: The Leuthold Group

years—a loss that would destroy much of the wealth they've been counting on for retirement and other purposes normally funded by saving current income? My good friend, Steve Leuthold of the Leuthold Group, calculated an excellent example of how devastating the loss would be (Table 13–1).

He assumes that in late 1991, a couple became convinced that the stock market was their one and only route to a comfortable retirement. Starting in January 1992, they diligently invested $2,500 each quarter in a 401(k) plan, all in equity mutual funds, and the total returns to date have matched S&P 500 performance (better than the vast majority of equity funds).

On December 31, 1998, including their 1998 fourth quarter contribution, the $72,500 invested for retirement had a portfolio value of about $164,603, a nice gain of $92,103, about 127 percent over cost. They more than doubled their money and can retire with ease if this trend continues.

But if the S&P 500 slides 25 percent over the next year and the couple continues to make disciplined quarterly investments, the $82,500 then contributed would have a portfolio value of $136,974, shaving the gain to $54,474, or about 66 percent over cost. This is a small reward compounded for eight years of diligent retirement saving.

And what's more, a 50 percent decline (a stock market retreat to closer to its median valuation levels) would shrink portfolio value to $105,762, only $23,262 more than the amount they had contributed over the last eight years, a gain over cost of 28 percent. CDs or money market funds would have done better. If stocks drop more, the gain is trivial. Money under the mattress would have been almost as good—even better on a risk-adjusted basis.

These losses may seem too big given the huge appreciation in stocks since 1991. Bear in mind, however, that in this example, the money was put in over time, so only the initial investment enjoyed the full gain and more recent deposits got only more recent appreciation. Nevertheless, all of the investment money suffers the losses. In real life, setbacks will probably be even bigger in the next bear market because most investors, attracted by the fabulous stock market appreciation in recent years, have invested much more in the last few years than in the early 1990s. Thanks, Steve, for the wonderful example of a bear market's devastation!

Most believe, of course, that investors in 401(k) and other retirement funds will never desert stocks, even in the worst of bear markets. Steve Leuthold's example and other factors discussed in Chapter 28 make me think otherwise. If investors become disillusioned by a debilitating decline in U.S. stocks, they will also enhance the fall by liquidating mutual funds, which will force the funds to sell in order to meet redemptions. Investors didn't hesitate to dump international stock funds in 1997–1998 in reaction to the Asian markets' melt-down. Ditto for foreign investors. The great American bull market has drawn them in from abroad, but they'll leave when the bear arrives and that will depress stocks further in the process.

SAVING REAPPEARS . . .

A big bear market would be the shock we've been waiting for to switch consumers from borrowing and spending to saving. If a big chunk of their stock appreciation is wiped out, all the inducements for savings discussed in Chapter 12 will be unleashed with full fury—the desire to spend to maintain the good life notwithstanding. And a switch to saving will make a big difference in the U.S. economy. Since the early 1980s, the consumer saving rate has fallen by 10 percentage points from about 10 percent to zero, or about two-thirds of a percentage point per year on average (Figure 12–2). Conversely, the spending rate has risen the same amount.

Suppose a saving spree breaks out and the saving rate rises by a half percentage point per year for ten years. In a decade, this will bring savings back to 5 percent of after-tax income, still well below the earlier postwar average of about 8 percent. The shift from a two-thirds percent decline per year to a half-percent rise is obviously more than a one percentage point net increase in the saving rate—and over a one percentage point net fall per year in the spending rate.

... WITH BIG CONSEQUENCES

That's a huge shift, considering that real consumer spending has only been growing at a 2½ percent rate in the last decade, but it has plenty of precedence. Recall that the destruction of Japanese real wealth in stocks and real estate may have a lot to do with the recent leap in their saving rate (Figure 11–1). U.S. consumer spending is two-thirds of GDP, and a long-term change in consumer spending habits will have similar effects on the other one-third of spending. Housing will be directly dampened by consumer caution. Capital spending will grow more slowly, especially that which is oriented toward capacity expansion, because weaker consumer spending growth spawns excess capacity. Even government spending will rise more slowly if the zeal for balanced budgets survives, because slower economies and deflation hold back tax collections. To be sure, economic sluggishness will curtail imports to the benefit of GDP. Nevertheless, the rising dollar we foresee and business weakness abroad, to say nothing of possible protectionism (Chapter 17), work the other way by encouraging cheaper imports to the detriment of domestic production.

A 1 percent or so slower annual growth in real GDP will reduce it from the 2½ percent of the last decade to 1½ percent or even less. Let me be optimistic and move the forecast range up a bit to 1½ to 2 percent. Coming on top of the other 13 deflationary forces already at work (See Table I–2 and Chapters 1–11), this weakness ensures deflation in the United States—and throughout the world. American consumer spending plus residential construction accounts for almost three-quarters of U.S. GDP, which, in turn, is over 25 percent of the globe's total. So, more than 20 percent of all the goods and services produced in the world are bought by U.S. consumers.

Of course, we wouldn't want this global economic slowdown to get out of hand. The previously booming U.S. business-consulting business is showing signs of slowdown as businesses cut costs—in this case, consulting costs. We're delighted to say, however, that this dastardly development has not spread to economic consultants, at least not to this one. We're growing, maybe because financial institutions and industrial corporations want to hear more about our deflation forecast.

The shock of the transition for U.S. consumers from spenders to savers would undoubtedly precipitate a U.S. recession that would spread globally, as already weakening European economies are dragged down. It would also depress troubled developing countries, and could push China into devaluation with all of its negative complications, as discussed in Chapters 10 and 11.

BACK TO WAITING FOR THE FED

There is, of course, a slim, remote, infinitesimal, highly unlikely, insignificant, trivial chance that I'm dead wrong on the trigger mechanism for U.S. consumer retrenchment. Contrary to my belief, the Asian Contagion's detrimental effects on U.S. corporate profits may be laughed-off by the U.S. stock market. Maybe I'm wrong and recent rapid earnings growth is sustainable even with a spillover from Asia, Latin America, and other troubled areas. Then robust consumer confidence and spending would remain intact, but continuing tight labor markets would again threaten a future surge in inflation, at least in the Fed's eyes. Bear in mind that this reasoning caused the Fed to tighten credit in early 1997, and the credit authorities undoubtedly would have raised rates further had the Asian flu not threatened to infect the United States. So we'd be back to waiting for the credit authorities to raise interest rates and, as is normal, precipitate a recession.

As usual, a bear market in U.S. stocks would precede that recession. Given stocks' lofty levels, the sell-off would probably destroy enough individual wealth to chase consumers out of spending and into a saving spree. Then, as with the case of an

Asian-initiated bear market, the end result would be deflation. Damned if you do, damned if you don't. I see deflation in the cards one way or another.

It's even possible that we'll get the worst of both possible scenarios. The Fed tightens credit because it doesn't see any sign of the Asian flu infecting the United States. At that precise time, however, the Asian Contagion becomes an epidemic among American corporations, sending profits to the hospital. Stocks would be severely wounded by both rising interest rates and falling corporate earnings.

Regardless of how we get there, I see deflation in the cards. In the next chapter, you'll see how deflation reinforces itself.

PART TWO

THE WORLD ECONOMY UNDER DEFLATION

14
CHAPTER

Deflation is Self-Feeding

In Chapters 1 through 13, I've made the case for deflation. Yet, you, like most people today, may still think that deflation just isn't possible in the modern world. You may believe that private spending is predominately on services, which have an inflationary bias. Government spending in today's developed countries runs a third to a half or more of economic activity, so its very size and built-in stabilizers will prevent widespread falling prices, you think. Nevertheless, the self-feeding nature of deflation will offset these impediments.

When price declines are widespread and chronic, buyers anticipate further declines. They wait for even lower prices, and the resulting excess capacity and unwanted inventories force producers to cut prices further. Suspicions are confirmed, so buyers wait for still lower prices in a self-perpetuating spiral. Furthermore, as a saving spree by U.S. consumers reduces demand and, thereby, encourages deflation, that deflation in turn will foster saving as people wait for additional lower price cuts before buying. And, the likely high real returns on fixed income instruments during deflation (see Chapters 20 and 21) will further reward saving even more and discourage spending.

This self-feeding cycle applies to services as well as goods. An airplane full of empty seats is just as much an inducement to cutting prices as is a dealer's lot full of unsold cars. Services, which compose almost 60 percent of consumer spending, tend to have much more labor content than goods production. So, it's really quite amazing that service inflation is falling at a time when U.S. labor markets are drum-tight. Since 1991, the inflation rate for consumer services has fallen from over a 6 percent annual rate to 2.5 percent. Think of what will happen when jobs become less plentiful. Also, think about the many services that are destined for lower prices. As noted earlier, the Internet has collapsed the costs of banking transactions, and an online stock trade costs one-tenth as much as that serviced by a full-service broker. The prices of computer software, especially adjusted for increases in application power, continue to drop like rocks in deep water.

Housing is another big piece of consumer spending. Mortgage rates continue downward as inflation unwinds, and utility costs are falling with deregulation and plummeting fuel prices. Internet purchases can reduce the cost of furnishing and equipping a new house, and even eliminate brokerage commissions paid for its purchase. Telecommunications is another important service, and there, too, new technologies are slashing costs and prices, as noted in Chapter 5. All this evidence of service deflation has thus far been largely ignored.

Deflation is also self-feeding in the business arena as firms wait for lower prices before investing in inventories as well as new plant and equipment, and capital spending is also depressed by excess capacity. Weak investment spending then increases capacity among capital goods producers, promotes further price declines, etc. As building costs fall, cheaper new structures depress the prices of older buildings. In deflation it's obvious that cost-of-living adjustments, big self-perpetuators of inflation, are either eliminated or become de-escalators that reduce wages and other costs.

REINFORCING DEFLATION IN REAL ESTATE AND GOVERNMENT

In deflation, as prices of real estate and other heavily leveraged assets fall, defaults will be more common and lenders much more cautious. So, construction will be depressed, leading to more excess capacity in that industry and even weaker prices in real estate markets already subdued by deflation. Of course, bear markets in tangibles will discourage investment and speculation in that area, and turn attention to saving and productivity-enhancing investments. That, too, cuts costs and prices. Speculation in tangibles is further discouraged by the high real cost of borrowing.

Deflation is self-feeding in government as well. With flat or only small increases in money wages and salaries, and more muted capital gains than in recent years, personal tax collections grow more slowly and fewer people are pushed into higher tax brackets, as noted in Chapter 13. The effect will be powerful and reverse the effects that inflation had in past decades. In 1996, inflation wasn't all that robust with the CPI rising 2.9 percent from 1995. Yet that inflation, combined with personal income growth of 4.9 percent and the realized capital gains that flowed from booming stocks, pushed adjusted gross income, as defined by the Internal Revenue Service, ahead by 8.3 percent. Taxpayers were forced into higher brackets, as total individual income taxes rose 12 percent, or half again as much. IRS data is not yet available for 1997 and 1998, but with the fall in inflation, the government's tax take no doubt grew more in step with incomes.

Taxable corporate profits also rise more modestly in deflation, as basic earnings advances, in nominal terms, are slower. Also in deflation, inventory losses occur as prices fall and depreciation overstates the cost of replacement equipment. Both reverse the effects of inflation and reduce taxable earnings. Furthermore, the portion of capital gains that merely offsets inflation will no longer exist and be taxed. Quite the reverse, capital appreciation will be reduced by the extent of deflation. Assuming that voter zeal for balanced budgets persists, sluggish growth in federal revenues will force even more government spending restraint and further cut Washington's share of the economic pie—another deflationary process. Ditto for state and local governments, which will see deflation erode income tax collections and sales taxes as prices fall.

THE REVERSE OF INFLATIONARY EXPECTATIONS

To appreciate fully the self-feeding aspects of deflation, it may be helpful to recall the exact opposite, self-feeding inflation. During the high inflation of the 1970s, people became convinced that it would last indefinitely, and indeed that prices would accelerate. So they borrowed heavily to beat rising interest rates as well as price hikes and invested in rapidly appreciating homes and other tangibles. This strained credit supplies and pushed up interest rates, while rampant demand for real estate, coins, antiques, and art works propelled prices. Suspicions were confirmed, spawning more of the same. Furthermore, even though interest rates rose, they remained far below the returns on tangibles. In fact, in the mid- and late-1970s, long-term interest rates, adjusted for CPI inflation, were negative, as noted in Chapter 2.

Similarly, consumers and businesses bought more inventories than they needed to in anticipation of rising prices, and invested in plant and equipment far in advance of actual need. That put pressure on supplies, pushed up prices, and encouraged even bigger hedge buying. Productive work and investments gave way to speculation, so there was little productivity growth to offset rising costs. This, too, added fat to the fires of inflation. Business didn't care much what it paid for labor and materials because cost increases could be passed through with ease, and with markups to boot. This practice fed on itself because costs accelerated as they moved through the production system and encouraged even bigger markups. Meanwhile, the resulting inflation induced widespread cost-of-living adjustments for wages, and thus even higher labor costs.

During those years I told clients how I'd succumbed to inflationary expectations even though I was predicting their demise. After the October 1973 energy price leap, I knew that drastically higher fertilizer prices would follow because natural gas is used to make its nitrogen component. But my local garden center owner hadn't caught on. So, as he was closing at Thanksgiving for the winter, I bought his remaining supply, and he even gave me a discount to avoid holding the inventory over the winter.

There it was, stacked up in my garage from the floor almost to the ceiling. I used part of it on my lawn the next summer, but still had room for another stack, so I returned the following fall. His prices had risen, but not much, so I repeated the exercise. I'm sure I would have kept repeating it until prices broke and I was stuck with a ten-year supply of fertilizer, but fortunately, I ran out of garage space first.

HALF WAY THERE

Inflationary expectations ruled the 1970s and are the precise opposite of the deflationary expectations I see developing. Indeed, consumers are beginning to anticipate lower prices. Few any longer buy a car that does not carry a rebate, and recently Pepsi's attempt to increase prices in supermarkets led to lower sales. Also, the business attitude toward cost pass-through has already made at least half of the transition. Very few American businesses today expect their customers to cover their cost increases. It's gotten to the point that most suppliers don't even bother asking for price relief. And this doesn't just refer to manufacturers facing withering foreign competition. Medical services, lawyers, and regrettably, economic consultants, are in the same boat.

When a business can't get its customers to pay more, it in turn tells its suppliers that their cost increases are their problems, to be offset by their own cost cuts and productivity increases. In fact, the only price discussions many firms have today with their suppliers concern how much the vendors' prices will be cut. This, of course, is the introduction of price decline pass-through, which will expand considerably in deflation as widespread price drops are pushed backward through the supplier chain.

WHEN DO YOU KNOW THAT DEFLATION HAS ARRIVED?

Consumer retrenchment in reaction to a major bear market in U.S. stocks would undoubtedly precipitate a recession which, because American consumers are the only meaningful source of global demand today, would be global. On a widespread basis, prices would decline in that downturn but that wouldn't insure deflation, because prices always decelerate in business dips. If inflation is running at 10 percent, it drops to, say, 7 or 8 percent rates in a recession; if at 4 percent, it falls to 1 or 2 percent in a downturn. Inflation is now about zero, so price declines of 2 or 3 percent in the next recession are likely, but prices could stop falling when it's over. If, in the recovery that follows, however, U.S. consumers remain cautious and prices continue to fall 1 or 2 percent per year, then chronic deflation has arrived. That is likely, because at that point, all 14 deflationary forces will be in full force.

It will also probably take the jolt of the next recession to convince most people that deflation is for real and allow for the full development of their deflationary expectations. The vast majority of American consumers and businessmen have only known the inflation of the last 60 years. In fact, polls show that most think that current inflation is much higher than the CPI indicates (1.6 percent for 1998), despite the belief by most economists that CPI increases are overstated by more than one percentage point, as noted earlier.

UNACCEPTED PRICE DECLINES

Indeed, a lifetime of chronic inflation has a lot to do with America's unwillingness to accept the virtual disappearance of price increases, on average. Many seem to ignore price declines on things they buy and only remember the increases. This is easy to do on big ticket items that aren't purchased frequently because few recall what they spent the last time they bought the item. Our basement freezer gave up the ghost last summer, so I replaced that Amana with one of comparable size, a 21-cubic foot GE at a cost of $540. As a good economist, however, I kept the paperwork on the Amana that was purchased way back in 1974—after 24 years, that old baby didn't owe us a thing. Its price was less, $352, but CPI has risen 53.4 percent in the meanwhile. So, in inflation-adjusted terms, the new freezer was 55.7 percent cheaper—less than half the real price we paid in 1974!

In quality-adjusted terms, the new freezer was even less expensive because better insulation and a more efficient motor and cooling system make the new model much cheaper to run. Lack of proper accounting for quality improvements is, by the way, one reason why CPI inflation is overstated. It is also likely that Americans perceive more inflation than exists because they, too, don't account for improved products. The quality of cars has improved immensely in the last two decades. Thirty years ago, Detroit's autos rusted out in three or four years, if the engine didn't die before then. Today I still drive my 1988 Lincoln Town Car (dubbed "the barge" by my kids); its been driven 115,000 *careful* miles and has never seen the inside of my junk-stuffed garage, but doesn't have any body rust. Yet most consumers, if they remember at all what they paid for their last car, only recall that it was a lot cheaper and don't take into account its lower quality.

A trip last Christmas by my wife and me to the FAO Schwarz flagship store in Manhattan provided many examples of unappreciated quality improvements. Sure, they still have a few straight-

forward old board games like Monopoly, but most contain electronics of some sort, yet don't cost much more than plain board
games because semiconductor chips are so cheap. One we saw was
a wooden jigsaw puzzle map of the United States, which spoke the
name of each state as that piece was lifted. (Of course, you may argue that interactive electronic toys discourage thinking and therefore aren't improvements in quality.)

Furthermore, with most prices rising nonstop throughout
their personal pasts, most consumers have come to believe that
only their cunning and aggressive bargain hunting can achieve
lower prices, while market forces outside their control—probably
the works of the Devil himself—conspire to charge them more.
They seem to ignore even chronic and substantial price declines on
frequently purchased items that are indeed caused by outside
forces. The collapse in crude oil prices that started over a year ago
has steadily reduced gasoline prices at the pump. No one can be
oblivious to this fact because gasoline is purchased so often. Yet,
few motorists accept this as a sign of deflation.

The same is true of drug prices. Sure, drugs appear to be expensive, especially newly patented pharmaceuticals, and even
more so for people on Medicare without supplemental drug insurance coverage. But drugs are often much cheaper than surgical alternatives. Furthermore, the substitution of generics for branded
drugs is reducing the cost in many cases, but most consumers fail
to recognize it.

THINKING WILL CHANGE

Despite this huge mental bias in favor of inflation, however, thinking will change and sooner or later, American consumers and businesses will see that the inflation emperor has no clothes. The onset
of recession, with rapidly falling prices for goods and services, will
certainly push them toward accepting deflation. So will fears that
the recession will be a rerun of the 1930s. They'll also be inclined to
exercise deflationary expectations in the recession and the long-
term deflation that will follow because their incomes will be growing slowly, if at all. Similarly, the bear market's removal of the
capital appreciation many have been relying on in lieu of saving
will make them more willing to wait for lower prices, and force

prices down in the process. Ditto for those who lose jobs in firms that don't adapt to deflation. Many businesses are now under excruciating pressure to maintain, even cut, their selling prices, but they'll be fully aware that deflation has replaced inflation when they see their costs decline as well in areas they never dreamed possible.

To be sure, deflationary expectations will not work on every good and service. Even if you are convinced that a decline in shoe prices is in the offing, it may not be enough to make you wait to buy. Waiting could entail another trip to the shoe store, and besides, if you buy a pair now, you get the use of them in the meanwhile. Also, the cost and discretionary nature of a good or service influences your sensitivity to deflation. An expected 5 percent decline in car prices may make you wait. If you're spending $30,000, that's a cool $1,500 in your pocket, and you can probably nurse your old bus along for another year. (Recall how rebate programs push vehicle sales up and down like ping-pong balls.) But an expected 10 percent drop in toothpaste prices may not make you get out the pliers so you can, by vigorous squeezing, make the old tube last until the lower price is in effect.

THE TRIGGER POINT FOR DEFLATIONARY EXPECTATIONS

What will it take to trigger deflation expectations? Probably not as big a decline in prices as the 3 percent inflation rate level that seemed to touch off inflationary expectations in the 1970s. Even before that decade, folks had gained familiarity with rising prices throughout the postwar era, and were adjusted to the inflationary beast. Been there, done that. Deflation, however, is a different animal, not seen since the 1930s, and few of us today have had firsthand experience with it. Widespread and chronic falling prices would be such a shock to most that it probably would take less deflation today than it took inflation earlier to get people's attention.

My judgment is that ongoing declines of 1 to 2 percent per year in the prices of most goods and a fair number of services, averaged over future business cycles, will do the job.

I think we'll see this degree of deflation because, among other reasons, it's usual at this stage of the 50- to 60-year Kondratieff Wave, as you'll learn in the next chapter.

15 CHAPTER

Deflation and the Kondratieff Wave

Deflation isn't as new, strange, rare, or exotic as many believe. Indeed, as noted in the Introduction, it's the norm in the United States in peacetime. It's also usual for this stage of the *Kondratieff Wave*, a cyclic economic phenomenon named for the Russian economist, Nikolai Kondratieff.

As a result of his work in the 1920s, he correctly predicted big problems for the capitalist countries in the 1930s, but he made a strategic blunder for a Soviet by suggesting that the capitalist world would survive. The reaction of the Kremlin was predictable, and Kondratieff spent the rest of his career in Siberia—making little rocks out of big rocks, by some reports.

The Kondratieff Wave shows that capitalist countries have consistently been subject to 50-to-60–year cycles of extended growth and decline, commodity price peaks and troughs, and rising and falling interest rates. After studying more than 100 years of data on commodity prices in industrialized countries, Kondratieff found that after a long period of expansion—approximately 25 years—a long decline ensued, lasting about 30 years. To date, this Long Wave seems intact, with a few modifications. Figure 15–1 shows a stylized Kondratieff Wave and the dates of its four phases in the United States, as well as wholesale and stock prices.

FIGURE 15–1

Kondratieff Wave, 1800–1998

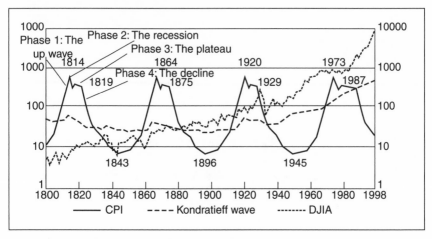

Source: U.S. Commerce Department and A. Gary Shilling & Co., Inc.

THE UPSWING

The upswing, or first phase, of the Long Wave starts with a popular war, which is typically short and inexpensive and serves to spur economic activity. It is fought against a weak foe at a time when public confidence is at its ebb, when the nation wants to be sure it can be victorious. The first U.S. trough war was the Mexican War, which started in 1846. The second was the Spanish-American War in 1898, and the third, World War II. This up-phase is dominated by strong growth and fairly mild recessions, and ends about two and a half decades later with an unpopular war—the War of 1812, the Civil War, World War I, and most recently, the Vietnam War. They all started at the height of public confidence and with the pursuit of some great cause, but ended in nothing but disillusionment.

The Civil War, World War I, and the Vietnam War all began with a "crusader" spirit. The Civil War, of course, was fought to end slavery. In the beginning of U.S. involvement in World War I, American soldiers marched off to war because, as Woodrow Wilson said, "the world must be made safe for democracy." The rationale for the Vietnam War was to prevent falling dominoes in

Southeast Asia and to stop the spread of communism. The enthusi-asm for all three wars evaporated quickly, and they became highly unpopular. Consider the draft riots of the Civil War and Lincoln's near reelection defeat in 1864 as well as the enormous trauma of the Vietnam War.

THE DOWNSWING

Those unpopular wars are followed by a surge in commodity prices and then collapse, and after that continuing price weakness for the balance of the downswing. This happened after the War of 1812, the Civil War, and World War I. The leap in prices in the early 1970s, at the end of the Vietnam War, and then the commodity price nose-dive were right on schedule. But widespread price declines have been delayed until now by two factors. First, the Cold War that began soon after World War II and didn't end until the late 1980s. Second, expanding government spending on social pro-grams, the legacy of the 1930s and the New Deal, which has only recently begun to be reversed. The voter tide against big govern-ment began to turn in the late 1970s, as you saw in Chapter 1, but restraints on public, medical, and welfare spending and the end of farm subsidies in the last several years are the first concrete evi-dence of federal government downsizing. As long as defense and non-defense spending were robust, the economy had a strong in-flationary bias.

The price explosion at the end of unpopular wars results in a self-feeding inventory building spree that ultimately breaks into the sharpest recession of the Wave, Phase 2, as excess inventories are liquidated and prices collapse. This was true after World War I, when the 1919 inventory explosion was promptly followed by the 1920–1921 recession, the fastest price decline on record. Similarly, the 1973–1975 recession, the sharpest and deepest of the postwar era, followed the gigantic inventory buildup of the early 1970s.

Then comes Phase 3, the plateau decade, when prices fall back and "normalcy" seems to return. Kondratieff called it "secondary prosperity." This was, of course, the "Roaring '20s" and the mid-1970s to mid-1980s decade of greed and glitz. It's also often an era of intense speculation—e.g., stocks in the 1920s; tangible assets in the inflation-persistent 1970s.

The final depression phase of the Kondratieff Wave starts with financial difficulties that usher in a period of slower economic growth and often some out-and-out hard times, like the "Hungry 1840s," the difficult years in the 1870s, and, of course, the 1930s. Deflation is a definite hallmark of this phase.

In the present Kondratieff Wave depression phase, which probably started in the late 1980s, the U.S. financial corrections of previous excesses have been spread out much more than in previous counterparts. As you'll learn in Chapter 17, the domestic economy during the 1980s and early 1990s saw a rolling correction of earlier agricultural, oil patch, and real estate over-exuberance. Now only over-leveraged consumers are still vulnerable. Note that farmland usually suffers earlier than other real estate in the downswing, and the plight of American farmers in the midst of the "Roaring '20s" and in the early 1980s is typical.

PROTECTIONISM IN THE DOWN PHASES

Protectionism and isolationism appear consistently during the Kondratieff depression phase. For instance, after the first Kondratieff cycle peak, tariffs were increased in 1816 and again in 1828—sometimes called the "tariffs of abomination." In the second down cycle, tariffs were raised once again. The McKinley Tariff Act of 1890, the Wilson tariffs of 1894, and the Kingsley tariffs of 1897 were blatantly protectionist.

The next cycle also had its protectionist legislation, of course, such as the Smoot-Hawley Tariff Act of 1930, involving more than 20,000 items. Whether protectionist legislation actually led to the Depression or not, the "beggar-thy-neighbor" policies that most governments pursued in the 1930s certainly made matters worse. As world economies slumped, many nations tried to export their problems to other countries, much as Asia is doing today.

Currencies were devalued in the Depression to make exports more competitive, and wealthy nations, particularly the United States, stopped extending credit to less-developed countries. This caused financially weak lands to default on their loans, which exacerbated the U.S. banking crisis and worsened deflation and depression. The reaction to the crisis by wealthy nations was to balance their budgets, reduce welfare payments (particularly in

Great Britain), and increase interest rates, thereby accelerating the downturn.

To be sure, memories of the tariff walls of the 1930s have spurred the postwar movement toward free trade and made it possible for technology and capital to move around the globe in search of the most cost-effective sites for production (Chapters 8 and 19). Nevertheless, the ongoing polarization of income in the United States and the growing trade deficits, especially with Japan and China, may well resurrect protectionism when jobs become less plentiful (Chapter 17).

GOLD

During the beginning of the upswing, the production of gold increases, probably swept along with rising prices and surging economic activity. But gold production declines during the down phase as prices in general fall, and there is no inflation against which it can serve as a hedge. Note that, recently, even central banks have been dumping gold as a sterile commodity that continues to fall in price and provides little return (see Chapter 26).

WHAT CREATES THE WAVE?

During Phase 3 and 4, the old technologies that drove the previous upswing have been fully exploited and overbuilt. The technologies that will drive the next upswing are already known, but not yet commercially exploited to their full degree. Kondratieff himself offered no causal explanation for the Long Wave, and his work was purely statistical. Yet this technology cycle offers an explanation of the Kondratieff Wave. The upswing is driven by the surge of investment in new technologies—canals and riverboats in the early 1800s, railroads and the American Industrial Revolution in the late 1800s, and autos and electricity in the early twentieth century.

Then, investment in these areas gets so excessive that it falters, and economic growth wanes. The investment in the next technology has already begun, but isn't yet big enough to sustain rapid overall business growth. The result are down phases of the Long Wave which are, in effect, the gaps between the full exploitation of one technology and the onset of massive investment in the next.

For example, railroads were developing in the early nineteenth century and pushing down transportation costs, but they did not become major economic driving forces until the second half of the century, when the transcontinental routes were built to open up the American West. But by late in the century, too many tracks had been laid and the sector consolidated. Similarly, autos made before the turn of the century but didn't dominate growth until decades later, and, then, finally saturated demand by the 1930s.

POSTWAR CATCH-UP IN SPENDING

The most recent upswing, beginning after World War II, was driven by postwar booms in construction, consumer durables, capital spending, Cold-War defense spending, and the flight to the suburbs. During the 1930s and 1940s, construction had been held down by the Depression and then the war, during which unspendable consumer purchasing power was channeled into war bonds. That liquidity fueled the huge postwar catch-up spending, especially in construction.

One reason for the postwar building surge was the proliferation of automobiles, another area of catch-up spending. With more cars came more roads, the interstate highway program, and the need for motels, diners, and service stations. Cars also enabled city dwellers, fed up with the annoyances of urban life, to move to the countryside, which soon became suburbs. That meant big spending on houses, furniture, appliances, and other durables. Needless to say, these Kondratieff Wave driving forces are long exhausted.

Similarly, the Cold War ended in the late 1980s, and with it, the huge postwar military buildup. The Cold War spawned entire industries, like aerospace, that have limited civilian counterparts. So, with the military stand-down, these industries atrophied, unable to move easily to production of civilian goods and services. Finally, the third big postwar stimulus, government social spending, appears to be waning, as mentioned earlier.

Granted, today's new technologies, such as telecommunications, computers, semiconductors, the Internet, and biotech, are mushrooming, but they aren't yet strong enough to drive the U.S. economy by themselves. Spending on high tech by consumers and business is hard to measure, but is still probably less than 10 percent of GDP, and has had little effect on overall economic growth until quite recently.

Nevertheless, this doesn't mean that the U.S. economy is about to collapse. Chapter 17 notes that a financial crisis, like that which initiated the Kondratieff Wave depression of the 1930s, is unlikely in Western countries any time soon.

In any event, the Kondratieff Wave has two points of current relevance. First, in the ongoing final down phase that we're now in, deflation is the norm. Second, the new technologies that will drive the next up phase are already well known and growing in importance. The first point is, of course, the thesis of this book. The second was touched on in Chapter 5 and will be fleshed out in the next and succeeding chapters.

16
CHAPTER

The Two Faces of Deflation

Whenever Americans hear the word "deflation," most immediately think of the Great Depression of the 1930s. Images of soup lines, shanty towns, and apple sellers are so vivid that any other idea of deflation pales by comparison. Indeed, the Great Depression did occur during the deflationary part of a Kondratieff Wave, with the typical attendant forces of excess capacity, fully exploited technologies, and new technologies only in the budding stage. Yet, the huge price declines in the early 1930s were the *result* of the financial collapse starting in 1929, not the *cause*. The stock market crash revealed quickly the over-leveraged nature of the financial system. Bankruptcies spread rapidly and were followed by massive layoffs and pay cuts for those still working. Deflation is, of course, the result of supply exceeding demand, and it is caused by either supply surging or demand dropping. In the 1930s, the fundamental cause was the shortfall of demand as incomes vanished.

THE 1930s COLLAPSE IN DEMAND

To be sure, the 1930s started with some excess capacity. It was already over-abundant in agriculture when the 1920s dawned. American farmers had hugely expanded acres in cultivation and production during World War I to feed Europe. After the war, however, European agriculture recovered. America was stuck with so much excess agricultural capacity—and farm debt—that farming entered a big deflation and financial crisis long before the Dust Bowl drought years in the 1930s augmented their woes.

Also in the 1920s, industries like electricity generation mushroomed as the nation got wired and developed considerable excess capacity in the process. The same was true in autos. Rapid overexpansion occurred at Ford, General Motors, and dozens of other manufacturers, whose names are now only found in history books and in the wonderful collection of antique cars in the Henry Ford museum in Dearborn, Michigan.

Nevertheless, it was the collapse in incomes and demand that primarily drove the bad deflation of the 1930s, not over-supply. Following the Crash, wholesale prices and employment (Figure 16–1) nose-dived in tandem as unemployment soared. The American Federation of Labor estimated that in October 1930 there were approximately 4.6 million unemployed workers. In October 1931, the number rose to 7.8 million, to 11.6 million in October

FIGURE 16–1

U.S. wholesale price index and employment rate, 1926–1940

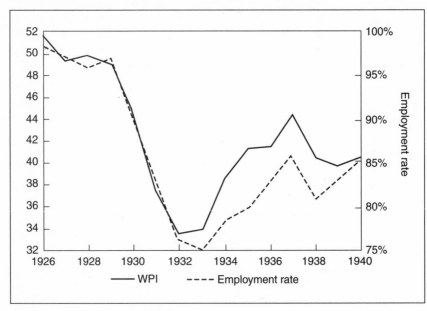

Source: *Historical Statistics of the United States*

1932, and early in 1933 to more than 13 million, almost 25 percent of the civilian labor force (Figure 16–2).

The wages of those still working fell faster than prices, even more so when periods of unemployment and short hours are included. Also, the declines had to be spread over a lot of unemployed people as well, especially at a time when government relief programs were tiny. My good friend John Farmer, a columnist for Newhouse newspapers, told me that in the Depression his family lived in Jersey City, New Jersey, and his father drove a bus from New York to Atlantic City. His mother's sister's husband was out of work quite a bit, so his father supported his own family and from time to time, helped his in-laws as well, until World War II started at the end of the decade and his brother-in-law got a job in a shipyard. Obviously, many people could only afford the bare necessities of life in the bleak days of the Depression. Of course, the United States was not alone in those dreadful years of the early 1930s. The Depression was global (Table 16–1).

FIGURE 16–2

U.S. civilian labor force unemployment rate, 1920–1940

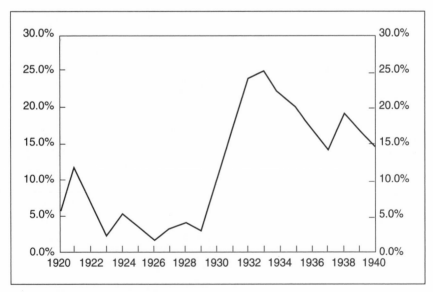

Source: *Historical Statistics of the United States*

T A B L E   16-1

Percentage Change in Industrial Production and
GDP (1929–1932)

Country	Industrial Production	GDP
Austria	−34.3%	−22.5%
Belgium	−27.1%	−7.1%
Denmark	−5.6%	4.0%
Finland	−20.0%	−5.9%
France	−25.6%	−11.0%
Germany	−40.8%	−15.7%
Italy	−22.7%	−6.1%
Netherlands	−9.8%	−8.2%
Norway	−7.9%	−0.9%
Spain	−11.6%	−8.0%
United Kingdom	−11.8%	−5.8%
United States	−44.7%	−28.0%
Czechoslovakia	−26.5%	−18.2%
Hungary	−19.2%	−11.5%
Poland	−37.0%	NA
Romania	−11.8%	NA

Source: United Nations

WORSE THAN ITS PREDECESSORS

To get a perspective on just how severe this shortfall in demand really was, compare changes in real consumption and real gross national product with changes occurring between 1839 and 1843, a similar depression phase of the first Kondratieff Wave, the "Hungry '40s" (Table 16–2). Even at the worst phase of that deflation, real consumption and real GNP increased. Notice that the declines in the money supply, prices, and number of banks were similar in the two periods. It's hard to pin the depth of the 1930s Depression solely on the decline in the money supply and on the Fed, as will be covered in Chapter 18.

It's also hard to pin it on American business or even the Hoover Administration. Because the federal government ran a

T A B L E   16–2

Comparison of 1839–1843 with 1929–1933 in United States

	1839–43	1929–33
Change in money stock	−34%	−27%
Change in prices	−42%	−32%
Change in number of banks	−23%	−42%
Change in real gross investment	−23%	−91%
Change in real consumption	+21%	−19%
Change in real gross national product	+15%	−30%

Source: 13-D Research

budget surplus in 1929, there was leeway to offset the weakening economy with fiscal stimulus. In November 1929, President Hoover called for tax cuts and expanded public works programs. He also gathered the captains of industry and made them promise to help sustain purchasing power by maintaining wage levels and increasing capital spending. After that meeting, Henry Ford raised the wages of his autoworkers from his celebrated $5 per day to $7 per day. Nevertheless, neither Ford nor other manufacturers could withstand the onslaught of the Depression. The average hourly wage of those production workers lucky enough to keep their jobs in manufacturing fell 21 percent from 1929 to 1932, and because hours were cut as well, average weekly earnings fell 32 percent. Many weren't so lucky. By 1932, 38 percent of those production jobs in manufacturing that existed in 1929 had been eliminated.

POST-CIVIL WAR DEFLATION WITHOUT COLLAPSE

Deflation, however, doesn't have to be the bad kind caused by deficient demand. In the down phases of the second Kondratieff wave (1864–1896), it was good deflation caused by excess supply. At the end of the Civil War, the country moved into the American Industrial Revolution, following the first to industrialize, the United Kingdom, by about 50 years. Agricultural value added was almost twice that of manufacturing at the beginning of that conflict, but the explosion of factory output equalized the shares of the two by the mid-1880s. At the end of the century, factories out-produced farms by almost two to one. Between 1860 and 1914, employment in manufacturing and construction tripled, and the physical output of manufacturing rose six times. Manufacturers in the steel, chemicals, glass, farm implements, cement, and machinery segments went almost overnight from cottage industries to full-blown factory production. Industrial growth was spurred, of course, by the needs of the Civil War, but after the war, the boom continued, fueled by rapidly changing industrial technology. The number of patents granted in the nation grew from 25,200 in the 1850s to 234,956 between 1890 and 1900.

Typical of what was happening to manufacturing in the United States between 1860 and 1890 is the pressed-glass industry. During that time, glass manufacturers of all kinds began to experiment with gas furnaces and continuous glass melting tanks. Coal was firmly established as the best glass-making fuel, but natural gas proved to be better because it burned at intense heat, left no residue, had no bad effects on the glass, and made continuous melting tanks possible in 1879. In addition to these general improvements, pressed-glass manufacturing benefited from new discoveries in glass chemistry. The use of lime instead of flint in the glass mixture reduced metal costs and gave rise to mechanical innovations that enhanced its properties.

HERE COMES THE TRAIN

At the same time, railroads pushed across the continent, uniting first North and South, then East and West. In 1860, the United States had 30,626 miles of track, mostly in the East, Midwest, and South. But Americans knew there was a vast land of resources stretching toward the Pacific Ocean, and in robust competition, railroad companies rushed to reach the West—with, to be sure, considerable government subsidies in the form of free land along the rights of way. The dramatic increase in miles of track occurred in three building spurts: in 1866–1873, 30,000 miles were built; in 1879–1883, 40,000 miles more; and in 1886–1892, 50,000 additional miles were constructed. By 1900, the United States had 198,964 miles of track (Figure 16–3).

FIGURE 16–3

Miles of railroad in operation in the United States, 1850–1950

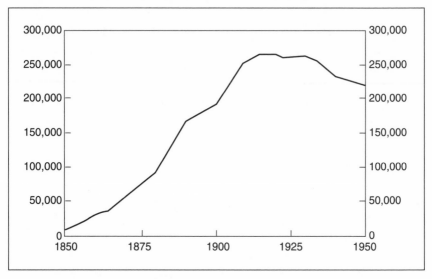

Source: *Historical Statistics of the United States*

Trains crisscrossed the nation, carrying people west and bringing agricultural products and minerals east, thus opening up vast
acreage for farmers, ranchers, and miners. Before the war, cattle and
hogs were primarily raised in the Ohio Valley, making Cincinnati
the leading center of pork packing, with the meat products moving
to market via the Ohio and Mississippi rivers. With railroads and
the invention of the refrigerated freight car, livestock production
shifted westward, and Chicago became a leading shipping point for
livestock and meat products. All of those cowboys that we see in
western movies weren't raising cattle for chuck wagon dinners, but
for Eastern markets that were only accessible by rail.

AGRICULTURE IN BLOOM

Accessibility of Eastern markets also caused a great expansion in
wheat growing, which, combined with cattle raising, fed the exploding labor force concentrated in industrialized cities. Food sur-

pluses created a marketable export, which became more important than cotton. After 1873, the American balance of trade turned favorable, because of wheat and wheat flour, meat products, and live cattle exports. Although agricultural products became a smaller percentage of U.S. output, agricultural productivity increased 40 percent from 1869 to 1899 as farm technology blossomed.

In the mid-1800s, John Deere of Illinois developed and sold a plow whose moldboard, share, and landslide were made of cast steel strong enough to break the tough sod of the prairies. In the late 1860s, John Oliver, also of Illinois, developed a plow of chilled iron (a soft-center steel), which was more durable and cheaper. Obed Hussey of Ohio and Cyrus H. McCormick of Virginia both came up with the same idea that would truly revolutionize the wheat-growing industry: the mechanical horse-drawn reaper. Hussey is credited with being first (1833), but McCormick was close behind (1834), and was a better marketer. When he began manufacturing in Chicago in 1847, he knew how to advertise and offer credit as well as instructions in maintenance and repairs. The number of reapers in use in the United States grew from 70,000 in 1858 to 250,000 in 1865. Improvement followed fast. Reaper and thresher were combined (hence the term "combine") in the 1890s.

An example of the productivity leap attributed to farm equipment is the drop in man-hours needed to prepare and harvest one acre of grain. In 1829–1830, the time required in Illinois was 61 hours, 5 minutes. By 1893, a Red River Valley spring-wheat farm took only 8 hours, 46 minutes to do the same thing.

The availability of so much output produced at such lower costs depressed prices considerably—even though the reduced prices vastly expanded sales. Ordinary Americans could afford meat on days other than holidays and manufactured goods for the first time ever. Innovations in glass manufacturing, mentioned earlier, compressed the retail prices of pressed-glassware by as much as 89 percent between 1864 and 1888, as shown in the top row of Table 16–3. Prices of food staples plunged dramatically. The overall Wholesale Price Index dropped at an annual rate of 2.6 percent for a total decline of 49.7 percent between 1870 and 1896, when the Spanish-American War, like any war, caused inflation (Figure 16–4). The wholesale price of a bushel of wheat fell from $1.58 in 1871 to 56 cents in 1894. Nails dropped from $4.52 for 50 pounds in 1871 to $2.00 in 1889.

T A B L E   16–3

Retail Prices per Dozen of Pressed-Glassware (1864–1888)

	1864	1874	1888	%Fall in Price 1864–1888
Goblets	$3.50	$0.78	$0.40	89
Tumblers	$1.30	$0.55	$0.37	72
Wine Glasses	$1.73	$0.50	$0.30	83

Source: National Glass Budget, May 6, 1899

F I G U R E 16–4

Post-Civil War deflation, wholesale price index, 1870–1900

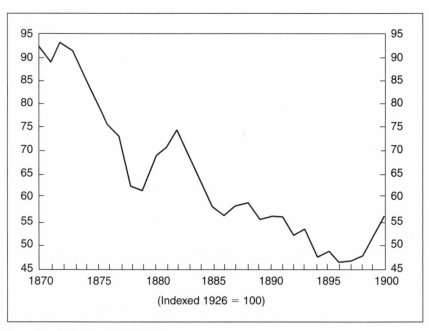

(Indexed 1926 = 100)

Source: *Historical Statistics of the United States*

Farm prices fell, but the prices farmers paid for supplies and services fell at least as fast. Rates for railroad transportation declined during the period despite concern over freight rate gouging. Between 1866 and 1897, the charge for carrying wheat from Chicago to New York fell from 65 cents per 100 pounds to 20 cents, or a 70 percent decline. Between 1870 and 1899, the charge for dressed beef transport declined from 90 to 40 cents, or 55 percent. Farm machinery prices also dropped by 60 percent between 1870 and 1900.

LOWER PRICES LEAD TO LOWER NOMINAL BUT HIGHER REAL WAGES

For many in service jobs, such as carpenters, painters, and blacksmiths, nominal, or money, wages after 1870 began to fall along with prices. Overall, non-farm employees saw their money pay decline from $489 per year in 1870 to $420 in 1894, a fall of 14 percent. But prices were falling faster than wages, so real pay grew 29 percent, or at a 1.1 percent annual rate, during those years. In an analysis conducted by the National Bureau of Economic Research, C.D. Long concluded that real wages in manufacturing went up 50 percent from 1860 to 1890.

The new technology of the late 1800s, then, mushroomed the supplies of agricultural and manufactured goods and that stimulated big leaps in demand. Still, supply outran demand on balance, because prices fell. At the same time, not only was productivity jumping in these new tech industries, but also their output enhanced the productivity of their customers. Mechanical farm equipment speeded planting and harvesting. Steel girders made it possible to build taller buildings than with wood. Steel ships with steam boilers were much more efficient than wooden vessels under sail. This, too, increased new tech output greatly. And even though prices were plunging in these new tech industries, output volume was growing faster, so their revenues exploded.

The net result was America's greatest period of sustained growth. Real GNP per capita grew at an average annual rate of 2.1 percent from 1869 to 1898, and the population rose at about the same rate, encouraged by waves of immigrants. Consequently, real GNP grew 4.3 percent per year, about twice today's sustainable growth rate, as prices sank 50 percent over a 26-year period. The good deflation of excess supply reigned supreme, even though this all occurred during the final down leg of the Kondratieff Wave (Figure 15–1).

GOOD DEFLATION IN THE 1920s

Although we'll probably never again see anything like the growth explosion of the Industrial Revolution and the opening of the West, good deflation has not been confined to that era. The "Roaring '20s" were also a time of deflation driven by supply growing faster than demand, even though rapid productivity advances knocked prices down and made goods affordable for many more buyers.

As the third Kondratieff Wave began its plateau after the 1920–1921 recession, the economy boomed. In the following eight years, industrial production almost doubled as wholesale prices fell on balance (Table 16–4). New technologies, especially electricity, were responsible for much of the boom. Electrification of factory power equipment grew from 33 percent in 1914 to 74 percent

T A B L E 16–4

U.S. Economic Growth (1921–1929)

Year	Industrial Production 1933–39=100	Wholesale Prices 1926=100	National Income (Billions)	Real Income per Capita (1929 Prices)
1921	58	97.6	$59.4	$522
1922	73	96.7	$60.7	$553
1923	88	100.6	$71.6	$634
1924	82	98.1	$72.1	$633
1925	90	103.5	$76.0	$644
1926	96	100.0	$81.6	$678
1927	95	95.4	$80.1	$674
1928	99	96.7	$81.7	$676
1929	110	95.3	$87.2	$716

Source: *Historical Statistics of the United States*

in 1929, as efficient motors replaced steam-driven overhead drive shafts with leather belts running to each machine.

Not to be left behind, the American housewife got her efficiency improved through electricity, as it ran such appliances as electric irons, vacuum cleaners, refrigerators and washing machines. The value of electrical appliance output gained 179 percent between 1921 and 1929; heating and cooking apparatuses, 86 percent; and radios, 200 percent. Housewives gave their washboards to museums and many laundresses became available for other work. Not surprisingly, the production of electric power more than doubled during this period.

Construction also took off during the 1920s. It had slowed during World War I, so builders were ready to go once money was available, and modern improvements made even recently constructed buildings old-fashioned. Building construction in 120 cities climbed from $373 million in 1918 to $3.4 billion in 1925, and one-third of it was in New York City.

Of course, the granddaddy of all boom industries during the 1920s was the automobile, and consumer auto sales rose 130 percent in the 1921–1929 years. The basis was laid earlier. Henry Ford's application of interchangeable parts and his introduction of the moving assembly line increased the production of cars by the whole industry from 65,000 in 1908 to 1 million in 1915. Between 1913 and 1914, the labor time required to put together a Model T chassis dropped from 2 hours and 38 minutes (down from an original 12 hours and 28 minutes) to 1 hour and 33 minutes. Consequently, the price of the Model T runabout dropped from $500 on August 1, 1913, to $260 on December 2, 1924.

As noted earlier, Henry Ford paid his workers an unprecedented $5 per day. He reasoned that if they couldn't afford to buy the cars they were assembling, he wouldn't sell many. I've known this for years, but never figured how $5 per day would buy anyone a car. Now I know. At $5 per day, 300 days a year (they worked Saturdays then), the assembler made $1,500 and paid few taxes. A Model T at $260 was definitely affordable.

Other prices fell as well in the 1920s, even after the 1920–1921 collapse, including items like home furnishings and apparel. Food prices rose a bit after plunging more than industrial prices during 1920–1921. Nevertheless, the weakness in the latter, even after the nose-dive at the beginning of the decade, made the "Roaring '20s" a time of overall deflation—the good deflation of excess supply.

If the deflation I see ahead is to be the good deflation of the post-Civil War era and the 1920s, not the bad deflation of the 1930s, overall demand needs to hold up. That, in turn, requires the nation's financial structure to remain intact. To see why this is likely, turn to Chapter 17.

17

C H A P T E R

The Looming Threat of Protectionism

Deflation has not always been linked to financial collapse, as you learned in Chapter 16. Will it be this time? Probably not in the Western world. Nevertheless, most people believe that any deflation in future years will be the bad deflation of the 1930s, which followed the demand-killing financial collapse, not the good deflation of the 1920s and the post-Civil War era, which resulted from mushrooming supply. Still, the good deflation I foresee, like its predecessors, does follow financial problems that result from over-expansion of capacity.

A STRING OF U.S. FINANCIAL PROBLEMS

In a sense—a Kondratieff Wave sense—in the United States it all started in the 1980s, as noted in Chapter 15. One by one the various sectors that had over-expanded and over-leveraged themselves in the 1970s heyday of inflation went through the deflationary wringer. Just like the collapse in agriculture in the 1920s, stratospheric farmland prices were the first to go in the early 1980s. Then followed the plummet in oil prices in the mid-1980s that took oil patch real estate and economies with it. By the late 1980s, it was overbuilt real estate nationwide that hit the fan when tax laws changed in 1986. In the process, the bank lenders, which were already weakened by bad Latin American loans, were humbled. The S&Ls were virtually wiped off the map.

This was a tough period and financial difficulties then domi-nated the American scene, but none of these crises sank the U.S. fi-nancial ship, maybe because they occurred in rotation—all the problems didn't erupt at once and compound each other. Also the federal government provided easy credit to avoid widespread foreclosures on farm mortgages. It filled the strategic oil reserve to limit the damage of oil price collapse. The S&Ls were, of course, bailed out by taxpayers to the tune of $500 billion. And the Fed kept short-term interest rates low in the early 1990s so banks could rebuild their capital by borrowing cheap and lending at much higher long-term rates.

IT'S THE 1930s IN ASIA

At present, the financial crisis is abroad, first in Japan, the else-where in Asia, and now in many other areas including Russia and Latin America. Because the economy is global, that crisis has global ramifications. In many ways, what's happening in those lands re-sembles events in Western countries in the 1930s. Then and now, over-expansion has given way to financial collapse, which, in turn, has dried-up credit and left unpayable debts, bankruptcies, and widespread unemployment in its wake. Then and now, countries have attempted to unload their troubles on others through com-petitive devaluation. Then and now, the net results are the aug-mentation of already considerable global gluts of almost everything. Back then, in the West, it came as a great shock to the multitude who expected the "Roaring '20s" to last forever. Now, it's disabusing those who had similar faith in the Asian miracle.

Look at Indonesia to see the similarity between the United States in the 1930s and Asia today. Basic domestic demand in early 1998 is ample. There is no shortage of hungry mouths to feed or backs on which to put clothes. With the rupiah's collapse from 2,500 per dollar in early 1997 to 16,000 at its low a year later, the op-portunities to sell in export markets became fabulous. At the same time, there is more than enough productive capacity to fulfill do-mestic demand and facilitate huge exports as well. What's lacking is financial confidence to ensure adequate credit to get supply and demand together. Perhaps an even better comparison is between Japan's bubble economy in the 1980s and the Roaring '20s in the

United States, followed by the deflationary depression of the 1990s in Japan, which parallels the American Great Depression of the 1930s, as noted in Chapter 11.

It may be even worse in Asia, Russia and Latin American now than it was during the American Depression, given their high dependence on exports to promote economic growth. The high tariffs and competitive devaluations of the 1930s certainly deepened the global depression, but at least at the time the United States was largely a self-sufficient economy. To be sure, the IMF is trying hard to contain today's problems by shoring up various countries financially. But, as you saw in Chapter 11, the IMF conditions may restrain growth in those lands and prolong their financial problems. Also, there is reluctance in many of those countries to accept the reforms urged on them by Western governments, as also noted in Chapter 11. And in this country, Congress is unwilling to keep pouring bailout money into them, either directly or through the IMF.

CAN IT SPREAD HERE?

Finally, even if the Asian Contagion is contained, it can still spread to the U.S. and other Western countries if Western financial institutions are vulnerable. I don't see this as the likely outcome, however. To begin, U.S. exposure to Asia's bad debt is limited. American banks have only about 1 percent of total loans in Asia and 2 percent in Latin America. This is far less than their relative exposure to Latin America, 6.3 percent of total loans, when it imploded in the mid-1980s and trapped many U.S. banks that were in the middle of the petro-dollar recycling game. In fact, European banks have more than twice as much exposure to Latin America as their U.S. counterparts. It is true that banks have been replaced as the primary lenders to developing countries by others, such as pension, mutual and hedge funds. U.S. banks' share of private lending fell from 83 percent in the 1980–84 period to 46 percent in 1992–98. Still, a hedge fund in trouble is not nearly the threat to public confidence that is a bank with closed doors—and ATMs. And, central banks are even willing to engineer the bailout of hedge funds if they threaten the financial structure, as discussed in Chapter 18. And back home on the ranch, most over-leveraged U.S. sectors already had their comeuppance in the 1980s and early 1990s, as noted earlier.

In the United States, it is true that business borrowing has been heavy recently, in large part to finance the capital-spending boom in the face of weakening cash flow. In 1998's first three quarters, non-financial company debt rose 11 percent from a year earlier, a much faster growth rate than the 4 to 5 percent in the early 1990s. Moreover, 41 percent of all newly issued bonds were below invest-ment grade, *i.e.*, junk bonds, up from just 30 percent in 1995. As a re-sult, corporate debt reached 43 percent of GDP, compared with 38 percent in the early 1990s and close to the highest level since 1960. Almost half of small businesses now use credit cards for financing, double the number two years ago, and that source now rivals bank loans. Credit cards may be more convenient than lining up bank borrowing, but they are obviously much more expensive, with in-terest rates often close to 20 percent.

U.S. BANKS ARE IN MUCH BETTER SHAPE

Still, the surge in business borrowing does not seem likely lead to a financial crisis, although it will hurt profits in the next business downturn. About half the new corporate bonds issued are replac-ing older, higher interest rate bonds. With the decline in interest rates, profits cover interest expenses four times over, compared to twice in 1989. And, most of the over-leveraged U.S. firms met their Waterloo in the 1980s and early 1990s. It's also important to note that U.S. banks and other lenders learned a lot from their near-death experience with bad loans in the early 1990s. Since 1990, re-turn on bank equity has risen from 10 percent to 20 percent, and the percentage of non-performing assets has fallen from 4.5 percent in 1991 to 0.5 percent as bad loans were written off. Shareholders and boards of directors have become much more active and vigilant. This doesn't mean that banks won't figure out ways to make big mistakes in the future, and they have repeatedly in the past, but at least they'll be starting from a position of strength.

Sure, the Federal Home Loan Bank System and other federal agencies have been borrowing heavily to finance housing, but else-where, the United States has also returned to a much better financial condition. Real estate debts are not big problems. The federal budget is in surplus and the Treasury is retiring debt. Overall, the annual net debt increase by non-financial sectors of the economy—consumers, businesses, and government—is even below the 10.4 percent ratio of GDP it has averaged in this century (Figure 17–1). Note that the climb that started in the late 1960s and peaked in the 1980s almost reached the heights of the two World Wars, when government borrowing was astronomical. The 1920's debt expansion pales in comparison—in part because, unlike the 1970s and 1980s, the federal government was then running a surplus, so private debt alone was in excess.

The only two sectors of the U.S. economy that remain vulnerable are consumers and stocks. But as noted in Chapter 13, I expect American consumers to retrench and reduce their excessive borrowing. That's part of our deflation scenario. Sure, credit card delinquencies and personal bankruptcies could leap even from current lofty levels, but massive foreclosures that would ignite a downward spiral in consumers' finances seem unlikely and politi-

F I G U R E 17–1

Ratio of total U.S. annual net borrowing of non-financial sectors to GDP, 1900–1997

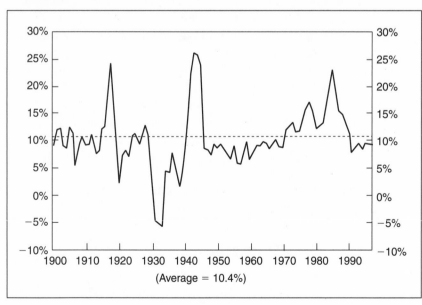

(Average = 10.4%)

Source: Federal Reserve Board

cally unacceptable. Indeed, there is evidence, in credit card delinquencies and other data, that consumers are already starting to
take a more cautious attitude toward debt.

Chapter 13 also notes my conviction that U.S. stocks are significantly overpriced and headed for a substantial fall. Still, a genuine bear market of the extent not seen since the early 1970s, with
a nose-dive of 40 to 50 percent in stock prices wouldn't in itself be
the end of the financial world. It's happened before without any financial catastrophe.

WHAT ABOUT OTHER DEVELOPED COUNTRIES?

Canada and Europe are about as exposed to Asia as the United
States in terms of imports or exports, as noted in Chapter 11. On the
financial side, European banks are more involved in Asia and Latin
America. Still, I don't think that any of these lands have big enough
financial or economic imbalances at home to collapse financially,
even though their economies have been infected by the Asian flu
and are weakening. Debt is about 34 percent of capital for the average European company, compared with 69 percent in the United
States. Canada will continue to suffer from falling commodity
prices, but her financial house is in fairly good order.

Japan will, of course, get the biggest fallout from Asia of any
developed country. She has the largest trade exposure and her
banks are the most involved. On top of this, as noted in Chapter 11,
Japan has considerable structural and financial problems at home.
We believe, however, that her high domestic saving rate and immense holdings of foreign exchange and assets abroad will protect
her from fallout from the Asian crisis. These factors should prevent
Japan's domestic difficulties from cascading into a financial
whirlpool, even though part of her savings has been lost on poor
real estate, stock, and other investments at home and abroad. (Recall
her Rockefeller Center and Pebble Beach investment disasters.)

A BIG CAVEAT—PROTECTIONISM

An important cause of the global demand collapse in the 1930s was
protectionism. To be sure, its aim was quite the opposite—limit imports and increase exports to spur domestic economic activity and

employment. But when all trading partners tried to accomplish this through competitive devaluation and tariff and non-tariff trade barriers, worldwide demand and every country's economic activity fell. Protectionism is definitely deflationary.

Largely because of memories of the derivative effects of protectionism in the Great Depression, free trade has been the global battle cry in the postwar period, especially in the United States and other developed Western countries. But even in those lands, and certainly in Japan and most developing countries, there has been plenty of heel-dragging. And by nature, free trade is fragile.

To begin, free trade is not the way God made the world. In fact, it is not natural to human beings and seems to require a single dominant global power who sees free trade in her interest. In recent centuries, there have been only two such periods—one when Britain ran the world from the middle of the nineteenth century through World War I; and the post-World War II period, when the United States dominated. Otherwise, protectionism, sprinkled with trade wars, prevailed.

The U.S. seems likely to remain the only superpower, at least for some years, but is free trade any longer in her interest? It definitely was during the Cold War, because it allowed Europe and Japan to concentrate on economic development and remain free of Communist control, often at the expense of the United States.

Now, however, the Cold War is over. The need to favor Japan is gone, including the acceptance of her mercantilism policy. We've seen Washington's fight against Japanese trade restrictions accelerate since the Berlin Wall came down. And China is no great favorite either, now that Beijing has made it clear that she wants to reduce U.S. influence in Asia and promote her own—American business involvement in China not withstanding. The potential there is for economic warfare to replace military confrontation.

SIMMERING PROTECTIONISM IN THE UNITED STATES

Furthermore, U.S. protectionist forces may now be subdued in an economy where anyone with any skills has multiple job offers—but what happens when the economy slows and a job surplus turns into a job glut? Pat Buchanan and Ross Perot on the right and Dick Gephardt on the left are beating opposite sides of the same protectionist drum, and their thumps will then be heard much more clearly.

Recall that only several years ago, when American jobs were much more scarce, organized labor was demanding that Washington cut off those slave labor-produced goods at the border so we could all go back to the lives we knew and loved. Note (Table 26–5) that as a result of higher productivity growth and slower economic advances, we foresee an 8.0 percent average U.S. unemployment rate in the next decade, compared to 6.0 percent in the last. Note also the ongoing polarization of American incomes, discussed in Chapter 12. To add insult to injury, the middle-class continues to see itself going down in a leaky barge while upper-income folks are sailing into the sunset in a beautiful new party yacht. It's no great surprise that the 1990 and 1993 federal tax hikes were "soak the rich" affairs.

Bear in mind that the benefits of free trade are subtle, broad, and long term. They often get lost as we, as human beings, credit ourselves and not our environment for our economic good fortune. Setbacks, however, are someone else's fault, and it's easy to blame outsiders for job losses and stagnant incomes. Politicians, pressed by special interest groups, find foreigners, who can't vote in U.S. elections, especially easy targets. Note also that even with strong support from the Republican majority in Congress and Fed Chairman Greenspan, President Clinton has repeatedly failed to win congressional approval for "fast-track" legislation to expand NAFTA and free trade.

Indeed, the storm clouds are already growing. The U.S. steel industry's perennial cry for more limits on imports is getting a more sympathetic response in Congress, and anti-dumping complaints against Japan, Russia, and Brazil are being processed faster than usual. Other industries—such as apparel and precision machine tools—are lining up behind steel for protection from imports. And they have popular support. A recent poll finds that 58 percent of Americans believe that foreign trade is bad for the country because it depresses wages and employment. The United States and Europe are mired in a banana war over E.U. policies that benefit their former colonies in the Caribbean in their exports of the fruit to Europe.

THE EURO MAY PROMOTE PROTECTIONISM

Protectionism remains rock-solid in Japan. Except for the United Kingdom, Europe has always been more protectionist than the

United States. Furthermore, there are signs that a Fortress Europe mentality is growing as the euro is introduced, and as new leftist leaders clearly favor jobs over free trade, as noted earlier.

Free trade in Europe has always been spurred by economies of scale. The United States was fortunate to have been settled largely after the advent of the railroad. This, plus Lincoln's decision to preserve the Union at all costs, has given us a huge country with a uniform culture and an economy so large that most businesses can achieve their full economies of scale within U.S. borders, even with today's gigantic productive potentials. Europe, in contrast, was settled when people moved by foot or horseback. That's heaven for American tourists. We can travel 100 miles in Europe and enjoy an entirely different culture. But it's hell for modern European businesses and has forced them to look beyond their own borders. Sweden, a country with two world-class auto companies but a population that can't support the output of even one large auto plant, has no choice but to be internationalist.

But with the euro, internationalism will atrophy as many more companies achieve their full-scale economies within Euroland without any currency risk. Individual European countries export a quarter or a third of their output, but much of it is to neighbors. Consequently, they export only about 15 percent outside Euroland. An Italian shoe manufacturer may be otherwise indifferent over exporting to America or Germany, but he'll choose Germany when he knows the euro is a riskless common currency. The likely wave of intra-European mergers and plans for a pan-European stock exchange also point to a more inward-looking orientation. And, it's a short step from being less internationalist to being more protectionist. Those with less need to export outside Euroland will be more likely to back limits on imports.

NEW THREATS FROM EMERGING LANDS

Developing countries have never been paragons of virtue in free trade development, and recent events are even more troubling. On September 1, 1998, Malaysian President Mahathir declared that "the free market has failed disastrously" and decreed that the Malaysian ringgit could no longer be traded outside the country. He was happy to see foreign money enter his country, but didn't want to let it check out of the roach motel. At around that time, Hong Kong authorities spent about $125 billion to buy around 12 percent of market-traded blue chip stocks and imposed surcharges on big holdings of equity futures contracts to curb short selling. Their aim was to bail out major local stockholders who were stuck with big positions, and to curb an attempted run on the pegged Hong Kong dollar.

Then Russia, after ending support of the ruble and defaulting on government securities, imposed tight controls on foreign currencies. Some Latin American countries enacted controls on foreign capital. In December 1998, Taiwan encouraged banks and insurers to buy stocks to help prop up the local market by allowing them to hide any resulting losses.

These reactions by countries that have been hit hard by the Asian Contagion are understandable. Whether they have devalued their currencies against the dollar or not, they are suffering from painfully high interest rates. And, their economies are in shambles after growing rapidly for decades. Many of these governments must be thinking, Why continue this sheer hell when high interest rates aren't retaining foreign capital, much less attracting it? Why not freeze the currency so interest rates can be cut?

The 1998 edition of the *Heritage Foundation/Wall Street Journal Annual Index of Economic Freedom* found that for the first time in the Index's five-year existence, more countries reduced economic freedom than increased it.

OMINOUS SIGNS OF LATENT PROTECTIONISM IN EUROPE

As developing countries impose controls on free markets, left-leaning Western politicians support them. France's socialist Premier, Lionel Jospin, wants greater regulation of world currency markets. Even centrist British Prime Minister Tony Blair called for some limits on freewheeling global capitalism. Japan's leaders are in the same camp. Senior Japanese financial official Eisuke Sakakibara wants a return to the Bretton Woods system of fixed exchange rates that was instituted after World War II, as does German Chancellor Gerhard Schroeder. "There needs to be better control of capital flows and of the financial system in general," the new Chancellor was quoted by *The Wall Street Journal* as saying, "or it could seriously impair economies and not just emerging economies."

French Finance Minister Strauss-Kahn and earlier German Finance Minister Oskar Lafontaine, in a joint statement, said, "markets need the guiding hand of government," according to the same publication. Japanese Prime Minister Obuchi has been meeting with his European counterparts to push for "tripartite cooperation" among Japan, Europe, and the United States to stabilize the exchange rates of the yen, euro, and dollar. Chancellor Schroeder said "the basic principle that laissez-faire is not a correct policy for those markets has established itself." French President Chirac also wants government involvement "to reduce fluctuation among the dollar, the euro, and the yen."

Proposals for controls on capital flows remind us that free movement of global capital is a relatively recent phenomenon, despite the support of economic theorists from Adam Smith to the present. The financial collapse in the 1930s produced a profound distrust of international as well as domestic financial markets. Consequently, Britain's John Maynard Keynes and America's Harry Dexter White, who engineered the Bretton Woods agreement establishing the post-World War II monetary system, feared that uninhibited capital flows could interfere with foreign trade. Keynes wrote, "It is widely held that control of capital movements, both inward and outward, should be a permanent feature of the system."

U.S. controls on capital outflow were imposed by President Johnson in 1967, in response to the weak dollar, and not removed until 1974, after the Bretton Woods system collapsed and floating exchange rates were introduced. By the early 1980s, only the United States, the United Kingdom, and Switzerland permitted free capital flows. Germany and Japan joined them later. But finally, with floating exchange rates among major countries, subsequent economic and financial stability, the removal of domestic interest rate controls, and the rapid economic growth in developing countries in Asia and elsewhere that was largely financed by foreign capital, the creed of free capital flow became widely accepted.

Will major developed countries impose limits on global capital flows, as a number of their leaders are proposing, or are their concerns simply a momentary reaction to current financial turmoil? Even more important, when the next recession among Western countries arrives, will their governments react as their emerging-country counterparts are now reacting by blaming it on foreigners and trying to isolate themselves by restricting foreign trade?

I don't believe that protectionism will become strong enough to depress global demand to the point that good deflation turns into bad. Still, the current trend toward capital and currency controls in developing countries, and the reaction in advanced lands and their latent protectionism are not encouraging.

Derivatives and Y2K are also threats to good deflation. You'll learn about them and also about why Western central banks and governments can contain financial problems but can't stop deflation in Chapter 18.

18

CHAPTER

Western Central Banks and Governments Can't Stop Deflation

A major bear market in U.S. stocks that spreads globally will probably not create financial chaos in the West—unless it touches off a forced unwinding of all the derivatives that have permeated the financial structures in recent years.

DERIVATIVES

Derivatives are a huge, multifaceted, interrelated market that few comprehend completely. I surely don't. I know something about the simpler forms, such as futures contracts on stocks, bonds, currencies, and commodities like soybeans, copper, and crude oil. I also know a bit about straightforward puts and calls. We use these in the portfolios we manage to implement our investment themes. They're dangerous enough because of their leverage. Just ask Nick Leeson, formerly of Barings and now behind bars. At the age of 25, he literally destroyed his 233-year-old firm in 1995 by accumulating a huge long position in futures on the Japanese Nikkei stock index. Then came the Kobe earthquake and the collapse in Japanese equities.

I haven't a clue, however, about all the exotic interest rate swaps and over-the-counter options on currencies or almost anything else you can think of, including abnormal weather. These are usually based on—*derived from*—real financial instruments like corporate loans and foreign currency obligations. They promise not only to convert long-term loans into short-term obligations, to eliminate foreign currency exposure, and to perform other feats of financial legerdemain, but to do so in almost riskless ways.

The names of some of these derivatives, however, suggest that they are less than riskless: "death-backed bonds," "heaven and hell bonds," "limbos," "harmful warrants," and "worthless warrants." Nevertheless, their creators assure the holders of these investments that they are based on mathematical models that precisely define the risks and ensure that those risks can be controlled. There's no such thing as a free lunch, however. Risk can be transferred, but not eliminated. The only question is, is it being transferred to weaker or stronger hands? My hunch is, and recent evidence suggests, that it's moving to weaker hands.

That was certainly true for derivatives-laden and unbelievably leveraged Long-Term Capital Management, which collapsed last year when Russia disintegrated financially and investors dumped junk bonds in favor of U.S. Treasuries. To be sure, no financial melt-down followed, thanks to a privately financed but Fed-led bailout and subsequent interest rate cuts. Nevertheless, other parts of the derivative realm are not yet tested.

THE NEW PORTFOLIO INSURANCE

For example, today's investors are so convinced that the put stock options they own against their long stock positions will preclude big losses that many have thrown caution to the wind. The Chicago Board Options Exchange has run large ads promoting puts on the Dow Jones Industrial Average as shields against market volatility. In other words the message is, don't sell your large capitalization stocks—simply buy puts on the Dow Jones to insulate them from a possible bear market.

Of course, someone must write those puts—i.e., sell them to investors—and whatever the put buyer gains in a falling stock market, the seller loses. The seller, many of them Wall Street houses, do get paid well for the insurance they provide, as long as stocks don't fall sharply. If they do, the sellers will enact their "dynamic hedging" programs, essentially selling stocks short to offset the puts they've written. This works fine in isolated cases, but if tons of stocks are sold under these programs, the result could be a self-reinforcing downward spiral, much like the portfolio insurance fiasco of 1987.

The odds of an options-driven stock market swoon are probably small, but certainly enhanced by the possibility, discussed in Chapter 13, that many green investors may eventually run for cover when the devastating effects of their first bear market sink in. Those who are leveraged may throw in the towel when they receive margin calls, and that selling would push stocks lower. And, as you'll learn in Chapter 28, many individual investors are carrying more leverage than they think. Even those without leverage may, as in the past, eventually panic and liquidate their mutual funds, forcing the funds to discard stocks in order to meet redemption.

Y2K

It's easy to conjure up a financial collapse from troubles with derivatives because no one knows the full size of the derivatives market, all of its interlocking features, and the extent to which it may have transferred risk from strong hands to weak hands. The same is true of the Y2K problem. Everyone knows of its existence, but no one can measure its size or the extent to which computer problems in one organization will spread to others when the calendar turns to the year 2000. I don't know either, but my hunch is that the concern is overdone, primarily because the fears of disaster are leading to corrective actions now. The analogy may not hold, but in markets, well-known problems are seldom as disruptive as feared because of prior reactions and adjustments.

If you really want to get into the swing of the Y2K phobia, however, just go back and read about how people felt a thousand years ago as the year 1000 approached. Many Christians in Europe expected the Second Coming of Christ with all the wars, earthquakes, famines, darkness of the sun and moon and falling of the stars forecast in the Gospels. Many did their best to get ready for the awful event, including Holy Roman Emperor Otto III, who spent two weeks in a hermit's cell. Scribes began correspondence with *"mundi terminum adpropinquante"* (now that we are approaching the end of the world). Of course, those who were cashing in on Y1K trade couldn't let a good business die even when the year 1000 came and went without disaster. Some simply postponed the end of the world to the millennium of Christ's death in 1033. Hey, given life expectancy at that time, they could then look forward to a whole lifetime of scare mongering.

One thing we might suggest is that whatever Y2K problems there are in the United States, they will be worse in Europe, which has been concentrating on the introduction of the euro. The switch to the new currency, however, may have helped prepare European firms to deal with the necessary computer reprogramming. Y2K may also be a big difficulty in Japan, where the ongoing deflationary depression and financial reform are consuming the bulk of attention. China may be different, however, where senior airline executives have been given plenty of incentive to solve their Y2K problem. They've been ordered to take flights on New Year's Day 2000.

I had a similar experience years ago while traveling around the world on a friend's father's oil tankers. One ship I was on had just come into Palermo, Sicily, for routine maintenance, and it had to be absolutely free of combustible gases before the welding torches and other dry-dock equipment were fired up. I'd been in-volved with the Chief Mate in supervising the cleaning of the oil tanks and was with him when the shipyard inspector came on board for a tour. As he looked down the hatches of several tanks, he asked us if they were gas free. We assured him they were, where-upon he pulled out a cigarette lighter, lighted the newspaper that was under his arm, dropped it down the tank, and ran off the ship like a scalded dog. With our word at stake, we couldn't follow him but, instead, had to stand there, sweating profusely. Well, the tank proved to be gas-free or I wouldn't be here to write this book.

In any event, if Y2K does prove to be a substantial problem and disrupts business here and abroad, it will only reinforce the al-ready plentiful forces of deflation.

CENTRAL BANKS TO THE RESCUE?

Another reason why I don't expect financial collapse in the West is because of the already demonstrated response of central banks to major problems. I noted in Chapter 2 that they are still fighting the last war, inflation, and not the next, deflation. Nevertheless, they aren't going to stand idly by while financial structures crumble.

After a gigantic burst of global leveraged lending and investing in earlier years, private capital started to withdraw from Asia when its collapse commenced in mid-1997. Foreigners and locals pulled out whatever money they could as $1 trillion in loans soured and $2 trillion in equity capital evaporated. Japanese banks continue to beat a retreat, not only from their domestic markets and the rest of Asia, but from the West as well. De-leveraging spread to Western financial institutions late last year after the financial demise of Russia slaughtered Long-Term Capital Management and other massively leveraged hedge funds. Not only hedge funds, but banks and other financial institutions eliminated their leveraged positions—and just to make sure they stayed de-leveraged, they fired the trading desks involved.

As noted earlier, the Fed moved to prevent global financial de-leveraging from drying up credit, and Euroland's 11 central banks followed with rate cuts. Meanwhile, the Bank of Japan was pumping money into the troubled Japanese commercial banks. Central banks can and will bail out their financial institutions. Nevertheless, they can't reverse the major deflationary forces at work in the world. The postwar era has been one of inflation, so demand has consistently exceeded supply. Consequently, when the Fed eased interest rates and more money, especially after having previously tightened them to slow the economy (usually to the point of precipitating a recession), pent-up and strong underlying demand was unleashed. Stocks anticipated this revival of sales and corporate earnings and rose once fears of further big profit slides had abated.

THEY CAN'T HOLD BACK THE DEFLATION TIDE

Now, however, there is no meaningful earlier Fed tightening to bottle up demand. Quite the contrary, the world is entering deflation. Supply exceeds demand, demand is more that satiated, and there's no pent-up demand to be cut loose by lower rates and more money. If you've already got too much of almost everything, lower financing costs and more readily affordable credit won't make you rush out to buy more. Instead, you're waiting for lower prices before buying. Anyway, as you'll learn in Chapter 20, real interest costs in deflation will be high even though nominal rates will be much lower.

Other deflationary forces are just too great for central banks to offset. Just ask yourself: Is it likely that even massive cuts in central-bank–controlled interest rates and floods of money in the West would reverse the stampede of capital out of Asia? Would they turn around the suitcases full of money that still flee Brazil after devaluation, or induce Japanese consumers to start spending like Americans? Or offset the deflationary effects of the end of the Cold War, the rapid rise of new technology, global outsourcing, new market economies, and the Internet?

Look at Japan, mired in eight years of bad deflation, to see how impotent a central bank can be. The overnight call rate has dropped from 8 percent to 0.01 percent, as noted in Chapter 11, but stocks are down two-thirds in this decade and remain depressed (Figure 11–2). Switzerland is also experiencing deflation, so her discount rate, cut from 7 percent in the early 1990s to 1 percent today, had done little to revive the economy. Recall the U.S. experience in the 1930s, when falling interest rates didn't help the economy much. Deflation brings on the classical Keynesian liquidity trap for monetary policy. Pulling on the monetary string by tightening credit can subdue economic activity, but pushing on that string gets no result when eager borrowers are few. Even dumping money out of airplanes probably would not cure global deflation.

MONEY SUPPLY GROWTH AND DEFLATION

Many argue that central banks can and will stop deflation with a flood of money. Some even worry that the recent rapid growth in the U.S. money supply will re-ignite inflation. Note the acceleration (Figure 18–1), starting with the onset of the Asian crisis in mid-1997, of the adjusted monetary base. It is composed of currency in circulation and commercial bank reserves with the Federal Reserve that support bank deposits and other forms of money. Part of its rapid growth is due to the leap in currency in circulation, as Russians, Argentines, and many others in shaky or worthless currency lands use the buck as their medium of exchange. The Fed estimates that in 1996, 60 percent of all the dollars in circulation were held overseas.

But note that the jump in currency in circulation isn't the explanation for the acceleration in the adjusted monetary base, or in the

FIGURE 18–1

Adjusted monetary base versus currency versus money supply (M2); year-to-year percentage changes, 1990–1999

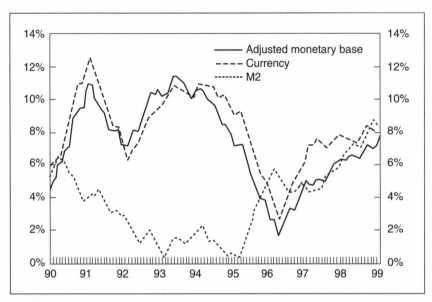

Source: Federal Reserve Board

M2 measure of money. All three growth rates are moving together (Figure 18–1). And they exceed the 5 percent growth in GDP in 1998. The United States is not alone in its money supply growth exceeding that of its economy. Much the same is true in Europe (Table 18–1). Before you leap to inflationary conclusions, however, note that the same is the case in deflationary Japan. The Bank of Japan may not have been overly aggressive earlier in this decade, but the money supply there has still been growing faster than the economy.

Table 18–2 shows that this has been the case during deflation in the United States—during the good U.S. deflation of 1870–1896 and the 1920s, and even during the bad deflation of the 1930s. Money then was barely growing, but, believe it or not, it still rose faster than GNP. Even though M2 fell in 1930, 1931, and 1932, GNP fell faster in each of those years. Many blast the Fed for not being aggressive enough in the 1930s—and blame the Bank of Japan for being too cau-

TABLE 18-1

Money Supply (M2) and Nominal GDP Growth in
Developed Countries (3 Qtr. 97–3 Qtr. 98)

	Money Supply	Nominal GDP
United States	7.4%	4.5%
France	8.0%	3.6%
Germany	5.3%	3.7%
Italy	7.2%	3.7%
United Kingdom	5.6%	4.1%
Japan	3.7%	−3.4%

Source: Haver Analytics and Federal Reserve Board

TABLE 18-2

Money and GDP Growth in Deflation and Inflation

	Money Supply	Nominal GNP	GNP Deflator
1870–1896	4.6%	2.0%	−1.8%
1920–1929	4.6%	2.3%	−1.3%
1929–1939	0.5%	−0.7%	−1.4%
1939–1980	8.2%	8.7%	4.6%
1980–1998*	6.5%	6.9%	4.1%

*Note: Figures for 1980–1998 represent GDP
Source: *The American Business Cycle* and Haver Analytics

tious in the 1990s, which is Japan's deflationary depression equivalent. I don't know if the criticism of the Bank of Japan is justified, at
least through Japanese eyes. They have a very different culture and
thought process than in the West. As for the Fed's actions in the
1930s, however, recall that the economy, and therefore the demand
for money, was collapsing faster than anyone realized as bankruptcies and layoffs spread. Banks were so shell-shocked that they didn't
want to lend, and businesses and consumers were too scared to borrow. It may be the same situation in Japan today.

MONEY IN GOOD DEFLATION

In bad deflation, many may be too scared to borrow and also may be so concerned over the outlook that they wanted to hold more money than usual, in and out of banks. But why would they also want surplus funds in good deflation when business was strong? That's why the recent Japanese decision to essentially hand out free money from every noodle shop across the country probably won't help. Furthermore, easier credit in Japan will continue to depress the yen, and Japanese leaders seem willing to accept a weaker currency. That will put pressure on other Asian currencies, including the Chinese yuan, and could spawn another round of competitive devaluations. Weaker Asian currencies might make those lands more competitive in global markets, but would raise the costs and servicing burdens of their dollar-denominated debts, chase away foreign investors who lose as currencies depreciate and force local interest rates higher to keep currencies from falling further.

When I first found that the money supply grew faster than the economy in deflation, especially in the bad U.S. deflation of the 1930s and in Japan in the 1990s, I was quite surprised. Maybe it's because the monetarists have been so critical of the Fed's behavior in the Depression that I, too, slipped into the belief that the Fed had at least contributed to the collapse in business. It's one thing to say that the credit authorities didn't do enough to revive business. It's quite another, however, to imply that they caused the downturn by constricting credit. With the economy falling much faster than the money supply, even in the darkest days of the early 1930s, that was hardly the case. Ditto for Japan in this decade.

There is another reason why the money supply grows faster than the economy in deflationary times, even in good deflation when borrowers and lenders aren't frightened, and mattress money has little appeal. Money is worth more as prices fall, and low interest rates mean that people don't have much opportunity costs on deposits that pay little or no interest. Of course, as I'll explore in Chapter 20, real interest rates are higher in deflation than inflation, but many depositors apparently look at their returns in nominal and not in real terms.

In any event, there is a rough correlation between short-term interest rates and the velocity of money, the ratio of GNP to the money supply (Figure 18–2). Long-term interest rates and money

FIGURE 18–2

U.S. short-term interest rates versus velocity of M2 money supply, 1870–1998

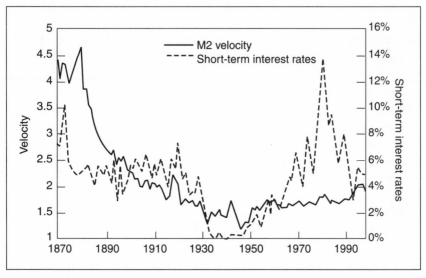

Source: Federal Reserve Board

velocity are similarly related. The turnover of money slows as interest rates fall, and vice versa. It's hard to explain, however, why
velocity didn't leap when interest rates spiked in the late 1960s and
1970s. Perhaps the elimination of caps on interest rates for bank
and S&L deposits convinced people to keep their funds in deposit
form. Still, that was the time when appreciation on real estate and
other tangible investments was far outdistancing the returns on deposits or any other financial assets. Furthermore, even though
nominal interest rates were high and rising, real interest returns
were negative in the mid- and late-1970s (Figure 20–2), and the de-
positor was a big loser.

Irrespective, the money supply grew more slowly than the
economy in the inflationary postwar era, both while prices were
accelerating in the 1939–1980 years and the deceleration since then
(Table 18–2). This is fascinating. The money supply grows faster
than the economy in deflation and slower than business activity in
inflation. This is exactly the reverse of what most investors—and

economists—believe. And it tells us that rapid money growth is no deterrent to deflation. At least it hasn't been in the past.

FISCAL POLICY IN DEFLATION

The bottom line is that, in deflation, central bankers, who genetically hate inflation, are generally unlikely to move far enough toward fighting deflation to offset it and probably couldn't if they tried their best. The same is true of fiscal policy. Many think that because government spending in today's developed countries runs a third to a half or more of total economic activity, and government employee salaries comprise a major part of that spending, its very size will prevent widespread falling prices because government pay cuts are rare. Then there are all of those built-in stabilizers, like unemployment insurance. Also, as you learned in Chapter 14, deflation curtails tax receipts, so if for no other reason than to stave off the dreadful possibility of reduced government income, governments will resort to massive anti-deflation fiscal stimulus, many reason.

But before you conclude that those pundits are right, recall from Chapters 1 and 14 that developed-country governments, backed by voter steel, are more interested in surpluses than deficits. Emerging market governments, with obvious exceptions, are broke so they can't embark on meaningful fiscal stimulus. Also, look at two real-life examples of deflation today—Japan and Switzerland. You already saw in Chapter 11 that Japan remains mired in a deflationary depression—the bad kind of deflation.

Switzerland, however, has suffered from benign deflation in recent years, in large part because of the strength of the Swiss franc as money sought a safe haven from the uncertainty over the new euro. Big deal, you may be thinking, Switzerland is just one big bank, and a strong currency attracts even more deposits, both cold and hot money. But Switzerland also relies heavily on manufactured exports and tourism, both of which are priced out of their markets by the robust Swiss franc. No wonder that, like Japan, she has seen nothing but economic weakness in the 1990s. Swiss joblessness used to be so low that they didn't count the unemployed, they named them. Then that rate jumped to previously unknown heights.

GOLD AND THE MONEY SUPPLY

The recent deflation experienced by Japan and Switzerland counter another argument that holds that deflation is impossible in today's world—there's no link between money and gold as in past deflations to prevent hog-wild increases in the money supply. It is true that money was still gold-based in the last serious deflation in the 1930s, and that since the early 1970s the gold tie is gone in most countries.

Note, however, that the Japanese yen isn't tied to gold and Japan has deflation. At the same time, the Swiss franc is linked to the yellow metal and Switzerland also has deflation. Also, recall that in past deflations, good and bad, the money supply grew faster than the economy. Maybe money wasn't being dumped out of covered wagons in the post-Civil War era or out of Model T's in the 1920s, but its link to gold didn't prevent the creation of big supplies in relation to the economy.

FEARS OF FALLING PRICES

Europeans are beginning to worry that declining prices will induce consumers to delay purchases in anticipation of still lower prices. Some are already calling for measures to promote inflation. Lars Heikensten, Deputy Governor of Sweden's central bank, was quoted in *The Wall Street Journal* after a recent interest rate cut as saying that this would "not be enough to push consumer prices back to the 2 percent target." An unusual statement for a normally inflation-fighting central banker, to say the least, although, as noted earlier, Sweden is experiencing deflation. In Japan, Taku Yamasaki, a former policy chief of the ruling Liberal Democratic Party, now favors "controlled inflation" to reverse deflationary trends and encourage consumers and businesses to spend. China is forming trade associations to set price floors on dozens of products ranging from autos to ostrich meat, and backing up the orders with fines. Interestingly, these measures are illegal in China, opposed by the State Planning and Development Commission, and unlikely to work. Nevertheless, deflation is rampant. China now has over 400 videodisk player manufacturers, compared to a handful three years ago. Excess capacity is so extreme that prices have dropped from $500 in 1995 to $200, and further declines seem unlikely to be negated by government directives. Overall, retail prices in China fell 3.2 percent in March 1999 from a year earlier, as noted in Chapter 10. A China-made VW Jetta now sells at $12,000, compared with $30,000 in 1995.

Despite these fears, I don't expect any coming deflation to be the bad variety. Even if big difficulties develop with excessive consumer debt, overblown stocks, lethal derivatives, or even Y2K, the odds are against a 1930s-style financial collapse. Table 16–2 shows that the depth of the first Kondratieff Wave depression, 1839–1843, witnessed economic growth despite widespread financial distress. Similarly, the worst years of the second Kondratieff Wave depression, 1873–1879, were mild compared to the early 1930s. A simple average of these three traumatic periods is much less severe than the early 1930s collapse. That average seems more appropriate as today's absolutely worst-case scenario than does a rerun of the Great Depression.

Good deflation requires not only a lack of financial collapse, but also a burst of supply. You see where that's coming from and why it will lead to years of good deflation in Chapter 19.

19

The Coming Era of Good Deflation

Good deflation requires not only a lack of a demand-depressing financial collapse, but also a leap in supply. In the late 1800s and in the 1920s, good deflation was driven by new technologies. It will be this time as well.

NEW TECH

As discussed in Chapter 15, computers, semiconductors, telecommunications, biotechnology, the Internet, and today's other new technologies have been growing rapidly for years, but aren't yet big enough to dominate the United States, much less other developed economies that are further behind in their application. Although the total size of today's new technologies is difficult to measure, it seems quite certain that they will soon be large enough to play the same role as did the railroad and machine technologies of the American Industrial Revolution in the late 1900s and electrification and the auto in the 1920s.

NEW OLD TECH

But that's not the only big source of price-depressing supply in the years ahead. The second is the exportation of the Industrial Revolution to developing countries in Asia, Latin America, and elsewhere. It's almost as though time stopped a hundred years ago when industrialization spread throughout Europe, the United States, Canada, and Japan; now it's started again, as the Industrial Revolution jumps to other shores and technologies like steel, autos and shipbuilding. The removal of many trade restraints in the post-war era has provided an open invitation for capital and technology to roam the world in search of the most cost-effective sites for the production of services as well as goods.

So, the Industrial Revolution has been exported to non-developed countries by advanced nations and the resulting low-cost output of goods and services has been imported in return. Businesses in Western developed countries and Japan have moved quickly to areas with even more cheap resources than the lush treasure trove of the American West in the nineteenth century—especially when you consider the cost of human capital.

This is even more true as the world's output contains less and less raw materials and more and more value added per pound. A century ago, the typical economic output was manufactured, like steel, or grown, like wheat. Steel requires coke, limestone, and iron ore as well as transport to ship out the finished product. Pittsburgh became the American steel center due to its strategic location in relation to all of those factors. Wheat takes good land and climate to grow and water or rail transport to move, and the American Midwest fit the bill beautifully. Today, in contrast, the typical new tech products are things like DRAM chips and software programming. Needless to say, their raw materials do not determine the production site. One 747 air freighter can move a lot of chips from South Korea to the United States, and all a programmer in India needs to move his output to America is a satellite disk.

In the middle of the 19th century, victims of the Irish potato famine and Chinese coolies were imported to build the U.S. transcontinental railroads. Now they're staying home but still working for U.S. companies at relatively cheap wages. The Irish are processing credit card transactions, and the Chinese are making tools and consumer electronics.

Furthermore, as noted, these developing countries aren't confined to just producing more old tech products like steel, autos, ships, basic chemicals, paper, glassware, basic capital equipment, and textiles. They are rapidly moving up the scale of sophistication. South Korea is a major supplier of computer chips. Taiwan makes many of the notebook/personal computers sold under U.S. labels, and is increasingly producing semiconductor chips for foreign companies in "foundry" operations. Hong Kong is a global financial center.

ON BALANCE, EXCESS SUPPLY

As you've seen in earlier chapters and Table I–2, excess capacity isn't just the result of the desire for better living standards in developing countries. It's also due to the spread of market economies, global sourcing, the booming buck, growing efficiencies in distribution, the mushrooming Internet, technology-induced productivity growth, ongoing deregulation, and the pressure on Asian and other developing countries to dump their exports in developed lands just to maintain, much less rekindle, employment. At the same time, there are constraints on demand caused by global defense spending cuts, relatively tight monetary and fiscal policies in developed countries, restructuring-related layoffs, the collapse in demand in emerging economies, G-7 retirement bulges, and soon, I think, big U.S. consumer saving. It's my judgment that, on balance, the supply increases will far outdistance the demand constraints. In other words, that the good deflation of excess supply will reign.

THE VIRTUES OF RISING PRODUCTIVITY

A major feature of new technology is the productivity that it promotes. Superior productivity growth is essential for a country's currency strength (discussed in Chapter 9), and it is also the key to increasing the economic pie that feeds consumers, corporate profits, and government spending. Rising output per unit of input allows all participants to get bigger slices without reducing anyone's share. Sure, more can be produced if a greater percentage of the population work and if people work more hours, but that approach soon runs out of steam. People become exhausted from overwork. Family life and leisure are disrupted and the pool of unemployed, but employable, people disappears.

Giving people more capital equipment to work with also increases output, but this, too, has its limits. Building capital equipment takes resources that otherwise could be devoted to raising living standards, and unless new equipment embodies more productivity, diminishing returns set in. Arming a construction worker with a second shovel won't help him dig faster. Both more hours and more capital equipment have been utilized in developing Asian lands, but the current crisis there shows that economic growth through simply adding more men and machines only goes so far.

Productivity is embedded in the inputs of labor, capital, technology, management, organization, infrastructure, regulation, and so on. Studies suggest that historically, about half of productivity growth comes from better trained, educated, and managed labor, and about half from more efficient equipment.

NO RECENT GLORY

Productivity growth in recent decades has been well below norm (Table 19–1). Notice that in every decade from the 1900s to the 1960s—even, surprisingly, in the 1930s—output per man-hour rose

T A B L E 19–1

Productivity in the U.S. Non-Farm Business Sector
(Average annual growth by decade)

	NBER*	BLS**
1901–1910	2.34%	NA
1911–1920	2.64%	NA
1921–1930	2.07%	NA
1931–1940	2.39%	NA
1941–1950	2.46%	NA
1951–1960	2.28%	1.94%
1961–1970	2.49%	2.55%
1971–1980	NA	1.28%
1981–1990	NA	1.03%
1991–1998	NA	1.26%

  * National Bureau of Economic Research
 ** U.S. Bureau of Labor Statistics, Department of Labor

2 percent to 2½ percent per year on average. Starting in the 1970s, however, growth faltered. No one's quite sure why, but there are clues.

The 1970s were disrupted by oil shocks and uncertainty that inhibited capital investment. Ample labor in the form of the postwar babies and married women was a substitute. But those newcomers to the labor force were inexperienced recruits, and the work ethic was poor. The growing share of government, due to its inherent inefficiency, deterred productivity as defense spending remained high and governments took over much of health care and other areas that otherwise would have gone to the bottom line-oriented private sector. High inflation in the 1970s discouraged productive work and investment in favor of tangible asset speculation.

The 1980s saw many of these productivity drags from the 1970s persist, even though disinflation was under way. Old habits die hard. Also, the restructuring that commenced in the mid-1980s, even though ultimately very conducive to productivity growth, was initially very disruptive. Think of the big corporate write-offs of restructuring costs and the difficulty people had in adapting to new, flatter corporate structures. Also, some of the productivity growth generated by American restructuring in the last decade has occurred not at home but in foreign emerging countries, as production moved to more cost-effective locations abroad. Some observers also argue that as the U.S. economy becomes more and more service-oriented, it is doomed to slower productivity growth because services are more labor intensive.

BUT THERE'S HOPE

Nevertheless, as I noted in Chapter 3, services are just as susceptible to restructuring and productivity advances as goods-producing industries. Also, the trend toward a service economy isn't new. In the postwar era, services' share of GDP has risen steadily from 33 percent to 55 percent. And, service productivity growth has been running well below trend (Figure 3–2), suggesting that a big catch-up is possible.

Think about what the Wal-Marts, Home Depots, and other mass distributors are doing to cut costs by increasing productivity, as discussed in Chapter 6. Consider what software is doing to eliminate secretaries, receptionists, and telephone operators—even typesetters, as desktop publishing becomes readily available and cheap. Galloping medical costs, seemingly with no hope of control in earlier years, are now being tamed as those that pay the bulk of the bills—government and businesses—demand efficiency. Note how airlines have changed route structures and procedures to improve productivity, including (ugh!) those telephone-recorded announcements of when your plane is supposed to take off.

In services as well as goods, not only new technology but also the expected surge in imports from Asia and elsewhere at lower prices will redouble American productivity-enhancing efforts. So, too, will weak export markets and the buck's long-term rally against the yen and the euro as well as emerging-country currencies. Less government involvement in the economy will work in the same direction (Chapter 1). The postwar babies are now fully absorbed in the work force and entering their most productive years, while younger inexperienced newcomers are few in numbers. Government surpluses and rising consumer saving will ensure more than ample funds for productivity-enhancing capital investment.

PRODUCTIVITY GROWTH AND DEFLATION

On balance, I foresee a return to productivity growth in the 2 to 2½ percent range. This is essential for the impending deflation to be the good kind because money wages are unlikely to fall. Nationwide sentiments against falling wages since the Depression have made general declines in wages nearly impossible. So, too, have minimum-wage laws, Social Security, welfare, and unemployment benefits. For the nation as a whole, labor costs account for over two-thirds of total costs. Consequently, if wages don't fall, the only way that overall prices can drop appreciably is for productivity to grow rapidly. Otherwise, profits would be wiped out, and that's bad deflation. Table 19–2 shows how this works.

If annual productivity growth is 2 percent and overall prices fall 1 percent per year, money compensation could rise 1 percent without disturbing equilibrium and normal corporate earning gains (Line 2, Column 3). A 2 percent deflation rate would work with flat labor compensation (Line 3, Column 3). In effect, each sec-

T A B L E 19–2

Deflation Math—Equilibrium Growth Rates for Compensation, Prices, and
Productivity

Annual Price Change	0	+1%	+2%	+3%
0	0	+1%	+2%	+3%
−1%	−1%	0	+1%	+2%
−2%	−2%	−1%	0	+1%

Numbers in boxes are equilibrium growth rates in labor compensation.
Source: A. Gary Shilling & Co., Inc.

tor of the economy would maintain its share of the overall pie,
which would grow with productivity, or 2 percent per year for all
participants. Real pay would rise 2 percent annually, even with
zero nominal wage gains because prices were falling 2 percent per
year. Real corporate profits would rise 4 to 4.5 percent per year (see
Chapter 20). If productivity grows 3 percent per year, 1 percent
money compensation gains would fit with 2 percent deflation
(Line 3, Column 4). In effect, then, 1 to 2 percent deflation rates are
consistent with money compensation not falling, maybe even rising a bit, as long as productivity growth is in the 2 percent or
greater range, which seems highly likely. This was very much the
pattern in the post-Civil War era, as shown in Table 19–3. Note that
money pay was flat, but real earnings rose 1.4 percent annually.

COMPENSATION CUTS WITHOUT CUTS IN MONEY WAGES

Another reason that deflation will not destroy corporate earnings is
the fact that money wages will continue to be cut without cuts in
money wages. Sure, in a few cases, money wages of individual
workers in specific jobs are being reduced, but the big action is elsewhere, as I discussed in Chapter 3. The compensation of specific individuals is falling—as their union shop jobs are outsourced, and
they end up working in lower-paying non-union organizations; as
they shift from full-time to part-time and temporary jobs, often

TABLE 19–3

U.S. Prices, Earnings, and Productivity
Growth (1870–1900) (Average annual
rates of change)

Consumer Prices	−1.3%
Nominal Earnings	0.0%
Real Earnings	1.4%
Productivity (1874–1900)	2.0%

Source: *Historical Statistics of the United States*

without benefits; and as jobs move to lower-cost areas and people move as well. Also, the greater reliance on bonuses and other forms of incentive pay is reducing total compensation for some.

From the employer's viewpoint, labor costs are also being cut by moving jobs offshore and replacing older, more expensive employees with younger, cheaper ones. And from the economy's perspective, money compensation is falling as jobs shift from high paying industries, such as manufacturing and transportation, to lower-wage industries, like retail trade and services.

KEEP YOUR PERSPECTIVE

In my judgment, the deflation ahead will be the good variety. It may not appear that way during the transition to deflation, which, admittedly, will probably be rough for many. More shocks, such a big devaluation or a financial crisis in China, are likely. So are major bear stock markets and recessions in Western developed countries. The Cassandras will then tell you that, indeed, the sun will darken, the moon will not give its light, and the stars will fall from heaven because the disaster of the 1930s is about to be repeated. This will certainly get your attention if, contrary to my advice in Chapter 22, you have stayed fully invested in stocks and suffered a 40 or 50 percent decline in what you though was the kids' college money and your retirement nest egg.

But the transitions to good deflation are always difficult. After the Civil War, the economy went through an uncertain transition and two recessions before the wonders of excess supply-driven deflation of 1870–1896 commenced. Recall from Chapter 15 that after World War I, the end of wartime price controls led to a 30 percent jump in wholesale prices in 1919–1920. This spawned an inventory building spree that was followed by a 50 percent drop in prices and the sharpest recession on record before the deflationary "Roaring '20s" commenced.

I only hope that if deflation continues to unfold in line with our forecasts, you will give credence to my further prediction of good deflation, and not be swayed by the doomsayers of financial collapse and bad deflation. It will probably take the passage of the next recession and well into the following recovery before many accept the fact that the stars aren't falling. For some, it will take longer. Recall that when the first millennium didn't bring the end of the world, some simply postponed their forecast of the apocalypse for 33 years.

HOW LONG WILL DEFLATION LAST?

I'm often asked "How long deflation will last?" Most of the questioners believe that even if deflation arrives, it will only last a few years. Then it's back to the good old inflation they may not have enjoyed but at least were accustomed to. The simple answer is: "Until the next war, and there's one out there waiting for us unless human nature has changed dramatically." Recall that, historically, inflation has been a wartime phenomenon, with deflation ruling during years of peace. But even war is likely to interrupt deflation only briefly. This may be hard to believe since we've all grown up in the last 60 years of inflation. That record-breaking stretch was to be expected, however, because it's been 60 years of wartime-World War II, the Cold War, punctuated by Korea and Vietnam, and the War on Poverty. Only now, for the first time since the late 1930s, is the world essentially at peace, and that's when deflation prevails. Regardless of your time horizon—3, 5, 10, 20, or 50 years—it's wise to anticipate deflation.

As a test, I've recently been asking clients if their office leases contain escalators to cover increases in property taxes, maintenance, utilities, etc. Invariably the answer is, yes. Then I ask if the escalators are symmetrical, so rent will fall when costs decline in deflation. None so far have thought about that possibility. But I have and am waiting for the day we send our landlord a smaller rent check. He'll undoubtedly yell bloody murder. I'll calmly direct him to the escalator clause in our lease. It's symmetrical.

To learn what many years of deflation will do to interest rates and corporate earnings, please turn to the next chapter.

20

Interest Rates and Profits

As deflation becomes established, interest rates obviously fall, but how far? The Fed won't hesitate to cut the short-term rates it controls once deflation is obvious, even though, as discussed in Chapter 18, lower borrowing costs probably won't do much to stimulate business or consumer spending. Figure 20–1 shows that U.S. short rates have been all over the place since 1835 and they can go low, virtually to zero, as they did in the deflationary 1930s and during World War II.

LOWER NOMINAL SHORT-TERM
INTEREST RATES, BUT HIGHER REAL RATES

I don't expect short rates to go to zero, but they could well fall to the 2 to 3 percent range in the period of 1 to 2 percent deflation we see ahead. That would put real short-term rates in the 3 to 5 percent range, not unusual by historical standards (Figure 20–2). Notice that in the pre–World War II era, real short rates were not only higher on average but also more volatile. Historical data compiled by my good friend Jim Bianco, President of Bianco Research, supports the range I'm forecasting. Real short rates have averaged 3.6 percent since 1831 and 1.4 percent in the postwar period (Table 20–1). In periods of mild deflation, when price declines were in the zero to 4 percent range, however, real short rates were 8.2 percent (since 1831) and 2.0 percent (since World War II). You may not be-

FIGURE 20–1

U.S. short-term interest rates, 1835–1998

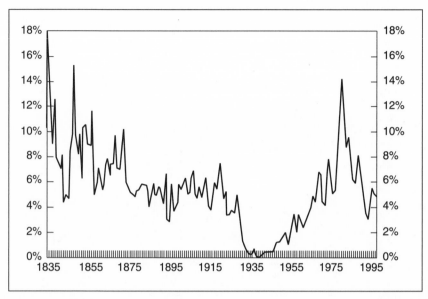

Source: Bianco Research

lieve it, but since World War II, there have been 26 year-over-year monthly periods when the CPI fell. (Year-over-year monthly periods is the measure used in Jim's study.) Deflation isn't a *complete* stranger.

Why were short-term rates lower in the post-World War II era? Probably because the Fed, living in the shadow of the Depression, worried more about high unemployment than inflation, as noted in Chapter 2. Consequently, the credit authorities held nominal short-term interest rates—hence, real short rates—below equilibrium, to prolong business expansion and promote strong employment.

In the late 1970s, the mood of the country and the politically sensitive Fed both shifted their concerns from unemployment to inflation. Nevertheless, even in the early 1990s, the Fed restrained short rates to help the bad-debt–ravaged banks rebuild their capital.

But now the Fed is fighting the last war, inflation, and not the next, deflation. Without the Asian crisis, the credit authorities un-

F I G U R E 20-2

U.S. real short-term interest rates (deflated by the consumer price index), 1835–1998

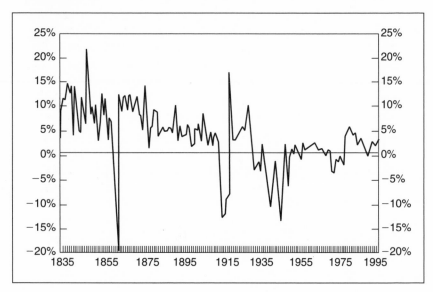

Source: Bianco Research

T A B L E 20-1

U.S. Real Median Short-Term Interest Rates

	All Periods	**Periods With Mild Deflation (CPI Year/Year 0 to –4%)**
1831–1998	3.6%	8.2%
1831–1913*	6.4%	8.7%
1913–1998**	1.4%	4.0%
1945–1998***	1.4%	2.0%

  * Before creation of the Federal Reserve
 ** After creation of the Federal Reserve
*** Post World War II

Source: Bianco Research

doubtedly would presently be busily jacking up short rates out of fear that tight labor markets will spawn inflation. This attitude, common among central bankers in developed countries, may keep short-term real interest rates higher than my 3 to 4 percent forecast range for some time and more in line with pre-World War II levels.

In any event, high real short-term rates are in the cards if for no other reason than that nominal rates are unlikely to go below zero, regardless of how severe deflation becomes. If deflation averages 1 to 2 percent in coming years, there will be times of 4 to 5 percent price declines. Then nominal rates of only 1 percent would return 5 to 6 percent in real terms.

THE SAME FOR LONG-TERM INTEREST RATES

Real long-term interest rates, *i.e.*, long-term bond yields, were also much more erratic before World War II (Figure 20–3) and generally higher, especially in times of deflation. In fact, the gyrations we've all sweated out since the end of the tranquil 1950s and 1960s pale in the face of earlier volatility. Nevertheless, the 1970s were a big shock to bond investors as surging inflation and the financing of big private and government borrowing pushed real long-term Treasury bond yields negative. Investors got a double dose of pain. They were hurt first as nominal bond yields rose (Figure 20–4) and the prices of existing bonds in their portfolios fell, and then a second time as those higher yields failed to offset inflation (Figure 20–3). Not wishing to go through the meat grinder again, they demanded, and got, real yield protection—9 percent in the early 1980s—which has slowly declined as concerns over resurgent inflation have proved unjustified. Nevertheless, real yields have not fallen as much as inflation has abated.

Like everyone else, bond holders after World War II expected prices to fall back to prewar levels. After all, that had been true in the past when wartime bulges in commodity prices were retraced with the return of peace. Little did they realize that the world had just begun a 60-year period of inflation, fueled after World War II by the Cold War, the Korean and Vietnam wars, and the War on Poverty. Consequently, for much of the postwar years, bond investors were behind the inflation curve. Even though they finally awakened to the true depth of the inflation problem—ironically in

FIGURE 20–3

U.S. real long-term interest rates, 1880–1998

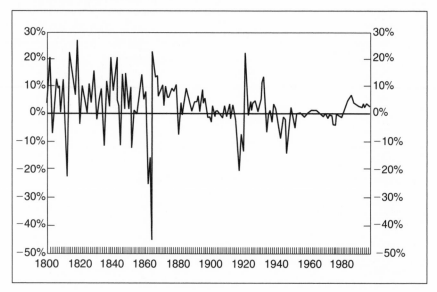

Source: Bianco Research

the early 1980s when it was starting to fade—and demanded high real returns, real interest rates on average in the postwar period have been low.

Real yields on high quality bonds averaged 4.5 percent in the 197-year period since 1801 and 8.2 percent in the mild deflation years, as shown in Table 20–2 (again using Jim Bianco's insightful data). Since the Fed was formed in 1913, real bond yields have run 2.5 percent in all the rolling 12-month periods and 5.1 percent in those when the CPI was flat to falling 4 percent. In the postwar period, the average was 2.5 percent overall and 3.5 percent in mild deflation years.

If deflation in the years ahead is in the 1 to 2 percent range and real bond yields run at the 5.1 percent average for mild deflation periods since 1913, nominal Treasury bond yields would be 3.1 to 4.1 percent. The 3.5 percent real yield average for the postwar era would push them even lower, to the 1½ to 2½ percent range.

This latter range seems too low for future years, however, even with deflation accompanied by higher consumer saving and gov-

F I G U R E 20–4

U.S. long-term interest rates, 1800–1998

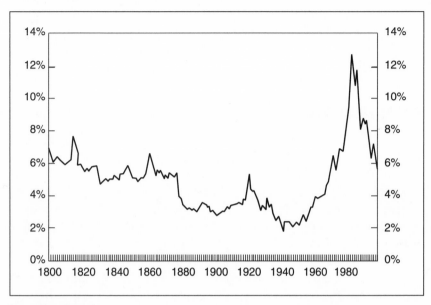

Source: Bianco Research

T A B L E 20–2

U.S. Real Median Long-Term Interest Rates

	All Periods	**Periods With Mild Deflation (CPI Year/Year 0 to –4%)**
1801–1998	4.5%	8.2%
1801–1913*	7.2%	8.7%
1913–1998**	2.5%	5.1%
1945–1998***	2.5%	3.5%

  * Before creation of the Federal Reserve
 ** After creation of the Federal Reserve
*** Post World War II

Source: Bianco Research

ernment surpluses resulting in debt retirement. Even in the 1930s, and then during World War II when interest rates were pegged by the Treasury and the Fed, long-term Treasury yields dipped below 2 percent only in 1940. In my judgment, the 3 percent target we've been using since the early 1980s for the final low for Treasury bond yields still seems valid after deflation is established. With 1 to 2 percent deflation, that will produce real yields of 4 to 5 percent.

A FLAT YIELD CURVE

It may strike you as odd that I'm forecasting short- and long-term interest rates at about the same levels in the deflationary years ahead. After all, long rates are normally above short rates, or at least they have been in the postwar era. That's why the yield curve graph of Treasury obligation interest rates, ranging from 3-month Treasury bills on the left to 30-year bonds on the right is called *normal* or *positive* when it slopes upward from left to right. And that's been the case 86 percent of the months in postwar years.

As noted earlier, however, the Fed, for most of that time, was deliberately suppressing short-term interest rates. Only when an inflationary bulge was a clear and present danger did the Fed push up short rates so rapidly that they exceeded long rates, which also rose as bond investors worried about inflation. The result is an "inverted" yield curve with short rates above long rates that persists until the credit authorities' inflation fears abate and they reverse their policy, usually because their tight credit had precipitated a recession.

At present, however, the yield curve is quite flat, even after the Fed cut short-term rates three-quarters of a percentage point in late 1998 (Figure 20–5). Bond investors smell deflation and have pushed long-term rates lower, while the Fed is more concerned with inflation than deflation and is no longer deliberately holding short rates down. In the future, a flat yield curve is likely, on average. Even though it was inverted only 14 percent of the months in the postwar era, from 1790 to the late 1930s, when inflation took off, short rates exceeded long rates about half the time, so, on average, it was flat. This will have profound effects on investment and business strategies, as you'll learn in Chapters 21 and 30.

F I G U R E 20–5

U.S. Treasury yield curve, as of April 1, 1999

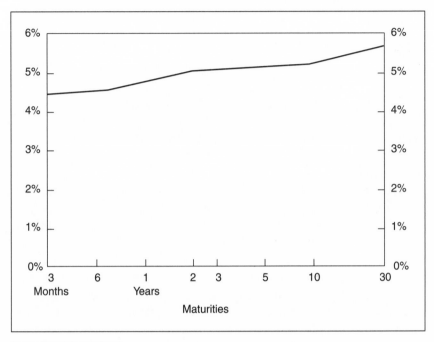

Source: Federal Reserve Board

PROFITS IN THE TRANSITION TO DEFLATION

In contrast to bonds, a not so funny thing will happen to U.S. corporate profits on the way to deflation. As noted in Chapter 13, the Asian flu will probably squeeze U.S. corporate profits and precipitate a serious stock market slide. This, in turn, will slash individuals' assets and induce consumer retrenchment and recession, which will depress profits further. Alternatively, even if the Asian crisis proves to be a non-event for the United States, it's only a matter of time until tight labor markets push the Fed to tighten credit to the recession-triggering level. The anticipated bear market would have the same net effect on individuals' portfolios and spending, and ultimately, on corporate earnings. Finally, even without a clearly identified mechanism, it seems likely that the shock of deflation, after

60 years of inflation, will be disruptive enough to disturb corporate earnings. One way or the other, the transition to deflation will involve a setback for profits.

AFTER THE TRANSITION

But what happens to corporate earnings after that recession if American consumers remain cautious and chronic deflation sets in? We constructed a statistical model, which relates pretax corporate profits to real GDP, the GDP price deflator, and unit labor costs. The model may seem simplistic, but it does pick up the major determinants of earnings. Furthermore, simplistic models have worked at least as well as much more complicated ones in my decades of forecasting. This model also makes sense because real GDP represents physical volume and the deflator stands for prices, so together they represent a proxy for total business sales. Unit labor costs represent compensation, the lion's share of business outlays, after those costs are offset by productivity improvements.

According to our model, a 1 percent rise in real GDP increases profits by 2.9 percent, quantifying the well-known leverage effect of production on earnings. In other words, profits rise about three times as fast as physical volume. Similarly, a 1 percent hike in the GDP price deflator (prices) raises nominal profits by 2.1 percent, all other things being equal. Of course, higher unit labor costs have the opposite effect, with a 1 percent rise depressing profits by 2.4 percent.

It's not surprising that the effects on profits of the deflator and unit labor costs are offsetting and similar in magnitude. The first represents the prices of goods and services sold, and the second, the costs incurred in producing those items. So, the two would be expected to move in parallel and they do (Figure 20–6). Higher unit costs are usually pushed through to higher prices, pretty much one-for-one.

Table 20–3 shows various model simulations. The top row depicts no inflation, with both the GDP deflator and unit labor costs unchanged year-by-year. To get to zero inflation probably will require a somewhat more restrained consumer than in recent years and, as a result, slower real GDP growth. We assume a 2.0 percent annual rise in real GDP, compared with 2½ percent in the past

F I G U R E 20–6

U.S. GDP deflator and unit labor costs, 1960–1998

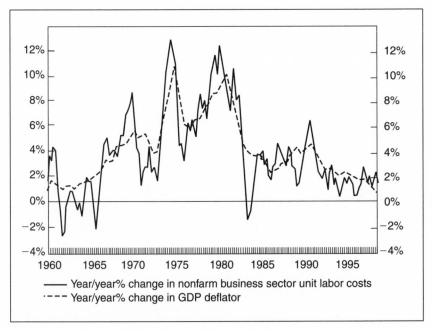

Year/year% change in nonfarm business sector unit labor costs
Year/year% change in GDP deflator

Source: U.S. Bureau of Labor Statistics and U.S. Bureau of Economic Analysis

T A B L E 20–3

U.S. Pretax Corporate Profit in Deflation (Annual Changes)

	GDP Deflator	Real GDP	Unit Labor Cost	Pretax Nominal Profits	Real Profits
	0	2.0%	0	4.4%	4.4%
	−1%	1.8%	−1%	3.2%	4.2%
	−2%	1.8%	−2%	2.4%	4.4%
1992–98	2.0%	3.2%	1.8%	9.9%	7.8%

Source: A. Gary Shilling & Co., Inc.

decade. As shown, our model translates these assumptions into a
4.4 percent nominal profit increase.

WHAT IF PRICES FALL?

If deflation sets in and the GDP deflator and unit labor costs each
fall 1 percent per year (Line 2), the general decline in the prices of
goods and labor will probably be accompanied by an even slower
growth in consumer spending. As discussed in Chapter 13, if consumers really get serious about saving, they may well increase
their saving rate by about ½ percent per year for the next decade, a
switch from the roughly two-third percent decline per year of the
past two decades. This will reduce real GDP annual growth from
the 2½ percent average of the last decade to the 1½ to 2 percent
range. I think 1.8 percent is a reasonable growth number for real
GDP. Using these inputs, annual profit increases drop to 3.2 percent (Line 2). With the same GDP growth, but 2 percent deflation
per year and a 2 percent annual decline in unit labor costs, profit
growth declines further to 2.4 percent per year.

In deflation, of course, real corporate profits grow faster than
nominal earnings, about 4 to 4.5 percent per year, as shown in the
last column. Still, both nominal and real growths are a far cry from
the results of recent years (Line 4). In addition, our simulation results might be on the high side for a condition of deflation. Our
model is based on the 1982-to-present era, one that saw corporations enjoy a substantial rise in their share of national income. This
climb might be difficult to sustain politically in deflation due to the
implied pinch in labor compensation's share.

Furthermore, slow sales growth during deflation would limit
the spreading of overhead costs, and this may not be adequately reflected in a model based on a period of much more rapid sales
gains. Also, as we've seen recently in Japan, deflation uncovers a
multitude of corporate sins that were previously hidden by inflation. In addition, our model's 15-year sample period, except for the
last several, was one of a weak dollar and gains for U.S. firms with
foreign operations as the currency was translated abroad into dollars for earnings reporting. So, our model forecasts do not really reflect the switch of those gains to losses as the greenback rises.

UNSUSTAINABLE PROFIT MARGIN GAINS

In addition, some of the other forces, which have pushed profits ahead recently, may not be sustainable. Much of the recent growth in after-tax profits and margins is due to lower effective tax rates (Figure 20–7), declining depreciating expenses and interest costs (Figure 20–8), overly aggressive write-offs in the past, and the favorable effects of stock market gains on pension funds. Without the first three of these factors, profit growth in recent years would have been much lower (Figure 20–9).

Interestingly, Wall Street analysts are concerned with these extraneous effects on earnings, and some are favoring cash flow, or earnings before interest, taxes, depreciation and amortization. This measure will slow future growth for firms like Citigroup and Wells Fargo that had big merger related restructuring charges. For Sunbeam, an earnings gain in 1997 turns into a cash flow loss.

F I G U R E 20–7

Effective tax rate on U.S. non-financial corporate sector, 1960–1998

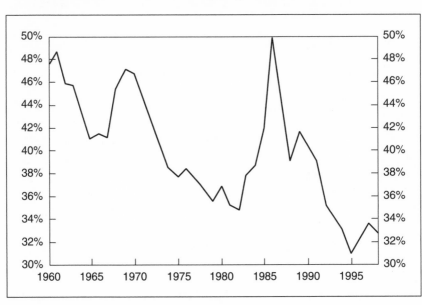

Source: U.S. Bureau of Economic Analysis

F I G U R E 20–8

Net interest expense and depreciation as a percentage of U.S. non-financial
corporate GDP, 1960–1998

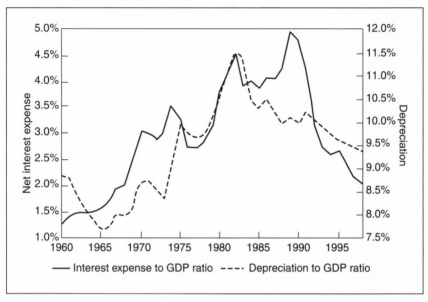

Source: U.S. Bureau of Economic Analysis

Will these salutary but non-operating influences on corporate
earnings continue? Interest rates will continue to fall, putting
downward pressure on interest expenses as deflation unfolds.
Nevertheless, the bulk of the rate decline that commenced in the
early 1980s is behind us, and the recent surge in corporate borrowing will increase interest costs for those with big new debts. Tax
rates have fallen because, among other reasons, corporations paid
29 percent tax on profits from leaping export sales in recent years,
compared to about 35 percent on slower growing domestic earnings. With weaker growth in exports in prospect, effective tax rates
may even rise unless Washington cuts U.S. corporate tax rates.

Depreciation has been falling in relation to gross corporate
product (essentially corporate sales) in recent years due to earlier
big write-offs of obsolete plants and equipment. That removed old
investments from balance sheets, and therefore further depreciation on them. But most of those write-offs are over, and deprecia-

F I G U R E 20–9

Profit trends for the U.S. non-financial corporate sector, 1965–1998

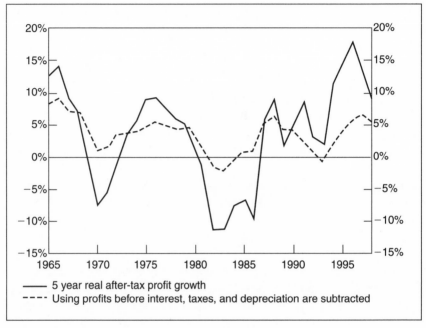

Source: U.S. Bureau of Economic Analysis

tion ratios will probably rise as the big recent purchases of new capital equipment are written off.

Profits also will be hurt as the overly aggressive write-offs of restructuring and other costs are terminated. In recent years, many firms have taken charges against their balance sheets for restructuring and other anticipated costs that exceeded the later actual expenses. These write-offs don't appear on their income statements until costs are actually incurred, so if the charges are too much, the firm can boost earnings in future years, often to fill in shortfalls and "manage" earnings for the benefit of Wall Street security analysts and investors. Lucent Technologies, for example, gained $300 million in the last two years as it revised some of its earlier restructuring charges. Other accounting gimmicks having to do with writing off the fruits of the in-process research and development of acquired companies have similar salutary effects on earnings. The

Securities and Exchange Commission, however, is on the warpath to end these practices. They also intend to eliminate write-offs for such normally expensed items as audit fees and Y2K costs.

As discussed in Chapters 3 and 28, corporations with deferred benefit pension plans must fund them so employees receive their promised payments upon retirement. In recent years, the roaring stock market has mushroomed the asset values of most of those pension plans and, therefore, reduced the annual employer contributions—in some cases, even reversing them to outflows back to the corporations. Lower or negative contributions mean more profits.

If we're right, however, and a big bear market lies ahead, companies will find their earnings depressed by increased pension fund contributions to make up for portfolio losses. Furthermore, once deflation settles in and stocks rise more slowly than in recent years (see Chapter 22), contributions will be larger.

RUNNING FAST TO STAND STILL

When taxes, interest, and depreciation are stripped away, to say nothing of the effects of overly aggressive write-offs and bull-market–restrained pension fund contributions, the rise in fundamental profit margins in recent years has been less than stellar (Figure 20–9). This suggests that American business has been running very fast just to stand still. It means that the tremendous restructuring that began in the early 1980s has been necessary to meet ongoing foreign and domestic competition. This is a sobering thought, because many believe that all the diligent earlier work by American business has finally begun to pay off. It's confirmed, though, by the spread between overall prices and unit labor costs, a rough measure of corporate profit margins (see Figure 20–6) that has actually gone from positive to negative in recent years. Deflation will intensify this competition and necessitate even more aggressive restructuring, which in turn will fuel deflation.

You've learned about the forces that are promoting deflation (Chapters 1 through 13) and its effects (Chapters 14 through 20). Now you're all set to delve into strategies for investors, businesses, and individuals wanting not only to survive but also to thrive in this new but perhaps not so brave world. Investors come first in the next eight—count 'em *eight*—chapters.

PART THREE

INVESTMENT STRATEGY FOR DEFLATION

21
CHAPTER

Bond-Based
Investment Strategy
for Deflation

Successful investment strategy in a deflationary climate will be very different than the postwar atmosphere of inflation. If you follow my 18 elements of deflationary investing, however, your portfolio should do well not only during deflation in the coming years, but also in the rough transition to it.

BONDS ARE BEAUTIFUL, ESPECIALLY
IN THE TRANSITION TO DEFLATION

With chronic deflation of 1 to 2 percent, I foresee 30-year Treasury bond yields returning to 3 percent, as discussed in Chapter 20. If so, then what we dubbed "the bond rally of a lifetime" back in the early 1980s is still underway (Figure 21–1) as yields fall further. As you're probably well aware, the prices of existing bonds rise as market yields falls because the interest they pay, their coupon, is fixed. Let's say that you buy a bond when market yields are 10 percent, so a newly issued bond at par would cost $1,000 and return, usually in two semi-annual installments, $100 per year. Even if interest rates suddenly drop to 5 percent, you still get $100 annually for the life of the bond. At the new, lower interest rate, how much would a buyer have to pay to get you to part with that bond? In this somewhat simplified example, it would take $2,000, because that's

FIGURE 21-1

U.S. long-term Treasury bond yields, 1952–1998

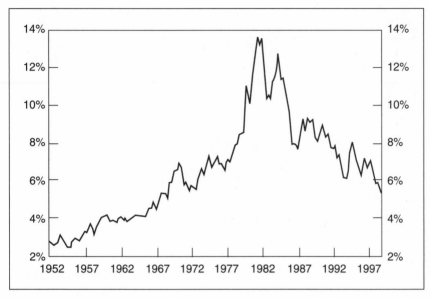

Source: Bianco Research

what it would take for you to get the same $100 per year by reinvesting that $2,000 in a new 5 percent coupon bond.

Note one very important fact. In this example, you can look on your bond investment as having doubled in price, or you can view it as having locked-in a 10 percent yield when market returns dropped to 5 percent. But you can't have it both ways. In other words, you can sell your bonds and take your 100 percent profit but then you've lost your 10 percent return and have to reinvest at 5 percent. If you keep the bond, you have a 10 percent return on your original investment but no realized profit.

Of course, you might think that the action in bonds is largely over because long-term yields have fallen from almost 15 percent in 1981 to about 5 percent. What's another two percentage points on top of a decline of nine already? Think again. A one percentage point decline from 15 to 14 percent increases the price of a 30-year bond by 7.0 percent, but a drop from 4 to 3 percent appreciates it by

19.6 percent (Table 21–1). To explain this phenomenon in over-simplified terms, a decline from 15 to 14 percent reduces interest rates by 6.7 percent, while a fall from 4 to 3 percent is a 25 percent decline. As shown in this table, the cumulative effect of the nose-dive in yields from 15 to 5 percent was a 167 percent gain, but a further fall to 3 percent would add another 40 percent.

MATURITY MATTERS

These returns and the numbers in the table actually understate the gains on bonds because they do not include the interest payments or assume that they will be reinvested. Due to the compounding of interest, this makes a very big difference in the total return, as

T A B L E 21–1

30-Year Treasury Bond Appreciation

Coupon @ Each Interest Rate Level	Price Appreciation for Each 1 Percentage Point Decline in Yield	Cumulative Price Appreciation	
		From 15%	From 5%
15%			
14%	7.0%	7.0%	
13%	7.5%	15.0%	
12%	8.0%	24.2%	
11%	8.7%	35.0%	
10%	9.3%	47.6%	
9%	10.3%	62.8%	
8%	11.3%	81.2%	
7%	12.4%	103.7%	
6%	13.7%	131.6%	
5%	15.4%	167.2%	
4%	17.3%	213.4%	17.3%
3%	19.6%	274.9%	40%
2%	22.3%	358.4%	72%
1%	25.7%	476.3%	116%

Source: A. Gary Shilling & Co., Inc.

you'll see later. It's also true that, because of the principle of compound interest, a 30-year bond, the longest maturity issued by the
Treasury, increases in value much more for each percentage point
decline in interest rates than does a shorter maturity bond.

Furthermore, you may be well aware of this, but perhaps not
the extent to which maturity matters. Note in Table 21–2 that at recent interest rates, a one percentage point fall in rates increases the
price of a 3-month Treasury bill by 0.2 percent, but a 10-year note
by 8.2 percent and a 30-year bond by 16.8 percent. Unfortunately,
this works both ways, so if interest rates go up, you'll lose much,
much more on the bond than the bill if rates rise the same for both.

As you can see, if you really believe that interest rates are going down, you want to own the longest maturity bond possible.
This is true even if short-term rates were to fall twice as much as
30-year bond yields. Many investors don't understand this and
want only to buy a longer maturity bond if its yield is higher.

Others only buy fixed-income securities that mature when
they need the money back. This strikes me as odd, especially for

T A B L E 21–2

Maturity Matters—Appreciation
for 1 Percentage Point Decline
in Yields From January 1999
Levels

Maturity	Appreciation
3 month	0.2%
6 month	0.5%
1 year	1.0%
2 year	1.9%
5 year	4.4%
10 year	8.2%
15 year	8.8%
20 year	11.8%
25 year	14.2%
30 year	16.8%

Source: A. Gary Shilling & Co., Inc.

Treasuries that trade hundreds of billions of dollars worth each day and can easily be bought and sold without disturbing the market price—by everyone but George Soros! Of course, when you need the cash, interest rates may have risen and you'll sell at a loss, whereas if you hold a bond until it matures, you'll get the full par value unless it defaults in the meanwhile. But what about stocks? They have no maturity so you're never sure you'll get back what you pay for them.

I saw this common investor attitude first-hand a number of years ago when we took over the management of my parents' securities. I don't think it was that they trusted our investment prowess as much as the fact that their broker of some 40 years retired. Soon after we restructured the portfolio, I got a call from my mother. "Gary," she said, "I see that you put Treasury bonds in our account that won't mature for 30 years." "That's right, Mom," I replied, "we think interest rates are going down and so they'll appreciate nicely." "But Gary," she rejoined, "Dad and I won't be around in 30 years." "Maybe, Mom," I noted, "but we won't necessarily still have them in your portfolio in 30 years even if you are still alive." And they may be—Dad's 91 and Mom's 89 and still going strong.

LOCKING IN HIGH YIELDS

I noted earlier the importance of reinvesting bond interest payments in boosting total return because of the compounding effect. As bond yields fall, though, the interest to be reinvested declines as well. When yields were 10 percent, the interest received could be reinvested at 10 percent. At a 5 percent interest rate, the reinvestment earns only half as much. The problem can be eliminated with *zero-coupon bonds*—also known as *stripped bonds* or *strips* because the coupons have been separated from the bond itself, or stripped. They pay no interest, only one final payment at maturity. They are bought at a discount to that fixed final price and, in effect, the current interest rate is locked in. At 5 percent yields, for example, a zero-coupon Treasury that matures in 30 years at $1000 sells at $228.60 because $228.60 compounded at 5 percent for 30 years equals $1000.

By eliminating this "reinvestment risk," zero-coupon bonds deliver much more bang per buck as interest rates fall than interest-paying bonds. If rates drop from 5 to 3 percent in the next two years, the 30-year coupon bond appreciates by 40 percent plus 10 percent interest in the interim for a total return of 50 percent. The 30-year zero, however, gains 91 percent.

OH, WHAT I COULD HAVE DONE!

Enticing as the return on zeros is in the transition to deflation and 3 percent Treasury bond yields, it still is small compared with what the astute bond investor could have made as long-term Treasury bond yields fell from their 14.7 percent yield peak in October 1981.

Suppose you had bought a 25-year zero-coupon bond then and kept rolling it over to maintain a 25-year maturity. That avoids the declining interest rate sensitivity of a bond as its maturity shortens with the passing years, as I discussed earlier. In December 1998, when 30-year Treasury yields had fallen to 5.1 percent, your investment would have gained 5,780 percent (Figure 21–2), according to data provided by Jim Bianco, my good friend at Bianco Research. In contrast, suppose you waited until stocks bottomed in July 1982 and then started to rally as equity investors began to realize that devastating inflation was abating. If at that time you bought a basket of stocks or a mutual fund that replicated the S&P 500 index and reinvested the dividends ever since, you would have gained 1,844 percent by December 1998, only one-third as much. If you had held off buying 25-year zeros until stocks bottomed, you would have foregone 75 percent appreciation. Still, between July 1982 and December 1998, your gains on the strips would have been 3,317 percent, 80 percent more than the return on stocks during the same period.

Of course, there's no free lunch. Like any long-dated bond, zero coupons are volatile on the upside when interest rates fall, but also on the downside when they rise, as they have occasionally in the last 17 years. In 1994's interest rate spike, those 25-year zeros lost 22 percent. They appreciated at a 27-percent year-end over year-end compound annual rate since October 1981, but the standard deviation around that fabulous return was high, 34 percent. This means that about two-thirds of the time the annual return fell in the −7 percent to +61 percent range. Pretty wide! In contrast, the total return on the S&P 500 index since 1982 was lower, 20 per-

F I G U R E 21–2

Comparative stock and bond performances, 1982–1998

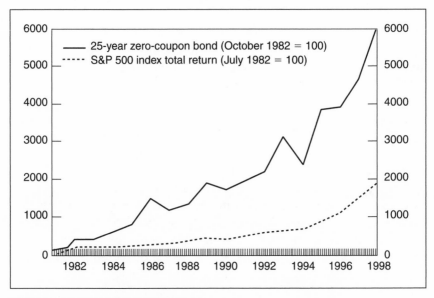

Source: Bianco Research and A. Gary Shilling & Co., Inc.

cent per year, but so was the 13 percent standard deviation. Note, however, that using year-end over year-end performance in these volatility calculations eliminates intra-year ups and downs, including the early 1987 stock spurt followed by the crash.

REMEMBER TAXES

It's also true that returns would have been lower in taxable portfolios. The appreciation in zeros in lieu of interest payments is taxed annually, even if they aren't sold. So, too, is the appreciation caused by falling interest rates when they're rolled over to maintain long maturities. They work best in tax-free accounts, and I used them for years in IRAs and pension portfolios we manage. Stocks that aren't sold avoid capital gains taxes, but their dividends suffer income levies. Small beer? Not so for long-term holders, because most of the gains racked up over a multiyear span come from the compounding effect on reinvestment dividends, and they get very big in relation to the original investment over time. I'll explore this in more detail in Chapter 22.

Treasury zero-coupon bonds are readily available from brokers in almost any amounts, and if you share my forecast of deflation and can stand the volatility, go for the 25–29-year maturities. Let 30-year zeros season a bit before you buy them. They can be erratic when initially created by stripping Treasury coupon bonds. The more risk-adverse will prefer shorter maturities or coupon bonds. Zero municipal and corporate bonds also exist. Even Amazon.com issued one. Like any zeros, however, they're an all-or-nothing bet on a single final payment. I'll take the wager on the Treasury, but not on a bookseller or a state or local government. Remember that New York City defaulted on its bonds in the mid-1970s.

I hope this discussion of zero-coupon bonds has disabused you of another popular misconception—that bonds are only for widows and orphans. There's plenty of bang-per-buck in long-term Treasuries, even more in long-term zeros, and if you're still bored, try Treasury bond futures. We use them often in portfolios we manage, and they are not for the faint-hearted.

SUPPLY AND DEMAND FOR TREASURIES

There's another reason why Treasury bonds should do well in the years ahead—the supply-demand balance. The federal budget, much to everyone's surprise, ran a surplus last year, and it is likely to stay there, on balance, in the deflationary years ahead. Sure, the booming stock market has generated lots of capital gains taxes as well as consumer enthusiasm and spending, higher taxable personal incomes, and higher corporate profits, but it won't last forever and the bull looks like he's on his last legs. Sure, deflation prevents the big tax gains that inflation created by pushing taxpayers into higher brackets, as noted in Chapters 1 and 14. Sure, Clinton wants to spend part of the surplus on new social programs. Sure, the Republicans want to reduce the surplus by cutting taxes. Sure, defense spending can't decline forever. Sure, the next recession will push the budget back into deficit as revenues fall and unemployment benefits and other spending jumps.

Nevertheless, American voters seem committed to reducing the size of federal spending. Barring massive tax cuts in the years ahead, surpluses will persist and reduce the supply of outstanding

Treasury obligations. Note that with the postwar babies now in their peak earnings years, Social Security revenues are far in excess of benefits. It's only later, about the year 2020, when they begin to retire in force that the big problems will be faced.

ONGOING DEMAND

At the same time, demand should remain strong from U.S. banks who use Treasuries for safety and liquidity, and from the postwar baby boomers who will buy more bonds as they age toward retirement and move toward more conservative portfolios. Foreigners will also continue to prefer the safe haven of Treasuries but many worry that foreign holders of $548 billion in Treasuries in late 1998, especially the Japanese, may do just the opposite. They may dump them and take the money home, or perhaps buy new euro-denominated securities. Indeed, there has been some recent selling by foreigners.

But before you conclude that this selling is the beginning of a long-term trend, note that Japan's investments in U.S. bonds, especially Treasuries, are much more rewarding than what's available at home and will be even more so if the dollar rises against the yen. Japanese insurance companies are obligated to pay policyholders 4 percent returns. They can't invest in domestic bonds at the current low yield of about 2 percent and make up the difference on volume! The zeal for American obligations may rise further now that Big Bang financial deregulation in Japan allows individual investors there to move funds abroad much more freely and enjoy returns that are vastly superior to those available in Japanese stocks, bonds, or real estate. Additionally, Japanese investors own only about 7 percent of U.S. Treasuries. And, while those investors, including the Bank of Japan, reduced their holdings slightly from $277.6 billion at the beginning of 1998 to $272.7 billion in November of that year, Treasury bond prices were going up, not down.

Japan was running a $119 billion current account surplus at annual rates in late 1998 and it isn't going to disappear anytime soon, especially with her traditional, and still dominant, policy of promoting economic growth by encouraging exports and retarding imports, as noted in Chapter 11. In addition, a weaker yen, which promotes bigger trade and current account surpluses, is part of her new easy money policy, as discussed in Chapter 18.

THE CURRENT ACCOUNT DEFICIT MUST COME HOME

A $119 billion current account surplus means that Japan ends up with $119 billion in foreign exchange in a year's time. What can she do with it? The only options I see are to convert it to paper currency, cut up the bills, and flush them down the toilet—or invest the surplus abroad. Of course, Japanese holders of dollars, the principal component of that surplus, don't have to buy Treasuries. They can buy U.S. stocks or, as in yesteryear, American farmland, hotels, Rockefeller Center, or build Honda plants in Ohio. They don't even have to invest in dollar assets. They may prefer German bonds—but then the Europeans end up with the dollars, and what will they do with them? As long as the United States has a current account deficit, one way or the other, foreigners must invest an equal amount in U.S. assets. Like chickens, the bucks come home to roost. And Treasuries will undoubtedly get their share of those returning greenbacks.

Furthermore, the U.S. current account deficit, $233 billion in 1998, is rising rapidly as confident American consumers buy more and more of the imports that desperate developing countries are sending here, while those lands purchase fewer and fewer U.S. exports. A U.S. recession and a switch by American consumers from borrowing and spending to saving will cut imports, but U.S. exports will also fall as the recession spreads globally. Furthermore, then, as in past conditions of worldwide uncertainty, risk-free and highly liquid Treasuries will be attractive. Recall the inflows of foreign money into Treasuries and the price rallies they have enjoyed in earlier foreign crises, such as Hong Kong in October 1997 and Russia in August 1998. In any event, the U.S. current account deficit is likely to persist for at least the next several years. If it doesn't, foreign countries that rely on the United States to buy their surplus production would be in deep, deep trouble, and that, too, would make Treasuries a safe haven in a sea of global woes.

TREASURIES AFTER DEFLATION IS ESTABLISHED

Once deflation is fully reflected in bond yields, the bond rally fun is over, because fairly steady yields can be expected to continue as long as economy-wide prices fall 1 to 2 percent a year. Notice in

Figure 20–4 that after deflation was established in the post-Civil War period, long-term bond yields remained fairly steady until inflation flared with the Spanish-American war at the end of the century. Real bond yields, similarly, were relatively quiet in that long deflationary era (Figure 20–3). Nevertheless, the 4 to 5 percent real returns on long-term Treasuries that I foresee after deflation becomes established will still be attractive and much higher than the postwar average of 2.5 percent, as discussed in Chapter 20. Furthermore, on a risk-adjusted basis, those real returns are excellent because of Treasuries' three sterling features—they are the highest quality securities in the world, they are highly liquid, and they cannot be called by the issuer, which might thereby limit price appreciation when interest rates fall.

At the same time, the yield curve is likely to be flat on average, in deflation, with long-term interest rates above short rates only half the time—unlike the previous postwar era when that was true 86 percent of the months, as also discussed in Chapter 20. So, you won't be able to play the old game of borrowing short term to finance long Treasuries and picking up the huge positive spread. Only when long rates are temporarily higher and likely to fall will this approach be attractive.

AVOID JUNK AND CORPORATE BONDS

There are bonds and then there are bonds. With the bond rally and the resulting lower yields in recent years, many investors have been so hungry for returns that they charged into junk bonds, those below investment grade obligations that are issued by companies here and abroad and by developing countries. They compressed the yield spreads in relation to Treasuries. Both professional investors and individuals, through mutual funds, were involved. In my recent book, *Deflation* (Lakeview Publishing Co., 1998), I advised investors to avoid them. Like any fixed-income investment, junk bonds are obligated to make regular interest payments, but their ability to do so is sometimes questionable due to the high financial leverage and uncertain prospects of their issuers. Consequently, in times of turmoil, they tend to trade more on company earnings prospects or country financial strength than in relation to interest rates. This is especially relevant in the difficult transition to deflation, as I noted in that recent book.

Since I finished writing *Deflation* in early 1998, junk bonds have been junked. The Russian financial collapse and adverse effects on hedge funds and other big holders of junk jumped the spreads between Treasuries and U.S. junk bond yields from 4 percentage points to over 7, while the difference in yields between Treasuries and emerging-market bonds leaped by 40 percentage points. Then, just as the fearless thought it was safe to go back in the water, they got clobbered again by the Brazilian currency devaluation. With further international financial crises in prospect as well as recessions in Western developed lands, I wouldn't touch junk bonds with the proverbial 10-foot pole. Junk may look attractive and some so-called sophisticated investors have returned to them, but it can get a lot more attractive. Don't get caught in the trap my good friend Ed Moos described when he says that these bonds can get cheap, cheaper, cheapest—and then you sell your holdings!

I'm also less than wild about investment-grade corporate bonds. It is true that a few corporates have 100-year maturities, and as you saw earlier, the longer the maturity, the more bonds appreciate as interest rates fall. Still the additional gain isn't that much. A 30-year coupon bond appreciates 17.3 percent if yields drop from 5 to 4 percent, but a bond of not 100 years but infinite maturity gains only a bit more, 20 percent. Furthermore, the IRS is concerned about very long maturity bonds, figuring they are more like stocks, which have no more maturity than debt instruments. IRS action to disallow the deduction of interest payments by the issuers would curtail their availability. Finally, the current spreads between even the best corporate bonds and Treasuries strike me as too narrow to offset the lower quality of corporate bonds, their lower liquidity, and their lack of call protection in most cases.

22
CHAPTER

Utilities and Stocks as Deflationary Investments

Utility stocks are aided by declining interest rates because of their high borrowing levels, but ongoing deregulation complicates the outlook, especially in the electric utility and telephone segments. So, too, does the reality that many electric utility managements have no better understanding of the competition that deregulation brings than did S&L managements when those institutions were deregulated. As you'll recall, most S&Ls were wiped out by poor investment decisions made when a competitive and volatile environment arrived.

Utility officers who are very good at dealing with regulators in rate-setting hearings and at being model civic leaders are not necessarily skillful in meeting competitors who can suddenly invade their territory. Furthermore, there's uncertainty over how regulators, state-by-state, will split stranded costs (the earlier investments in nuclear and other unprofitable facilities) between the electric utilities and their customers. Similarly, regulators and telephone companies are still wrestling over access to local and long distance markets.

In this turmoil of utility deregulation lies investor opportunity, but also risks. I suspect that the winners will be utilities led by managements that understand, and embrace, competition, and which are also operating in a reasonably hospitable regulatory climate. In the case of electricity, the industry is separating into generation, transmission, and distribution components, and competition can be expected in all three areas. In addition, firms like Enron are managing final customers' total energy needs—natural gas and/or electric—and buying and trading whatever generation, transmission, and distribution services it takes to get the job done. While telephone companies compete among themselves, they will also continue to collide with cable TV, satellites, wireless, PCs, and other telecommunications services.

Even after interest rates stabilize when deflation is firmly established, the transition to utility deregulation will continue.

STOCKS OVERALL ARE HURT BY THE TRANSITION TO DEFLATION, REASONABLY ATTRACTIVE THEREAFTER

Overblown U.S. equities may suffer a major fall of 40 to 50 percent in the transition to deflation. The spillover effect from Asia will seriously hurt corporate profits, as discussed in Chapters 13 and 20. Also, U.S. firms with exports and foreign business holdings will experience weak sales and currency translation losses as the dollar rises. And if Asia doesn't do the job, the ever inflation-wary Fed will, as it raises interest rates to head off wage inflation and ends up precipitating a recession. If neither of them disrupt stocks, then the rough transition to deflation will. Note that after 60 years of inflation, deflation will be new, rare, strange and exotic to almost every investor and business.

Furthermore, few are prepared for a major stock market decline, as discussed in detail in Chapter 13. Stocks have only been down in one of the last 16 years (1990), but historically equities have fallen in 25 to 30 percent of the years. It's as hard for those who have never sweated through a prolonged bear market to envision their psychological reaction to it, as it is for anyone who's never been in combat to mentally visit a foxhole with live bullets whizzing by.

If the next bear market will be your first, take yourself aside and try to picture your reaction to a 40 or 50 percent decline in your stock portfolio and no end of the sell-off in sight. Write down what you'll then be worth to make it as realistic as possible. Do you accept the loss as part of the game? Do you then worry about your retirement, especially if your holdings of stocks and mutual funds—directly and through 401(k) accounts—are the bulk of your net worth? Are you willing to buy more stocks, borrowing if necessary to do so, because they have become so cheap? Professional investors who are veterans of bull markets only might also ask themselves similar questions.

STOCK RETURNS IN DEFLATION

Beyond the transitional period lies deflation itself and, to many, this means curtains for stocks. They are thinking about the bad 1930s-style deep deflation, and a big interim sell-off in equities won't make them any more optimistic. At that point, few will think about how well stocks did in the moderate deflation days of the post-Civil War era and the 1920s. As events unfold, keep in mind the difference in stock performance in the modern day examples of bad and good deflation—Japan and Switzerland—touched on in Chapter 18. In Japan, bad deflation knocked the Nikkei stock average down 63 percent from its peak at the end of 1989 to the end of 1998 (Figure 11–2). In contrast, good deflation pushed Swiss stocks up 304 percent in that same period (Figure 22–1).

Misconceptions over the effects of deflation as well as on stock performance, aren't uncommon, though. Soon after I joined Merrill Lynch in 1967, we developed a statistical model to explain stock price movements. We used all the usual suspects as inputs—sales, profits, interest rates, and even a measure of speculation provided by my good friend Bob Farrell, now Merrill Lynch's Senior Investment Advisor, who I quoted back in Chapter 13. We also tried inflation rates, and much to our surprise, the model said that inflation was negative for stocks.

I say, "surprise," because at the time, stocks were considered to be great inflation hedges. Merrill Lynch even had poster-sized graphs mounted in its offices to remind investors that in the postwar era up until then, consumer prices and stocks had risen in parallel. Well, that was in 1967. It wasn't long until we found out why our model was correct, because rampant inflation murdered equities. I wish I had one of those posters today to constantly remind me just how wrong received doctrine can be.

FIGURE 22-1

Japanese and Swiss stock indices, 1990–1999, showing effect of good and bad deflation

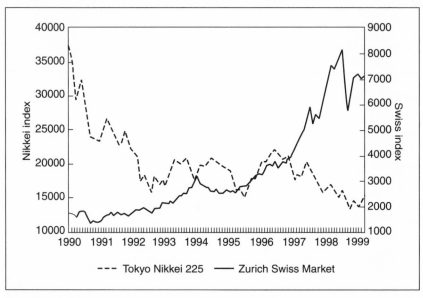

Source: Haver Analytics

REAL STOCK RETURNS IN DEFLATION

As noted in Chapter 20, with 1 to 2 percent steady deflation, corporate earnings will probably rise at around 2½ to 3½ per year in nominal terms and 4 to 4½ percent adjusted for inflation. Similar real appreciation in stock prices seems likely, and interestingly, this is in line with historic returns as compiled by Jim Bianco (Table 22–1). Notice how extraordinarily consistent the CPI-adjusted returns of 4¼ percent without dividends are for the Dow Jones Industrial since 1885 and earlier indexes compiled for stocks back to 1802. This is amazing. In the early 1800s, the U.S. was an agrarian economy concentrated on the East Coast. Canals and riverboats had yet to open up the plains east of the Mississippi. The heyday of railroads and the Industrial Revolution was still half a century away. Stocks were highly speculative and ownership was narrow. Anything that consistent over so much time and spanning so many big economic changes has got to get your attention!

Notice, too, the above-norm performance since 1974. This, in effect, made up for the miserable results during the earlier high-inflation years, because the total postwar result (1945–1997) of 4.21 percent was about in line with previous history. The make-up aspect of the ongoing stock rally is also shown in Table 22–2, which separates the postwar period into three parts: the initial post-Depression/postwar era of recovery and growth (1947–1968); the years of inflation that slaughtered stocks (1968–1982); and the pe-

T A B L E 22-1

Real U.S. Stock Index
Returns Since 1802*
(Average Annual Return)

1802–1998	4.34%
1802–1913	4.30%
1913–1998	4.38%
1945–1998	4.21%
1974–1998	4.99%

*Without dividends

Source: Bianco Research

T A B L E 22-2

Postwar S&P 500 Index Returns*

	Nominal		Real	
	Cumulative % Change	% Change Average Annual Rate	Cumulative % Change	%Change Average Annual Rate
Jan. 1947–Dec. 1968	600.1	9.2	322.8	6.8
Dec. 1968–July 1982	2.7	0.2	–62.5	–6.9
July 1982–Dec. 1998	988.0	15.6	544.9	12.0
Jan. 1947–Dec. 1998	7724.1	8.7	922.6	4.6

*Without dividends

Source: A. Gary Shilling & Co., Inc.

riod of disinflation (1982–1998). The average annual nominal gain for the total postwar era, 8.7 percent, is close to the 9.2 percent of the 1947–1968 pre-inflation years (Column 2), leaving the pounding stocks took during inflation (1968–1982) to be offset by the subsequent disinflation-related rebound. Notice also the 4.6 percent average real total return over the entire period (Column 4), with declines during inflation and subsequent strength as inflation abated. The rebound has been spectacular but so was the earlier decline, leaving performance over the entire postwar period in line with earlier history. From December 1968 to July 1982, the real S&P 500 fell 62 percent to below its real 1929 level.

Inflation comes and goes and it all averages out, apparently. In any event, our forecast of 4 to 4½ percent real stock appreciation, once deflation is established, is right in line with history.

CAVEATS

You should think about two caveats, however. Historically, the United States has been largely an internally-oriented country, and only recently have major American corporations earned 50 percent or more from foreign business. So currency translation gains or losses weren't generally important until the last decade or so. During that time, except for the last several years, there have been gains as the dollar fell, as noted in Chapters 13 and 20. But while the dollar appreciates in steady-state deflation, currency translation losses will persist and be substantial. Current thinking is quite to the contrary.

Note that when translation losses have been announced with no forewarning in the past several years by the likes of IBM, Coca-Cola, 3M, Kodak, and GM, their CEOs have said, in effect, "I'm shocked, shocked to learn that we lost money when the dollar rose." Equally shocked Wall Street analysts shuddered and the stocks dropped. If the dollar continues to rally, CEOs and analysts will eventually accept translation losses as an ongoing reality. In the meanwhile, shareholders will suffer from these shocks.

Second, as discussed in Chapter 20, U.S. corporate profit margins have been boosted in recent years by declining interest costs, falling depreciation expenses, lower effective tax rates, aggressive write-offs, and the favorable effects of the bull market on pension fund portfolios. Few investors seem to be aware of these salutary but unsustainable special factors.

NOMINAL TOTAL RETURNS IN DEFLATION

How about total returns, including dividends, in deflation? Many have almost forgotten about dividends in the ongoing 16-year stock rally, and with average dividend yields 1 percent (Figure 13.2), they hardly count when stocks are jumping 30 percent per year. But dividends have mattered in the past, as noted in Chapter 21, and will again. In the postwar era, from January 1946 through December 1998, the S&P 500, with dividend reinvestment, rose 55,352 percent, or at a 12.9 percent compound annual rate. Without dividend reinvestment, however, the total gain was much lower, 6,504 percent, or an 8.4 percent compound annual rate. This difference of 8.5 times in the final value of the portfolio may sound too large, given the dividend yield average of 3.9 percent in the postwar era and the even lower yields recently. Two powerful factors, however, have been at work.

First, reinvestment dividends have compounded as the additional shares of stock they bought appreciated. Second, more recent dividends are much, much greater than 1946 dividends, because of the 289-fold rise in the S&P 500. The S&P 500 was 4.25 in January 1946, so the annual 3.9 percent yield at that time returned the stockholder $0.17 that year. In contrast, in the beginning of 1998, the S&P 500 was 963, so the dividend yield of 1.5 percent that year meant a $14.25 payment to the investor, or 84 times the early 1946 payment. With some equities, long-term stockholders enjoy annual dividend payments that exceed the price they originally paid for their shares.

With an interim stock market decline of 40 to 50 percent, current dividend yields would rise to about 3 percent. Combined with 2½ to 3½ percent profit growth, this would give a nominal total return of about 5½ to 6½ percent, assuming that price/earning ratios (P/Es) remain unchanged. This, too, is in line with Jim Bianco's historical data going back to 1802.

To be sure, lower interest rates should push P/Es higher in the normal fashion, but bear in mind that I'm talking here about stock returns after deflation is established and after the decline in interest rates is over. At that point, P/Es should be steady. In the transition to deflation, falling interest rates will boost P/Es, but the effects will be more than offset by a key ingredient in that transition—the squeeze on profits, probably initiated by the Asian crisis but related to a recession in all likelihood. Lower interest rates may boost P/Es, but multiplying higher P/Es by much weaker earnings still results in lower stock prices. This is, of course, nothing new. Stocks normally fall well into recession as earnings weakness initially overpowers the decline in interest rates that typically starts soon after the downturn commences.

It seems reasonable, then, that the total nominal return to stocks during a steady state of deflation will be in the 5½ to 6½ percent area, and in real terms, 1 to 2 percent higher. Again, this is normal by historical standards, but be prepared so it's not a big shock to you after the 30 percent returns of recent years. It will be even more of a shock if you expected a return to the earlier investment salad days after having suffered through a severe bear market.

In any event, in the long run, interest in U.S. stocks will be strong because of the higher rates of consumer saving (Chapters 12 and 13) and the limited alternative investments in a deflationary world. Although the postwar babies' need to save for retirement is only one of many reasons for much higher saving in future years, it's fascinating to note the high correlation between U.S. stock prices and the number of people in the 45–49 age bracket (Figure 22–2). Please don't interpret this graph as guaranteeing that you can't miss in stocks until 2007, however. We tried every age bracket against stocks and this one showed the best correlation. One way to lie with statistics is to try enough things until you find one that fits. If you check enough sample sets of toothbrushers, sooner or later you'll find, sure enough, one with fewer cavities that brushed with Crest. Also in the lying with statistics department, note that statistical correlation doesn't prove causality. I absolutely positively guarantee that if you beat a drum every time there is an eclipse of the sun, it will go away.

BONDS VERSUS STOCKS

It's abundantly clear that I favor bonds over stocks in the transition to deflation. A possible 50 percent appreciation in 30-year Treasury

FIGURE 22-2

Population of 45- to 49-year-olds versus real S&P 500 index, 1947–2007

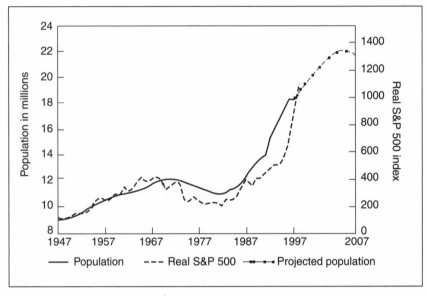

Source: Haver Analytics and U.S. Department of Commerce

coupon bonds and close to 100 percent in zero-coupon bonds over the next several years compared with a 40 to 50 percent fall in the S&P 500 makes the choice simple. This would continue the vastly superior performance in zeros compared with stocks since the early 1980s, as discussed in Chapter 21.

Bonds also look relatively attractive once deflation sets in. To be sure, at that point a 5½ to 6½ percent total return on stocks compares favorably with a 3 percent yield on bonds, which are unlikely to experience further meaningful appreciation. Nevertheless, on a quality-adjusted basis, the spread narrows considerably. As noted earlier, nothing beats the high quality or liquidity of Treasuries. And, also, as noted earlier, deflation may provide weaker profit growth than I'm assuming here, serving up some other unpleasant corporate surprises in the process.

23 CHAPTER

The Myth of Global Diversification

No one diversifies his portfolio to hold down his returns. Yet many accept the lower returns that diversification normally brings in the name of reducing volatility, and especially in the hope of offsetting big losses.

As an undergraduate major in physics, I learned a lot about the law of large numbers. Let's say you flip a perfectly symmetrical coin. You know that the probability of its landing with heads up is 50 percent, but if you flip it only once, the results will be zero or 100 percent heads. Further flips could give the same result—that's the hope that attracts people to casinos despite the unfavorable odds—but the law of large numbers says that the more you flip the coin, the closer the results will be to 50 percent heads. Note, however, one very, very important thing. There is absolutely no relationship, causal or otherwise, between one flip and another. The dice have no memory, as gamblers say.

INTERRELATED ECONOMIES AND BONDS

This last point explains why global diversification of bond and stock portfolios is much less successful than its proponents believe. Relationships do exist among markets. This is clearly true for government and other high-quality bonds issued by developed countries. Developing-country bonds are something else, either the residue of previous financial disasters, like Latin American Brady

Bonds, or pieces of paper whose prices depend largely on the actions of the local potentate or the economy's stage in its boom-bust cycle (noted in Chapter 21).

G-7 bond yields generally move in close correlation. You invest in one, you've invested in all—not surprising, because the same major forces affect them all. Inflation in the 1970s pushed up their yields. Disinflation and the recent universal zeal for lower deficits and control of government spending pushed them down. Sure, there are some significant differences but they are usually transitory. The Continental countries went into recessions in the early 1990s, later than English-speaking countries, and they recovered later, with some small differential effects on yields. Canadian yields were above the pack in earlier years when Quebec separatism was a serious threat; Italian yields jumped in the early 1990s when it looked like every politician, and half the rest of the country, was destined for jail during the anti-corruption binge. Japanese bonds strayed because of the strong yen and the 1990s deflationary depression there. But these are exceptions.

Furthermore, as global economies become increasingly interdependent, the value of global bond diversification will fall further. It's sort of like foreign travel. Outside of scenic wonders (like in the American West, the Andes, and the Alps) or historic sites (like London and Athens), the only places you want to visit are underdeveloped countries with strange, exotic cultures. As a tourist, who wants to visit a modern city like Frankfurt with virtually no historic buildings left after World War II and inhabited by folks who look a lot like those you see in Chicago? Ireland is still interesting, but becoming less so as trucks and cars replace horse-drawn carts. As economic development rolls on, the list of exciting tourist destinations shrinks. Antarctica, anyone?

ARBITRAGE AND INFLATION DIFFERENCES LIMIT SPREADS

G-7 bond yields also tend to move in lock step due to the reaction of arbitrageurs. Any openings of the normal spreads among bonds of similar quality issued by governments with similar policies and running economies on similar tracks don't last long.

These yields are even more closely correlated when inflation differences are removed, as they should be because these differences in inflation rates are normally reflected in exchange rate movements. If the United Kingdom has bond yields one percentage point above U.S. yields, it's probably because inflation rates there are one percentage point higher as well and sterling is falling 1 percent against the buck per year, thereby removing the yield spread advantage for U.S. bond holders. This phenomenon was especially true of Japanese bonds for years. Lower inflation rates there than in the United States spawned lower-than-normal government bond yields, but the rising yen against the dollar made up the difference for American investors.

G-7 STOCKS MOVE TOGETHER AS WELL

For similar reasons, G-7 stocks also move in close correlation. This isn't to say that U.S. stocks have always been world-beaters. In the 1970s, they had a total gain of just 5 percent while Chilean equities soared 2,351 percent as that country shook off socialism. In fact, virtually all equity markets, except those in Southern Europe, beat the U.S. in that miserable decade of major inflation. The unwinding of inflation and restructuring pushed the United States' rank up in the 1980s. Even in 1990–1997, however, Brazil, Chile, Mexico, Hong Kong, and Switzerland outshone the excellent results in the United States in the equity department.

WHERE ARE LOW CORRELATIONS WHEN YOU NEED THEM?

Furthermore, there is evidence (Table 23–1) that year-by-year performances in some high-flying foreign stock markets have relatively low correlations with U.S. equities. Hong Kong, for example, grew 29.1 percent per year on average between 1969 and 1998, compared with 13.9 percent in the United States (Column 1), and had a correlation coefficient with the United States of 0.43 (Column 2). Mexican stocks had a 23.2 percent annual rise and an even lower correlation, 0.18. (A zero coefficient means no statistical relationship between two markets; 1.00 would signify complete year-by-year lock-step movement in the two stock markets; -1.00 would mean complete offsets in volatility.) This may suggest that you can get better performance in some foreign markets without compounding the volatility of your U.S. portfolio very much.

T A B L E 23–1

Global Stock Markets 1969–1998 (In Local Currencies)

	Average Gain	Correlation with U.S.	Standard Deviation of Gain	Standard Deviation ÷ Average Gain
Australia	10.9%	0.54	26%	2.4
Canada	10.5%	0.60	17%	1.6
France	16.4%	0.45	29%	1.8
Germany	15.7%	0.39	29%	1.9
Hong Kong	29.1%	0.43	51%	1.8
Italy	13.8%	0.39	40%	2.9
Japan	17.6%	0.18	36%	2.1
Mexico	23.2%	0.18	50%	2.2
Netherlands	19.2%	0.75	19%	1.0
Singapore	19.8%	0.27	50%	2.5
Spain	14.9%	0.19	32%	2.2
Switzerland	17.3%	0.54	25%	1.5
United Kingdom	17.3%	0.56	30%	1.7
United States	13.9%	1.00	16%	1.2

Source: A. Gary Shilling & Co., Inc.

No way! Like many other soaring stock markets, Hong Kong's was much more volatile than America's. The standard deviation of its annual growth, 51 percent, was much higher than the 16 percent in the United States (Column 3), and Mexico had a similar high standard deviation, 50 percent. The ratio of the standard deviation to average annual growth (Column 4), a good measure of risk–reward, shows that you paid 1.8 percent in volatility in Hong Kong for every 1 percent of appreciation, and even more in Mexico (2.2 percent), compared with 1.2 percent in the United States. From this standpoint, the Netherlands' market would have been better—19.2 percent annual growth and a 1.0 ratio. But Dutch and American stocks were much more highly correlated, with a 0.75 coefficient, so bad years in Dutch stocks were usually bad years in Wall Street. In addition, these annual averages over the past 29 years hide a lot of variations, and some real cliff-hangers. There's no free lunch.

In another recent analysis of global diversification, Morningstar, Inc. set up three model portfolios. One held 100 percent U.S. stocks; the second held 70 percent in U.S. stocks, 20 percent in developed market stocks, and 10 percent in emerging market equities; and the third held 50 percent in U.S. stocks, 30 percent in developed market stocks, and 20 percent in emerging market stocks. Performance was measured for 1-, 5-, and 10-year periods. The 100 percent U.S. portfolio performed the best in all three time periods, and the more the international exposure in the other portfolios, the worse the outcome. Even after accounting for the greater volatility of the 100 percent U.S. portfolio, as measured by its standard deviation, it still was the best place to be in each of the three time periods.

A study by researchers at Hautes Etudes Commerciales, a leading French university, shows that the correlations among U.S. and foreign stock markets are low when market volatilities are low. These are often times of steadily rising stock prices, like the rampant bull U.S. market in the 1990 to mid-1997 years, the longest stretch with no setbacks of 10 percent or more in over a century. But that's the time you'd like to have all markets in sync, so the wonderful gains in the United States won't be offset by the fall of over 50 percent in your Japanese stock holdings in that period.

Even worse, much worse, correlations among markets jump to the sky in periods of big volatility—read, during bear markets. That certainly was true in the 1962 and 1973–1974 bear markets and, of course, in the 1987 crash, which started in the United States and precipitated a global melt-down. They simply shut down the Hong Kong market on October 19, the day of the crash and let the bulls sweat it out for seven days until it reopened 33 percent lower. More recently, in October 1997, Russian and Eastern European stock markets were shut when stocks worldwide were being dumped with gay abandon. When the Russian market reopened, it promptly fell 20 percent more. More recently, in 1998, when stocks sold off in the midst of the Russian melt-down and the Long-Term Capital Management demise, they dropped universally. Figure 23–1 shows the action for the big boys. Many emerging markets that were already full of holes simply submerged further. In 1998, the average emerging markets mutual funds lost 27 percent and the Latin American funds were the worst of that litter of mongrels, down 38 percent. The Brazilian devaluation in January 1999 was another example of stock markets moving together when they're falling.

FIGURE 23–1

International stock indices compared, April 1998–March 1999

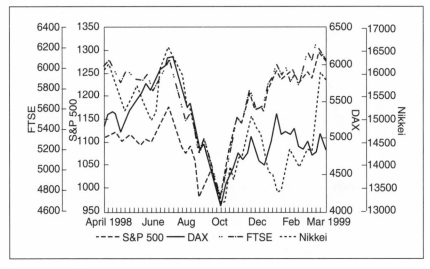

Source: Haver Analytics

A ONE-WAY STREET

Diversification doesn't work for American investors because bear markets tend to be global but bull markets aren't as consistently so. In other words, global stock diversification works when you don't want it and doesn't work when you do. The Hautes Etudes Commerciales research found that in the 1973–1974 and 1987 sell-offs, the correlations between the U.S. and major foreign markets jumped to 70 percent, and even more so for the Hong Kongs of the world. Similarly, a recent study by Sanford Bernstein & Co. reveals that in six of the last seven U.S. bear markets in the 1970–1990 years, sell-offs followed in major foreign markets. Furthermore, the correlation between the FT S&P World index, including the United States and the S&P 500, has risen sharply since 1995.

None of this should really surprise you. When financial difficulties are absent, investors can concentrate on country-by-country differences in economic growth, business regulations, and other factors that lead to lower correlations among stock markets around the world. But crises, regardless of where they start, tend to spread globally in today's financially interconnected world. This is especially true when they start in the United States, as did the 1987 crash. America is an important market for many foreign companies, so when U.S. stocks tumble, perhaps anticipating a weakening economy, stockholders of foreign multinationals get nervous. At the same time, in foreign markets, outsiders, especially Americans, own big chunks of those stocks—36 percent of French stocks and 45 percent of Italian in 1997. When money mangers retrench, they often sell first what they understand least—foreign holdings.

Furthermore, when any market slides, the investors' urge for liquidity results in selling everything in every market at any price, and with today's telecommunications, they can do so almost instantly. Limited liquidity in some markets adds fat to the fire. If an investor has a big position in Hong Kong stocks and can't get out because there are few buyers, he'll dump U.S. shares to reduce his overall portfolio risk.

The law of large numbers doesn't apply because stock markets around the world aren't independent. Ironically, the widespread use of global stock diversification has increased the interrelations and volatilities of markets and, therefore, is largely responsible for its useless, even lethal, nature.

HEDGING PROBLEMS

Global stock diversification also encounters currency risks. Normally, when there is trouble in the world, even if the United States starts it, the dollar benefits. If stocks fall globally as well, foreign losses can turn into disasters in dollar terms. U.S. investors obviously took a punishing when Asian stocks nose-dived and their currencies collapsed in 1997–1998. Currency hedging is possible against developed countries' money and a few others, like the Hong Kong dollar. But it's difficult against many other thinly traded emerging country currencies, and impossible against controlled currencies like the Chinese yuan. Outside of the yen, few Asian currency exposures are hedged by professional portfolio managers.

In any case, hedging is an expensive insurance policy. Sure, it's relatively cheap when all is calm. You pay a reasonable premium when your house isn't burning. But what happens to the premium when your neighbor's house is ablaze and yours is downwind? The guys selling you the hedge aren't stupid. As the flames and wind rise, they probably charge you about as much for the hedge as you'd lose without it as foreign currencies drop, plus a risk-enhanced profit. There's no such thing as a free lunch. (I love that phrase: I'm going to have it engraved on my tombstone, not only because my Midwest upbringing and puritanical nature wants to believe it, but also because it sums up the essence of economics—the allocation of scarce, *i.e.*, not free, resources.)

Furthermore, when you're told that a company hedges its foreign exposure, don't accept it on face value. There are many ways of hedging. Matching foreign assets and liabilities is one, but that doesn't protect sales and earnings. Hedging sales and earnings can leave assets exposed. This quarter's expected earnings might be hedged, but what about next quarter's and next year's? The farther out a company goes in currency hedging, the more expensive it gets. Few Wall Street analysts or other experts truly understand what companies really do in hedging foreign currency exposures, much less how to compare the unhedged exposures among corporations. Rest assured, though, that total hedging of all of a firm's foreign exposure is prohibitively expensive.

OTHER RISKS TO GLOBAL DIVERSIFICATION

Other risks in global diversification abound, especially in developing-country markets. Company disclosure of key financial data is often nonexistent, if not distorted. So, deteriorating conditions can be hidden until it's too late for investors to exit with anything left. In some countries, companies can't be forced into bankruptcy, so managements can run them down to the last won, rupiah, or dong.

Here's another problem. South Korea earlier limited foreign ownership of a company's stock to 26 percent, so shares available to outsiders sold at premiums of as much as 50 percent. That average disappeared when Korean stocks tanked and foreigners dumped their stocks. Another double whammy. The same was true for investors in emerging debt markets. Earlier, tranquillity lulled them into leveraged positions to magnify their yields. But it also magnified their losses when Asia came unglued and those bonds collapsed. The pain intensified further as banks that had lent as much as 90 percent on developing country bonds cut their limits to about 75 percent, and forced investors to sell out or come up with the difference. The IMF and investor pressures may remove some of these emerging market pitfalls, as noted in Chapter 11, but that remains to be seen.

Finally, don't confuse global diversification with foreign investing. Those with superior knowledge of developments abroad that will influence security prices significantly can achieve superior results. But this is far different from diversification solely to reduce volatility. One way to achieve global investment exposure is to own American multinational companies like GE or IBM. Then, in effect, you're letting them pick the best areas for long-term growth, and enjoying the benefits of U.S. securities regulation and accounting standards at the same time.

24

CHAPTER

New Technologies Win in Deflation

New technologies are great generators of deflation, as you saw in Chapter 5. They will also be great beneficiaries of deflation, especially in relation to old technologies whose sales will be muted as buyers wait for lower prices. In effect, deflation will further separate the sheep from the goats by further opening the sales and profits growth gaps between new and old tech industries.

As you learned in Chapter 15, new tech is nothing new. Many think computers and the Internet are more important than the Industrial Revolution or even the invention of movable type printing, but they play the same role now that steel and chemicals did in the late 1800s and autos and electrification did in the 1920s. Same play, different actors. New tech industries always have five important characteristics, as touched on in Chapter 5.

FIVE HIGH TECH CHARACTERISTICS

The first characteristic of new technologies is that they are no strangers to deflation. Prices always fall as the innovation and productivity of new tech unfolds, and as the economies of scale in new tech production come into play as output mushrooms. Look at computer prices (Figure 5–2) as an example.

The second characteristic of new technologies is that sales volume soars, in part because lower prices open up new markets. As discussed in Chapter 16, in the post-Civil War era, huge declines in prices vastly expanded markets to include those who, for the first time, could afford manufactured products. The drop in the price of a Model T runabout from $500 in 1913 to $260 in 1924 had a similar effect. As in earlier times, this pattern of high tech advances leading to more demand should persist in the years ahead. Today this holds true for semiconductors and computers, and it will also probably prove true in telecommunications, biotechnology, and the Internet.

Third, volume also expands for new tech firms because much of their output boosts the productivity of their customers, often in revolutionary ways, as I also noted in Chapter 16. Concrete eliminated many stone masons in the late 1800s, and trucks and cars were more efficient than the horse-drawn vehicles they replaced early in this century, just as the Internet is removing legions of salesmen and other marketing costs today. Even seemingly mundane companies involved in old technology are turning to new tech. International Paper is using computer automated machinery to cut in half the time needed to shift shipping carton machines from one sized box to another. McDonald's uses computers to direct the cooking of hamburgers and fries and to forecast supply needs during busy times of the day. GM has used computer-aided designs to cut the time it takes to design a new car from 40 months to 24 months and possibly 18 months soon. Drug companies employ computers to do thousands of tests at once and tally the results automatically. CAT is installing sensors on earth moving machines that relay information by satellite to its headquarters in Peoria, Illinois, that allows technicians to monitor engine temperature, oil pressure, and other measures needed to head-off major breakdowns.

Fax machines and e-mail are much more efficient than today's post office (if it ever was efficient), but ease of correspondence can get too easy. Before e-mail was common, I got few responses to my *Forbes* columns because readers had to write to me in care of the magazine's office. That not only took time to get a letter to me and a reply back, but also necessitated typing the letter, finding an envelope and stamp, and mailing it. Now readers pound out kudos or criticisms of my columns on their computers and send them by e-mail in seconds—although some are lengthy enough to require hours to read and respond to. The volume of comments has exploded, but I still answer them all.

Of course, volume explosion in response to price cuts doesn't guarantee success. Price cuts of 80 percent at a going-out-of-business sale generates big volume, but the firm still goes out of business. What's necessary is for price cuts to generate such big increases in volume that revenues rise. Then, if economies of scale are substantial, profits zoom. This is normally the case with high tech, but there are exceptions. When PCs priced under $1,000 were introduced last year, for example, sales volume jumped at Christmas, but not enough for some retailers to see big gains in revenues and earnings.

Cases like this, however, are the exceptions, as I learned years ago when making annual speeches to the Semiconductor Equipment and Materials Institute, a trade group of suppliers to the semiconductor industry. Every year I heard about big price cuts in semiconductors, and I wondered how the producers could make any money. Then the economics of the business dawned on me, and I bought a number of their stocks.

The fourth characteristic of new tech is its rapid obsolescence. This, too, is nothing new. The launching of the British battleship *HMS Dreadnought* a century ago instantly reduced the value of the rest of the world's battlewagons to scrap metal. So, even though buyers know that prices for new tech products will be lower later, they have to buy now. The speedy technological advances in autos in the early decades of this century meant that even though prices were falling, buyers couldn't wait for still lower prices. Who wanted to keep cranking the old Tin Lizzy by hand after cars with electric starters were available?

To be sure, Detroit tried to keep the game going long after its technological advances slowed by instituting planned obsolescence. A new tail fin here, a few portholes there, and earlier models were supposed to look hopelessly out of date. But American car buyers, aided and abetted by the VW Beetle and then high-quality Japanese imports that seldom changed designs, thought otherwise. It's fascinating that Volkswagen is now reintroducing the Beetle.

In contrast, look at your own PC. You know from years of experience that you'll get more computer power per buck next year, but you can't wait until then to give your current machine to the church rummage sale and buy a new one, or at least replace a lot of its guts. By then it will be hopelessly obsolete. I know this firsthand from experience in my own shop.

Our in-house computer czar trots into my office every month or so to announce that we need to upgrade a machine or two.

"Why?" I ask. "Are we going to make better forecasts and more insightful portfolio decisions with more powerful and faster machines? I don't think we're calling 'em any better than 20 years ago when we didn't even know what a Wang was, much less a PC."

In reply, he carefully explains that among other advances, the new machines have lots more memory, which we may not need but which the software boys use in writing their new programs. In the process, they stopped updating our current software, which, for reasons known only to them and to God, develops bugs over time. Have they taken a leaf from Detroit's book on planned obsolescence and built in time-release viruses? Regardless, we have no choice but to jack up the old machines and run new ones under them—and you don't either. Our computer czar has added a new argument for new machines: Some of our old clunkers aren't Y2K compatible and can't be made so. Oh, well.

NEW REPLACES OLD

A fifth feature of new technology is that it often replaces old tech. When furniture started being made by machinery in factories in about 1840, many skilled craftsmen, who had taken years to learn their trades, were obsolete—a sad development for my wife and me and other lovers of hand-made pieces. Similarly, the advent of automobiles and trucks sent many horses to the glue factories and buggy whip workers to bankruptcy court. John Henry may have beat the steam machine in driving railway spikes, but he died in the effort and no one challenged the machine afterwards. Electric and gas refrigerators relegated the iceman to Eugene O'Neill's play. The telephone and other modern forms of telecommunications killed Western Union.

LOWER INTEREST RATES HELP HIGH TECH

There is another plus in deflation for high tech investment—lower interest rates. As is well known, lower interest rates make future earnings worth more today on a present value basis. This works especially to the advantage of firms with rapid profit growth, and consequently, earnings that will be much bigger years from now. New tech companies are usually in this category, so as interest rates fall in the transition to deflation, their P/Es tend to expand faster than do those of old tech companies with slower profit gains.

Indeed, the P/E leaps that have accompanied declining interest rates since the early 1980s have a lot to do with the rise in stock prices in general. Since 1982, S&P 500 earnings have risen 8 percent per year, and the rest of the 16 percent annual average gain came from the rise in the P/Es from 9 to 26. Meanwhile, 30-year Treasury bond yields fell from almost 15 percent in 1981 to close to 5 percent.

Of course, after deflation settles in and interest rates stabilize, the P/E play is over. And earnings growth still has to be adequate to justify the P/Es, as discussed in Chapter 22. In terms of justifying current out-of-sight P/Es on many new tech stocks and infinite P/Es for Internet stocks with no earnings, never, never forget that for investment success, you need some earnings to which to apply the P/E. Long-term government bond yields in Japan have fallen from 8 percent to a low of less than 1 percent in this decade, but with the deflationary depression there killing corporate earnings, stocks have still fallen by two-thirds. On balance, I still think U.S. stocks are over-valued.

Regardless, new tech, as in the past, thrives in deflation. In fact, it is the driving force of the good deflation we foresee as it promotes productivity and mushrooms supply. Note also that new tech isn't just confined to high tech industries like computers and the Internet. As you'll learn in Chapter 26, manufactured housing is on our investment winners list, in part because its cost-advantage construction in a controlled factory setting is more efficient than building site construction where weather and other uncontrollable factors are common. As a result, manufactured houses cost one-half per square foot as much as site-built single-family homes but look almost the same when finished on the lot. These units now account for one-third of single-family housing starts, and are not only substituting for site-built houses, especially in the low-priced area, but are also pressuring site-built contractors to improve their efficiency.

WATCH THE NEW TECH INVESTMENT CYCLE

As I've expressed repeatedly so far in this book, new tech is of tremendous significance, especially in promoting productivity growth, economic advancement, and deflation. Yet successfully navigating your way through the new tech waves can be tricky if you want to avoid being drenched or even sunk. History, however, shows that new technologies normally go through similar investment cycles, and the latest example, Internet stocks, will probably tread that timeworn path.

OVER-ENTHUSIASM

The first step in the new technology investment cycle is investor over-enthusiasm. To be sure, the Internet, like its predecessors over the last 150 years, is solidly based, here to stay, and growing like crazy. Nevertheless, eager investors get carried away and, as noted in Chapter 13, their enthusiasm builds on itself to tulipomania proportions as the stocks skyrocket (Figure 24–1). At this stage, the sky is literally the limit, and antediluvian concepts like profits and cash flow, even revenues, only cloud up the unlimited horizon.

FIGURE 24–1

Internet insanity sector index, 1993–1999

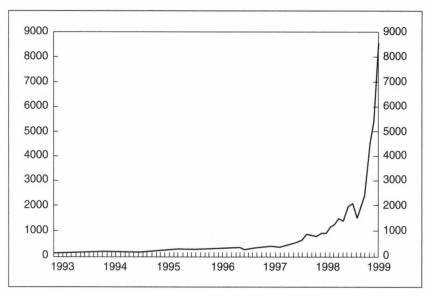

Source: The Leuthold Group

This, of course, attracts scads of new entrants, zealous to cash-in on the opportunities to raise money cheaply, develop personal and company wealth quickly, and participate in the mushrooming business. That was as true in the glass industry in the late 1800s, in autos in the early 1900s, and in computers in recent decades as it is in Internet companies and their suppliers today. At the same time, at that early stage of the new tech cycle, growth, current and antici-pated, is so robust and new investment money is so plentiful that costs are of little concern. Today, people with Internet experience are being pursued with fabulous salaries and stock options, and the great demand for them only makes them scarcer and more valuable.

NASTY COMPETITION

Then comes the competition. Initial public offerings become so prolific that even wildly enthusiastic investors become satiated. In the first five weeks of 1999, nine Internet companies raised more money through public offerings than was raised in the last five months of 1998. The $1.7 billion exceeded the total raised in all of 1995. The pipeline remains clogged with new offerings as well as potential sales by insiders who own an unusually high 27 percent of 30 Internet-commerce firms with a market value of $57 billion. Note that over 50 percent of all high tech initial public offerings in 1992–1998 finished last year trading below their offering prices.

Competition for the products being offered starts to erode prices. Amazon.com is now competing with the online arms of Barnes & Noble, Borders Group, and other booksellers. Will Amazon.com itself become a middleman that is eliminated as pub-lishers sell directly to consumers via the Internet? Home Depot, Lowe's, and Costco have started selling on the Internet, in part to prevent online sellers from invading their turf but also, no doubt, to squeeze that competition. OnSale.com has gone the limit by launching its At Cost service, which offers computers and acces-sories at the price it pays the manufacturers and distributors, and the firm hopes to make a profit from small handling fees, charges for credit card use, fees for service contracts and leases, and ads on its Web site. Meanwhile, "autonomous agents" scan the Web for the lowest prices of a particular product.

Costs also begin to matter at this stage as competition heats up and growth slows down. Note that, today, online brokers are

faced with expensive technology upgrades and increasing demands for extra services from customers. At the same time, NAS-
DAQ market makers who want their business have been squeezed
by new SEC trading rules and have cut their trading rebates to online brokers by as much as 70 percent.

PREDECESSORS

At the same time, the new tech participants and investors begin to
question whether the new product will indeed be the best thing
since sliced bread—which, I understand, created no lasting investment bonanza for bakery stocks when it was introduced. In 1882,
investors in London rushed into shares of companies involved in
electric lighting, a promising new technology, after the invention of
the light bulb. Nevertheless, the boom turned to bust as much of
the money went into fraudulent inventions, worthless patent fees,
and promotion expenses while regulators delayed electrification in
favor of municipal gas lighting companies.

This phase mimics the California gold rush, where it was the
guys selling picks and shovels, not the gold miners, who made the
money. Maybe the Internet search engines like Yahoo! and
Altavista will thrive. But are advertisers going to support all those
web sites if Internet users avoid their ads in favor of jumping to
hard information or confine their attention to searching for low
prices on products?

Also, think about all the data, reports, and more that is available free with the providers' hopes that users will get hooked and
be willing to pay later. Good luck, guys! I experienced this reality
several years ago in a slightly different context. I appeared on a TV
business show hosted by my good friends, Ken and Daria Dolan.
On the air, we talked about our investment strategy, which was
performing very well at the time. We also offered a complimentary
copy of our monthly newsletter, *Insight*, which the Dolans heartily
endorsed, to anyone who called our offices. The show was aired
live in the evening when our offices are closed; in our antediluvian
frame of mind, we didn't (and still don't) have voice mail but rely
on real live people to answer the phone during business hours.

The next morning we were deluged with requests for free
*Insight*s. One particularly exasperated caller said he was glad he fi-

nally got through, because he'd phoned all night and only got a busy signal. Now our phone system jumps incoming calls from one line to the next, and the only way a caller can get a busy signal is for all 15 lines to be full. Apparently, they were, even in the middle of the night. We mailed out about 1,000 copies of *Insight* and had to reprint it to do so. The number of paying new subscribers that resulted, however, was trivial.

We obviously wanted to avoid a repeat of all of this disruption and expense with little to show for it, so on my next appearance on the Dolans' show, Ken suggested that we again offer free *Insights*, but ask for a trivial $5 to cover shipping and handling. The requests went from over a thousand to a handful. I wonder if the purveyors of free Internet information and data aren't going to have a similar experience when they try to charge for their now free wares?

CONSOLIDATION

As overly enthusiastic expectations for a new technology are disappointed, financing dries up. But new technologies grow so rapidly and require so much capital in the process that a closing of the money tap creates big trouble. Inevitably, consolidation follows and it's the companies with the deep pockets and steadfast sources of finance that ultimately survive.

In the late 1800s, the American steel industry, a new technology of the day, had grown far too rapidly and was being killed by price-cutting and competition. Furthermore, Andrew Carnegie's Carnegie Steel was so efficient that no one else could successfully compete. So, J. P. Morgan, the moneyman, bought out Carnegie and combined his operations with other less successful firms to form U.S. Steel. The company was a huge financial success. Cutthroat competition was curtailed as demand for steel mushroomed.

Similarly, big consolidation can be expected among Internet companies when investor disappointment curbs capital sources. Already, many Internet firms realize that their growth will be limited unless they link up with TV networks and cable companies. Many firms will simply disappear or be merged into a relatively few strong survivors. But, the fundamental prospects for rapid growth and eventual financial success in the Internet will not have changed, only investor's perceptions of them. Consequently, that is precisely the time, after the initial bubble has broken, that Internet stocks will be the most attractive, especially on a risk-adjusted basis. They will have been beaten down to levels that make them very cheap in relation to their prospects.

This cycle of initial over-enthusiasm and over-expansion, followed by disappointment and consolidation before the basis of long-lasting financial success is laid, is the classic pattern for new technologies over the last 150 years. Keep it in mind as you consider investments in the Internet or any other new tech area.

AVOID OLD TECHNOLOGIES

Unfortunately for their makers, autos are now an old technology with relatively few big advances, regardless of how much the industry's annual advertising blitz tries to convince you that anything produced earlier is of Flintstone vintage. They, and other old tech goods and services, have no rapid technological advances to create instant obsolescence and no big price declines to open new markets. (Henry Ford, where are you when Detroit needs you most?)

Figure 5–1 drives home this existing disadvantage of old tech versus new from an investment perspective. Old tech still dominates overall production, which has hardly grown in the last two decades compared to new tech.

The gap between old technologies—flat to rising costs because of limited technological advances, aging work forces, and slow growth in saturated markets—and new technologies' declining costs because of rapid technological advances opening big new markets and swift obsolescence, is nothing new. What is new is deflation. It will further open the investment gap between them. New technology industries won't be much different. But old technology industries will suffer as buyers expect lower prices and wait for them, and as new tech literally wipes out many of them.

CONSUMER DISCRETIONARY SPENDING LOSES, ESPECIALLY OLD TECH PRODUCTS

The disadvantages of old technologies will be magnified for consumer discretionary items, as people turn down their spending flames and add fuel to their saving fires. Goods like cars, appliances, extra big houses, and non-essential apparel are obviously destined for disappointing sales and earnings. Even with quotas in place, apparel imports have already virtually eliminated the ability of that industry to offset sales weakness with price increases in recent years. U.S. automakers will be noticeably vulnerable as consumers save more, wait for lower prices, and see their suspicions confirmed as rising-dollar–inspired cheaper imports force Detroit to follow suit.

So will airlines. Let's say that deflation has set in and airline ticket prices are falling. You want to visit your dear Aunt Suzy who lives across the continent. She's still in good health, so you say to yourself, I'll wait until next year. Airfares will be even cheaper then and besides, I'm trying to save and can do so by making the trip later. Because you and lots of others reason this way and postpone trips, airlines will fly half empty. So, they'll cut ticket prices to try to induce travelers and to meet their competitors' price reductions. When that year's wait is over, you'll notice the drop in fares and, because Aunt Suzy's still in great shape, you'll postpone your trip again and call her occasionally instead. And so it will go for airlines and other old technologies that produce consumer discretionary items as they're hit with the double whammy of consumer zeal to save and self-feeding deflationary expectations.

DUCKING HENRY FORD'S REALITY

As I mentioned several times in earlier chapters, Henry Ford paid his Model T assemblers an unprecedented $5 per day so that they could afford to buy the cars they were building. Many American producers of consumer discretionary goods and services have been able to avoid Ford's economics in recent years. They have restructured and, along with many other employers, curtailed wages and middle-income purchasing power growth in the process. But they have not been faced with the weak demand that could have followed. Consumers have continued their spending spree, regardless of their income growth, and have covered the gap by reducing saving and increasing borrowing (see Chapter 12).

This situation is unsustainable. I'm not suggesting that American companies involved in the domestic production and distribution of non-essential consumer items should or will increase employee compensation to provide the wherewithal to buy their products. That might be in their best interest, and it might work if those firms were organized as cartels and walled off from imports, but foreign and domestic competition won't allow it. Instead I'm saying that they will find that the years of middle-income stagnation, spawned in part by their own restructuring, will come back to haunt them.

Consumers will not only stop increasing their spending faster than their income growth, but will cut back spending and increase saving rates to make up for past year's excesses (see Chapter 13). This will be very rough on the sales and earnings of the firms involved. As spelled out in Chapter 25, meaningful sales growth is necessary for good profit performance. Continual restructuring alone can't do the job, with or without mergers.

WHERE CONSUMERS MAY CUT BACK

Table 24–1 lists the changes in various categories of consumer spending in the 1973–1975 recession, the worst since the 1930s. It may give a rough guide to the nature of future consumer entrenchment. Notice the weakness in autos, appliances, foreign travel, clothing, and even tobacco. Utility spending rose due to surging oil prices, and medical spending was out of control. What's interesting is the switch from foreign to domestic air travel in times of consumer caution. The movies also thrived—cheap entertainment and escape from economic worries. They also played that role in the 1930s, you may recall. But how about movies for worried economists?

Not just airline travel but many other services can be just as discretionary as goods. Maybe more so. Just ask my Dad, who started practicing dentistry in 1931 in Toledo, Ohio, reportedly the hardest-hit American city in the Depression. Postponing dental work was common back then. As you're well aware, we expect no depression, but even if service prices don't drop enough to encourage people to wait to buy, consumers will still postpone or even eliminate non-essential services as they strive to save. They will probably hold back on dining out and taking vacations, to the detriment of restaurants, gasoline sales and oil companies, hotels and motels, middlebrow cruise ships and their builders, and airlines

T A B L E   24–1

Percent Change in U.S. Real Consumer Spending
(November 1973 to March 1975 Recession)

Total	–0.9%
Movies	37.9%
Medical	6.8%
Household Utilities	6.4%
Domestic Air Travel	3.7%
Video, Audio & Computing Equipment	2.7%
Alcohol	2.5%
Home Prepared Meals	0.6%
Dining	0.6%
Spectator Sports	–1.8%
Clothing & Shoes	–2.3%
Books & Maps	–2.8%
Foreign Travel	–3.5%
Tobacco	–5.5%
Kitchen & Other Appliances	–13.0%
New Cars	–27.4%

Source: U.S. Bureau of Economic Analysis

and aircraft manufacturers. As mentioned earlier, Boeing, like any other capital-equipment maker, gets a magnified effect from any fall-off in demand for the goods or services that utilize its equipment. If airline traffic falls and excess airline capacity mounts, new aircraft orders will collapse. Ditto for hotels and motels as consumers retrench and business use of teleconferencing explodes.

Naturally, retailers and related firms benefit from declining costs of goods, especially imports and domestic products that compete heavily with imports, assuming they're not forced to pass on the lower costs. But those who handle consumer discretionary items will see their volumes and profit margins squeezed, as increasingly thrifty consumers wait for still lower prices. Shopping malls may suffer as consumers retrench and as Internet shopping explodes. Furthermore, as consumers switch from borrowing and spending to saving, credit card issuers will be damaged. Sub-prime lenders will suffer as higher productivity growth and weaker economic advances push the unemployment rate up to an average 8 percent over the next decade (see Table 26–5), and people with low skills lose their jobs. To make matters worse, some of these people have recently become homeowners with very small down payments and large mortgages in relation to their incomes (discussed in Chapter 30). If they become unemployed and the prices of their houses are falling, all of their debts become highly questionable.

25
C H A P T E R

Consumer Spending Winners

Even with increased saving among individuals, there will be some winners in the consumer spending area during deflation. With the strong dollar, imports will decline in cost, and those that are essential to consumers will enjoy success. Also included are goods and services with strong brand identifications or patent protection that will limit competitive price erosion, and proprietary products and luxury goods with status appeal. This group includes high-priced items preferred by those with the bucks, as the national income continues to move into higher-income hands. Note, however, that those sold globally could still suffer. The collapse of Asian economies has hurt Rolls-Royce, diamonds, cognac, and luxury watches.

Lower-cost status symbols may sell well to those who can't afford much, but want the very best of what they can afford. Surveys show that lower-income people often drink higher-priced liquors than those with more pay and assets. Upscale recreational travel and other services that higher-income people favor will also be winners. So, too, will be banks, insurers, securities firms, financial planners, and others that provided financial services to individual savers who need help in investing their rapidly growing funds, once deflation is established, as shown in Table 25–1. Nevertheless, nominal returns on financial assets will be much lower in deflation, as noted in Chapters 20, 21, and 22. Consequently, broker commissions and asset management fees will be forced down. If stocks are rising 30 percent per year, a 1½ percent mutual fund fee takes only

T A B L E   25–1

Financial Institutions

Financial Institutions in the Transition to Deflation:	
Winners will be:	**Losers will be:**
Those with net long Treasury portfolios	Stock brokers
• Life insurance companies	Investment bankers
Those that borrow short and lend long	Credit card issuers
• Mortgage-oriented REITs	Sub-par lenders
Bond-oriented mutual funds	Stock-oriented mutual funds
Financial Institutions in Deflation:	
Winners will be:	**Losers will be:**
Those that assist savers and investors	Credit card issuers
• Stock brokers	Sub-par lenders
• Financial planners	
• Asset managers	Those that rely on hard assets as collateral
• Trust companies	
• Banks oriented toward high net worth customers	• Residential
	• Commercial real estate, especially older buildings
• Mutual funds	• Inventories
• Life insurance companies	Those that borrow short and lend long
Those with U.S. orientations as the dollar rises	
	Commercial real estate insurers
	Those with heavy exposure in developing countries
	Spread lenders

5 percent of the gain, but if they rise 5 percent per year, it reduces the investor's net gain by 20 percent.

Regional banks will probably continue to be bought as the banking industry consolidates. Mutual fund advisors are pursuing shareholders by diversifying into brokerage and banking services. The insurance industry will continue to consolidate due to persistent intra-industry competition and the expansion into insurance by banks, brokers, and other financial service providers, as discussed in Chapter 7. Stock insurance companies will keep buying one another and mutuals as well, as they become available for sale through mutual holding companies and demutualization. More mergers that cut across banking, insurance, and security industry lines can be expected, following the announced combination of Citicorp and Travelers Group.

Nevertheless, a major bear market in U.S. stocks during the transition to deflation could disrupt many of these plans, especially for securities-related firms (see Table 25–1). Declining equity prices dry up trading volume and profits, causing initial public offerings and other investment banking as well as merger and acquisition activity to atrophy. Bear markets reduce the value and fees of managed assets and ultimately drive individual investors out of managed accounts and mutual funds.

In recent years, many Wall Street firms have shifted emphasis from commission-based businesses and trading activities to asset management, underwriting, and other activities that generate fee income on the assumption that fees will produce a more stable and predictable income stream. With this in mind, Merrill Lynch bought Britain's Mercury Asset Management in 1997, Morgan Stanley Dean Witter purchased Van Kampen American Capital in 1996, and Credit Suisse acquired Warburg Pincus Asset Management in early 1999. Fee-based business will smooth income in the short run, but as a major bear market in stocks will prove, virtually everything on Wall Street except commodities is ultimately dependent on equity prices. Consequently, the stocks of all of those firms are simply leveraged plays on overall equity prices, and they will fall much more than the average when stocks take a tumble. Even worse hit will be the livery cars in New York City that haul around all of those brokers and investment bankers and, occasionally, their clients.

Although financial institutions that help savers will benefit in deflation, those that concentrate on lending will suffer. As noted in Chapter 24, credit card and sub-prime lenders are in for trouble. Ditto for those whose loans are backed by residential and nonresidential real estate, which will probably fall in value and, thereby, increase loan risk exposure. This will be especially true of old buildings, because lower building costs will make new structures cheaper and force down the values and rents of older ones, as discussed in Chapter 26. Loans on inventories that are declining in value will also have increasing risk exposure.

To offset these increased risks, financial intermediaries will need wider spreads between their borrowing and lending rates. But after long-term interest rates decline in the transition to deflation, they won't be able to get them from borrowing short term and lending long term because the yield curve will be flat on average (see Chapter 20). Furthermore, the likely high real interest rates in deflation won't help them because nominal rates will be lower, putting pressure on interest rate spreads. Even if banks end up paying zero for deposits, for example, the interest rates they earn on loans and investments may not cover their costs. Paying less than zero for funds is possible by assessing fees on deposits, but also politically difficult in the United States.

Property insurers may also be under fire from declining real estate values, because this will probably force premiums down on residential and commercial buildings. Also, falling building costs and the pressure they will put on older buildings' values and rents could create problems, perhaps even arson in some cases.

MANUFACTURED HOUSING AND MAYBE RENTAL APARTMENTS WIN

We've been bullish on manufactured housing ever since we foresaw disinflation killing the investment appeal of housing many years ago. In the high inflation of the 1970s, people combined great investments with places to live. Get a bigger, more expensive house regardless of your needs, mortgage it to the hilt, and clean up as inflation propels the price, was the philosophy. But house prices are no longer zooming.

So people are now separating their abodes from their investments, and manufactured houses fill the bill. They tend to be smaller than site-built houses, and with advances in design and quality, look almost identical when two or more units are attached and finished. Their improved quality has also led to the repeal of zoning restrictions in many locales, and multi-wide units no longer carry a "trailer park" image. More important, manufactured housing is about one-half the cost of site-built units per square foot, as noted in Chapter 24. They also appeal to retirees and middle income

Americans, who continue to be restructured into tough economic straits, as well as those seeking moderately priced second homes.

Deflation, including lower prices on houses, and newfound consumer zeal to save will only add to the comparative advantage of factory-built over site-constructed housing. People will be even less likely to buy unneeded housing, but for those who need it, the choice seems clear to me—but then I'm a director of a major manufactured home company, Palm Harbor Homes.

Rental apartments may also be in strong demand in an environment in which people increasingly separate their living quarters from their investments. Now, I'm not suggesting that Americans will give up on single-family owner-occupied housing. The idea of a single-family home of your own is just too deeply embedded in the American culture. Consider me as Exhibit Number One in that department. I'm a dedicated gardener and do-it-yourselfer who plans to be carried out feet-first from the suburban house we've owned, remodeled, and re-remodeled for 30 years—much to the consternation of my wife, who'd love to move on, even into an apartment some day.

But many who have no pride of home ownership and who would vastly prefer to yell for the "super" (New Yorkese for the building superintendent) than to apply a wrench to a leaky pipe have bought houses and apartments in past decades only to participate in capital appreciation. If I'm right, they'll be more inclined in future years to occupy rental apartments. This might be especially true of empty-nesters who don't like to mow their lawns and who decide to unload their money pits—especially because these homes are no longer appreciating rapidly. At the front-end of the life cycle, young couples may decide that because houses are no longer great investments, there's no reason to strain their financial, physical, and emotional resources to buy big expensive houses as soon as possible. So, they'll stay in rental apartments a bit longer and wait until their kids are of the age that a single-family house makes sense.

It will take a surprisingly small shift in housing patterns to make a big difference in the demand for and construction of rental apartments. Today there are 117 million housing units in the United States, about 46 million of them apartments, of which 35 million are rental. If only 1 percent of total existing households decided to move to rentals, the demand for apartments would increase by over one million, most of which would need to be newly built, given current low vacancy rates. This is a big number compared to new apartment starts of 300,000 last year.

Investors can participate in rental apartments, either through direct ownership or through REIT stocks. There are also REITs that concentrate on rental sites for manufactured houses. Still, this may be a tricky area for investment. As discussed in the next chapter, deflation will depress building costs, putting old apartments at a competitive disadvantage to new buildings and forcing down the rents on older units, unless demand is strong enough to keep all apartments occupied. Confining your investments to new buildings won't solve the problems either, because today's new apartments will be tomorrow's old apartments as soon as the leases expire.

PRODUCTIVITY ENHANCERS WILL BE EVEN MORE ATTRACTIVE

The deflationary world that I see ahead will be even more competitive than the disinflationary climate we're leaving. So the need to cut costs and improve productivity will be even more pressing.

We first looked at this phenomenon from an investment viewpoint back in the mid-1980s and developed the concept, "bottom-line growth stocks." These were companies that proved so effective at enhancing productivity and carrying the fruits to their bottom lines that investors eventually perceived them as growth companies, even though they lacked the rapid sales advances normally associated with growth stocks. As a result, their stock prices gained from both rapid earnings growth and rising P/Es as investors awarded them growth-stock status.

We went so far as to conduct an extensive study of all major U.S. industries, ranking them by such characteristics as evidence that they were already taking concrete restructuring steps, the proprietary value of their products, the pressure on the various industries to cut costs, the size of costs that could be cut, and the extent to which domestic and foreign competition might force them to restructure massively just to keep profits intact. The concept seemed sound, and the resulting industry, as well as company, rankings were intriguing. We found inorganic chemicals, rubber, photographic equipment, tobacco, aerospace, engines and turbines, aircraft, iron and steel, foundries, drugs, and communications equipment especially interesting.

With the recession and slow economic recovery of the early 1990s, however, it became apparent that restructuring alone, even of the most heroic and persistent dimensions cannot produce rapid and consistent profit growth. That's still true today, with or without mergers. It takes meaningful top-line growth as well, and many of our bottom-line growth stock companies did not and probably cannot, produce that growth consistently, especially in an era of deflation and excess supply in most industries.

Consequently, we haven't abandoned the concept but shifted to the other side, to those that help others restructure, cut costs, and promote productivity. Even if their customers end up running very fast to stand still, these productivity enhancers will thrive, assuming they're not servicing only failing industries.

When I think about this category, computers, telecommunications, and many of the other new technology industries discussed earlier in Chapter 24 certainly come to mind. But so do low tech or even no tech sectors. Temporary help agencies that provide workers only when needed certainly are productivity enhancers. So, too, are consultants who often achieve economies of scale by communicating research, expertise and best business practices to a wide variety of clients. First and foremost in the category are, naturally, good economic consultants, and please don't think that's an oxymoron, like honest politicians.

THE DOLLAR WILL RALLY

Chapter 9 spells out all the reasons I expect a strong greenback for many years. But how do you invest in it? One way is to favor the stocks of domestically oriented companies, which are often, but not always, smaller. Small stocks have under-performed their larger brethren in recent years (Figure 25–1) and probably for good reason. Our research shows that all things being equal, investors prefer large companies whose names and products they recognize. Only when those big firms are under fire, as they were when raging inflation and lousy productivity growth killed their earnings in the late 1960s and again in the 1970s, did they fall from favor.

FIGURE 25-1

Ratio of small cap median P/E to large cap weighted P/E, 1973–1998

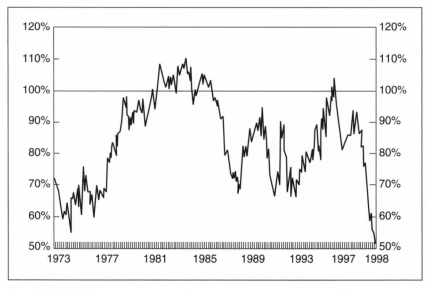

Source: The Leuthold Group

In the future, the problem won't be inflation. Instead, it will be the difficulty that multinationals, usually large companies, will have because of their foreign exposure. Large firms usually need global markets to accommodate their size and will be constantly beset by currency translation losses, weak exports, and probably depressed sales in developing economies for some years to come. Also, as noted earlier in Chapter 23, currency hedging can be prohibitively expensive. But, in addition to multinationals, watch out for domestic firms that compete with imports, and note that even small companies can have most of their business abroad.

You can, of course, also take advantage of dollar strength directly through currency futures and forward markets. I see the yen and euro currency in long-run bear markets, but am much less convinced that the Anglo-Saxon currencies—British sterling and the Canadian, New Zealand, and Australian dollars—will fall further against the greenback.

Y2K—IT'S TOO LATE

I can't discuss investment strategy without at least mentioning opportunities to benefit from Y2K. It is true that a great deal is being spent to correct Y2K problems. After reviewing the plans of Fortune 500 companies, the Federal Reserve estimates they will spend $50 billion. This will hurt the profits of many corporations, adding another blow to the effects of the Asian Contagion discussed in Chapter 13. Of course, that spending will help someone else, but the beneficiaries are less likely to be public companies. In our portfolios, we've been involved in a few Y2K stock plays in the last several years, but most of the beneficiaries like accountants and consultants are private concerns. And you can't buy stock in all the guys who are writing scare books about Y2K either.

At this point, the problem with Y2K stocks is that it was all over but the shouting before 1999 even began. Figure 25–2 shows the Leuthold Group's Y2K index of stocks. Talk about anticipation of their 15 minutes in the sun! They rose 90 percent in 1994, 77 percent in 1995, 122 percent in 1996, and 64 percent in 1997, but then dropped 35 percent in 1998.

FIGURE 25–2

Y2K company stock price index, 1994–1999

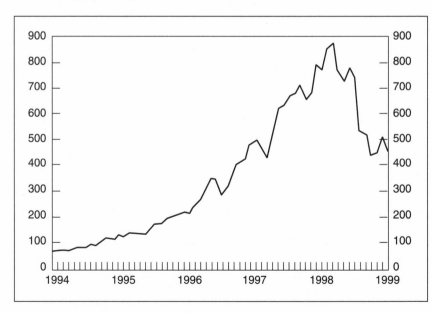

26 CHAPTER

Avoid Commodities and Real Estate

As you're well aware by now, disinflation cut commodities prices, in some cases dramatically, as a world of surpluses emerged in the last decade. The decline in commodities ranging from agricultural products like sugar to industrial commodities like crude oil has been dramatic. The price of gold has also collapsed, much to the dismay of its devotees.

In fact, even the central banks now see gold as a non-earning asset—falling in price and tying up money that could be better spent balancing government budgets or earning returns. Central banks hold 30 percent of the world's gold that's above ground, and many are slashing their holdings (Table 26–1), except the gold-passionate French and a few others. For the last decade, central bank sales have averaged 9.3 million troy ounces per year. Much to the dismay of gold devotees, the new European Central Bank elected to keep only 15 percent of its reserves in gold. Furthermore, almost all major country governments, even in France, are pushing the IMF to sell gold and use the proceeds to help developing countries repay their foreign debts.

DEFLATION'S EFFECTS ON COMMODITY PRICES

Expect more of the same commodity price weakness with deflation. Agricultural prices are also likely to fall further as deregulated U.S. farmers plant fence-row to fence-row. (Where are the pheasants I

TABLE 26–1

National Gold Holdings (In Billions of U.S. Dollars)

	1980	1997	% Change
United States	264.3	261.9	–0.9%
Germany	95.2	95.1	–0.2%
Switzerland	83.3	83.3	0.0%
France	81.9	81.9	0.0%
Italy	66.7	66.7	0.0%
Netherlands	43.9	27.1	–38.3%
Belgium	34.2	15.3	–55.3%
Japan	24.2	24.2	0.0%
Portugal	22.2	16.1	–27.5%
Austria	21.1	9.3	–55.9%
Canada	21.0	3.1	–85.2%
United Kingdom	18.8	18.4	–2.1%
Spain	14.6	15.6	6.8%
Australia	7.9	3.2	–59.5%
Sweden	6.1	4.7	–23.0%

Source: The IMF and The Bank of Canada

love to hunt going to find cover? Private game preserves that raise and release the birds for hunters may be the only answer.) Other developed countries will also expand output and exports as agricultural deregulation spreads, albeit slowly, to Europe and Japan.

Many believe that commodity prices can't go much lower because many producers of raw materials, ranging from sugar to copper to crude oil, are losing money. Price floors, however, depend much more on where a commodity is produced, than on the breakeven point of its producers. To see this, consider two similar metals, copper and aluminum.

Two Similar but Different Metals

Copper production costs have dropped more than 30 percent since the 1980s, but the plummet in prices has pushed them below breakeven levels in many countries. True, in developed countries, where production is in private hands, producers won't operate at losses, at least not for long and, in classic economics textbook fashion, are closing down production. But not so in developing lands, where production is usually controlled directly or indirectly by governments. There they will keep operating indefinitely, even at losses, in order to support employment and to earn the foreign exchange needed to service their huge foreign debts. In fact, they will probably increase production and exports as prices fall in order to maintain their foreign exchange receipts. So, the lower the price, the more they produce, and the more they produce, the lower the price. This is not what you call a normal economic response to price declines!

Note (Figure 26–1) that copper is largely produced in developing countries, and even China, a previous importer, is now exporting. Advanced lands, principally Australia, Canada, and the United States, only account for 28 percent of the total. Production, which rose sharply in 1997 and 1998, may grow even faster in the years ahead as desperate producing countries try to offset the effects of

F I G U R E 26–1

Mine production of recoverable copper in the world, 1997

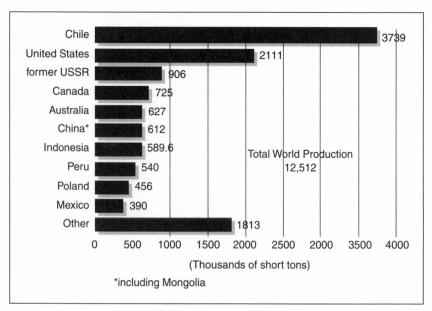

Source: U.S. Department of the Interior

FIGURE 26–2

Prices of aluminum and copper, 1996–1999

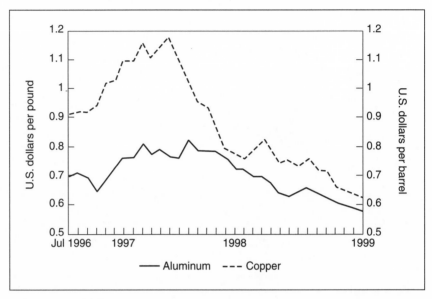

Source: Haver Analytics

lower prices on export earnings with even greater output. In 1998, Codelco, the government-owned Chilean copper producer, increased its copper production 13 percent in the face of falling prices and its lowest earnings since 1993.

In contrast, 54 percent of aluminum is produced in developed countries, where production is cut promptly when prices slide. In fact, at least part of the reason that Aluminum Co. of America, the world's largest aluminum company, recently acquired both Alumax (the third biggest U.S. producer) and Inespal is to control output. Small wonder that copper prices have fallen much more than aluminum prices since the Asian crisis commenced in mid-1997 (Figure 26–2).

BYE-BYE OPEC

Cane sugar is easy to produce in Brazil and almost every other tropical country using slash-and-burn techniques, and it has simi-

FIGURE 26-3

Arabian light crude oil prices, 1996–1999

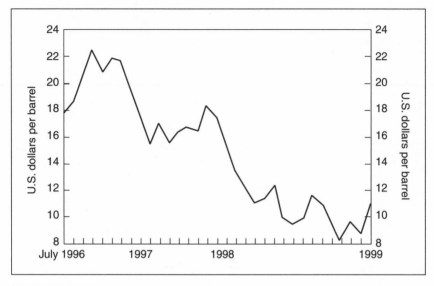

Source: Haver Analytics

lar economics. It's the same with citrus, palm oil, coffee, and many other agricultural and non-agricultural commodities. It's also true of crude oil. Even though prices have collapsed since early 1997 (Figure 26–3), more drops lie ahead. Development and production costs are much lower than when crude oil prices dropped below $10 per barrel in the mid-1980s due to technological advances such as 3-D seismic surveys and horizontal drilling. In the Middle East, it costs only about $1 per barrel to get the stuff out of the ground with new technology, but even that ridiculously low number won't halt production in a country that desperately needs the foreign exchange. Note that the once financially mighty Saudis are now in debt and were apparently forced to borrow from the tiny United Arab Emirates in 1998.

OPEC increased its quotas in November 1997 to legitimize Venezuela, Qatar, Nigeria, and other cheaters, but that hasn't held them back and won't in the future. In 1998, OPEC raised production 600,000 barrels a day, to 27.8 million, more than double the growth in global demand. Each dollar decline in oil prices cuts Venezuelan export and tax revenues by $1.7 billion, money she requires to service large foreign and domestic debts. Venezuela is now America's biggest foreign crude oil supplier, in part because she's closer and safer than Middle East oil exporters. When she cheats and exports more to the United States, the Saudis lose. Indonesia, another big debt-laden oil producer, also has plenty of incentive to step up output. The Saudis are exceeding their new quota. Russia, also heavily dependent on oil for export earnings, is trying to raise production and exports. The recent OPEC agreement to cut production will, undoubtedly, meet the same fate as earlier attempts—rampant cheating.

The world's proven oil reserves are up 40 percent since the mid-1980s, with much of it in non-OPEC lands, due in part to developments in areas like Turkmenistan (Chapter 8) and also due to new technology. Contrast this with current and impending demand weakness from Asia and elsewhere. The nine Asian Tigers accounted for only 7 percent of oil consumption in 1986 and 13 percent in 1996, but for 52 percent of consumption's growth in that decade. It is time to say bye-bye to OPEC, at least as an effective cartel. What a difference this is from the frightening early 1970s oil embargo when the world quaked at every Saudi whisper. Oil can hardly prosper in this climate, assuming no new major Middle East war or other big oil supply disruptions.

You can easily see the vicious circle in globally traded commodities. For example, Asia consumes 34 percent of the world's copper. So, as the Asian economies and their needs for copper collapse, prices nose-dive. This, in turn, depresses the export earnings of developing-country producers, who then produce and export more copper in response, further depressing prices.

COMMODITY PRICE WEAKNESS—NOT A ZERO SUM GAME

Obviously, commodity price declines are not only deflationary, but also produce winners and losers. In the case of petroleum, the winners include A. Gary Shilling & Co., with our deflation forecast; consumers who pay less for gasoline, electricity, and heating oil; energy users like airlines, railroads, bus lines, and ship operators; and those energy-intense producers of such items as cars, cement, rubber, steel, and petrochemicals. Oil producers and those who drill and service oil wells are the obvious losers. It may appear to be a zero sum game with everything the losers lose being gained by winners, but it isn't—not on an individual consumer, company, and even country basis.

An oil producer's whole business is involved with petroleum, but the gasoline consumer buys many other things as well. So, the loss to an individual oil company exceeds the gain to the individual consumer. The same is true at the country level. Developing countries that export oil rely heavily on it, while oil is much less important to developing countries that import oil (Table 26–2). The distinction is even greater for developed countries where oil and other raw materials imports, directly or as parts of finished products, are small. The same is true within advanced lands. In 1981, 21 percent of Texas' gross state product came from energy. Now it's only 11 percent.

This shrinking importance of oil and other commodities in developed countries isn't surprising because as products—both goods and services—become more sophisticated, they contain less in raw materials, as noted in Chapter 19. Former Saudi oil minister Sheik Yamani put it succinctly when he said, according to *The Wall Street Journal*, "The oil industry will not contract because the world

T A B L E   26–2

Relative Importance of Crude Oil Exports/Imports to Developing Nations (1998) (Crude oil exports as a % of GDP)

Ecuador	10.0%	Brazil	0.5%
Venezuela	19.5%	Chile	1.4%
Iran	18.1%	Turkey	2.0%
Kuwait	32.5%	Czech Republic	1.9%
Saudi Arabia	38.2%	Hungary	1.9%
United Arab Emirates	39.6%	Poland	1.4%
Algeria	12.8%	South Korea	2.6%
Nigeria	46.4%	Taiwan	1.6%
		Thailand	1.8%

Source: Haver Analytics

is running out of oil, but because the world is becoming less and less interested in what oil has to offer."

WILL CARTELS DEVELOP?

OPEC may be irrelevant, but some think that, as in the past, weak commodity prices and global excess capacity may spawn cartels that might not only arrest price declines but promote increases. At the same time, others see the recent rash of mergers, discussed in Chapter 4, aimed not only at cutting costs but also at reducing supply and establishing cartels or oligopolies. Note, too, the famous quote from Adam Smith in *The Wealth of Nations*, published in 1776. "People in the same trade seldom meet together, even for merriment or diversion, but the conversation ends in a conspiracy against the public, or in some contrivance to raise prices."

It's certainly possible that the Exxon-Mobil merger is aimed, at least in part, at re-establishing the global control of crude oil that major oil companies exercised before the now terminally ill OPEC took over as an effective cartel. Similarly, the government-forced restructuring of the South Korean chaebols is leading to concentration in the Korean auto and semiconductor industries with global ramifications. Before joining this camp, however, note that successful cartels have three important characteristics.

Cartel Characteristics

First, successful cartels require strong and patient leaders. A cartel's purpose is to keep prices above equilibrium by curtailing supply. This creates excessive profits and encourages cheating by those who want to exceed their quotas. The leader's function is to discourage the cheaters and to accommodate them when necessary by cutting back its own output. The Saudis earlier served as OPEC's leader when they had ample financial reserves, but now they have huge international debts to service and have switched from being the leader to joining the cheaters. Other commodities and industries that face economic excess supply also appear to lack strong potential cartel leaders.

Second, for a cartel to succeed for any length of time, the alternative to dumping excess supply on the market must be leaving it in the ground, not holding it in inventory. Historically, cartels in metal have worked periodically because if zinc or lead isn't mined, little expense is incurred. That's why the OPEC cartel worked for so many years. According to *The Gartman Letter*, Douglas C. Vearley, President of Phelps Dodge, said of copper in a recent interview, "We are mining a resource that is depleting with no profit. . . . The more you dig out and make nothing on, the less you have when you might have a better price."

In contrast, it is hard to imagine a cartel among PC manufacturers, which have high overhead costs and make things that are expensive to store and that become obsolete quickly. Many, but certainly not all, of the current and likely large mergers that might suggest movement toward cartels are in industries like drugs and financial services with similar characteristics. At the same time, most "leave them in the ground" commodities like oil and copper are found primarily in developing countries that desperately want to produce and export them to create jobs and earn foreign exchange.

Third, a cartel works best when both buyers and sellers want prices to rise. Cartels that produce lasting assets, like diamonds, led by deBeers, and Hong Kong land, controlled by the government, have buyers as well as sellers rooting for higher prices. (I'm indebted to our good friend and client Charles W. Hastings of Bessemer Trust Company for making this point.) This is certainly not the case with oil, steel, banking, autos, or any other industries whose products are consumed or depreciate rapidly. Few other products fit in this category.

This doesn't mean that cartels cannot be formed as they were in the past to keep falling prices from falling further—and for other purposes as well. In the 1920s, Winston Churchill, in a speech to the House of Commons, advocated a cartel in natural rubber, in which Britain has huge interests, to soak the Americans in order to help repay World War I debts owed to the Yankees. The rubber and other raw material cartels set up then lasted for a few years, because in the good-deflation era of the 1920s, demand was strong enough to prevent rampant cheating. They collapsed in the global depression of the early 1930s, however, and attempts to revive them were unsuccessful because demand continued to be too weak. In any event, I doubt that any cartels attempted in the deflationary years ahead will be widespread enough or have strong enough leaders to offset the deflationary forces of worldwide excess supply.

Finally, note that the global consolidations now going on in industries such as automobiles, telecommunications, energy, semiconductors and financial services may actually stimulate competition and reduce prices. Small grocery stores, even if located on every street corner, tend to be less competitive than supermarkets.

From an investment standpoint, falling commodity prices are good news for business users who aren't forced to pass through all of the decreases in their materials costs sooner or later, if there are any. But they will be bad news for not only commodity producers, but also their suppliers—such as makers of farm implements and fertilizer companies as well as mining equipment manufacturers. The oil field equipment and services industry is more problematic because little new drilling has been done since the 1980s and equipment is presently close to being fully utilized, while promising new oil fields in the former Soviet Union and elsewhere are being developed. Nevertheless, caution is warranted there as well during deflation, because weak energy prices persist.

REAL ESTATE AND OTHER TANGIBLES GENERALLY AREN'T ATTRACTIVE

Real estate excesses of the 1970s came to grief in the 1980s, as discussed in Chapter 17, but that area has since stabilized and revived. In the late 1980s and early 1990s, foreclosures and write-downs cut the prices of many structures down to profitable size, especially those that are well-located high-quality buildings with prime tenants. Think about it. As long as rent covers ongoing costs for utilities, maintenance, and repairs, the building is worth something. All that's needed to make it economically viable is to wipe out the mortgage, *i.e.*, give the lenders a bath and take the equity participants into the hot tub with them. Bulldozers take care of the remaining real estate excesses.

Additional forces helped real-estate–troubled sectors revive. As also noted in Chapter 17, government spending aided the agriculture and oil patch rebounds; the Midwest ceased to be the rust belt as manufacturers restructured and regained competitiveness against foreign invaders; and the East and West coasts bounced back as the late-1980s–early-1990s financial crisis and defense cutbacks were absorbed. More recently, the booming U.S. economy and falling mortgage rates have revived real estate demand and property is floating on a sea of stock appreciation. Still, it's not back to the heady days of the 1970s and early 1980s when real estate served as the hedge of choice against high inflation.

Fundamentally, real estate, farmland, and other tangibles are not great investments in deflation, regardless of local pockets of strength. The same holds for companies involved in the business as lenders, developers, and builders. If the price of everything else is falling, why should the price of land and structures resist? Especially in a time of excess capacity, when:

- Few need more buildings;
- Businesses are looking for ways to put more people in a given office space and encouraging telecommuting and teleconferences in place of hotel-utilizing business trips;
- Consumers are visiting malls less frequently and buying less;
- People are cutting down on discretionary leisure travel and the hotel and motel use involved;
- The postwar babies are all housed and those who will be in the prime home-buying age brackets are few in numbers;
- People are trying to save, postpone new houses, and more efficiently utilize already ample space; and
- Agricultural price supports are being phased out and farmers are free to over-expand production to their hearts' content.

Real Estate and Lower Interest Rates

But, ah, you may be thinking, lower interest rates will make real estate and other tangibles much cheaper to finance and, therefore, more attractive. That's what I heard from a group of real estate clients in the early 1980s when I first forecast 3 percent yields on 30-year Treasury bonds. I meet periodically for dinner in Los Angeles with this group of developers, builders, and other real estate specialists, and they were so overjoyed with my forecast back then that one of them even offered to pick up the dinner tab.

But then I delivered the bad news. Sure, I acknowledged lower interest rates would reduce the rates at which real estate is capitalized and therefore push prices up—all other things being equal, as economists are wont to say. But, I went on, the key to lower interest rates (then in double digits), was disinflation, and an important enabler of declining overall inflation rates would be a collapse in real estate prices. Those guys were assuming that real estate would continue to appreciate, with interest rates falling in a vacuum. It didn't quite work out that way; California subsequently went through the real estate wringer.

If I'm right and long-term Treasury yields drop to 3 percent, mortgage rates will be about 4 percent. If overall prices are falling 1 to 2 percent annually, real estate prices in general—buildings and land—will probably decline at about these same rates. (Real estate has followed inflation rates closely in the past.) Hence, the real cost of real estate financing won't be negative, as in the 1970s, but positive and quite high, 5 to 6 percent. Recall from Chapter 20 that real long-term interest rates are likely to be about twice as high as the average of the earlier postwar years. A real estate investment will be profitable if the net income from it exceeds 5 to 6 percent, but its attractiveness will be based on income, not appreciation, which is likely to be negative. In effect, rental income must be big enough to cover ongoing costs, high real interest charges, and an annual decline in the property's value of 1 to 2 percent, on average—and still provide an acceptable return on the investment. In deflation, gone are the days when real estate investors could only cover current costs with rents and count on making a profit through appreciation of the property's value.

In addition, the prices of building materials will fall with deflation, cutting the cost of new buildings below those of old ones. This will encourage new construction and put added downward pressure on rents in existing buildings as their vacancies rise—as they will when tenants move to new offices with cheaper rents, as noted in Chapter 25. Obviously, landlords will want to nail down the longest leases possible, especially if they own old buildings, warehouses, hotels or shopping malls. Lower rents will, in turn, depress land values, already under pressure from deflation.

This is a very different situation from that which existed in past times of excess real estate capacity. When crude oil prices collapsed in the mid-1980s, for example, jobless oil industry workers fled Texas and apartment rents nose-dived. Excess capacity in old buildings with low rents curtailed new construction until, with economic revival in the Lone Star State, rents rose enough to make new apartments attractive. In deflation, it's existing buildings' rents that will feel the heat as new buildings benefit from cheaper construction costs and lower land prices.

ANTIQUES AND COLLECTIBLES

To be sure, the continuing polarization of American income will put more purchasing power in the hands of those high-income people who tend to be the buyers of coins, antiques, and artwork. But will they want to "invest" more of their increased saving in these items in a deflationary era, when antiques, like other tangibles, will tend to fall in price? Are they, by and large, true appreciators of beauty for its own sake? Or are they quasi-appreciators who want to believe that their treasures will rise in value, irrespective of whether they ever intend to sell—or could sell at profitable prices, given the huge spreads between the bid and ask prices of many tangibles? Don't get me wrong. My wife and I love eighteenth century English and American furniture, but we see it as gorgeous furniture, not appreciating assets.

Real estate's tax angle will also reverse in deflation. Inflation created capital gains, which weren't taxed until the property was sold. Meanwhile, real interest rates were low or negative and nominal interest costs were deducted year-by-year. In deflation, nominal interest will still be deducted on an average basis, but they will be low while real interest costs will be high, and capital losses will only be deductible when the property is liquidated.

"Chubb's Antiques Roadshow" on Public Television travels around the country so people in various cities can bring in their antiques to be evaluated by experts. The pros give lengthy and interesting discussions of the backgrounds of selected pieces of furniture, porcelains, paintings, and memorabilia, their designers, and where, when, and how they were made. They also occasionally point out that people's treasures are fakes, and fakes are proliferating, given today's high prices for antiques and the technical advances that can make foolproof copies while you wait. But otherwise the high point of "Antiques Roadshow" is always the same. The expert asks the owner how much she thinks her antique is worth and then shocks her with its huge value, as the television camera zooms in for a close-up of the overjoyed collector. I hope this fine program will survive in deflation days.

OTHER INVESTMENT GUIDEPOSTS

Many, but certainly not all, of the elements of our investment strategy are imbedded in our long-term U.S. economic forecast (Table 26–3). These numbers reflect the expected shift of American consumers from a 20-year borrowing and spending binge to a saving spree. Because consumers now account for 68 percent of GDP, and 72 percent when residential construction is included, their retrenching will have profound effects in slowing overall economic growth. At the same time, government spending, especially de-

TABLE 26–3

Long-Term Forecast of Real GDP Growth

	1987–1997	1996–2007
Gross Domestic Product	2.6%	1.8%
Personal Consumption Expenditures	2.5%	1.4%
Durable goods	3.9%	1.0%
Non-durable goods	1.8%	1.3%
Services	2.6%	1.5%
Non-residential Fixed Investment	4.7%	4.4%
Structures	0.4%	0.0%
Producers' durable equipment	6.7%	5.4%
Residential Fixed Investment	0.9%	0.5%
Change in Inventories (BN$92)	26.3%	15.0%
Government Purchases	1.0%	0.8%
Federal	−1.5%	−0.7%
National defense	−2.8%	−1.0%
Non-defense	1.7%	0.0%
State & Local	2.7%	1.6%
Net Exports (BN$92)	−86.9%	−48.5*%
Exports	9.2%	5.0%
Imports	7.1%	3.2%

* Average for the decade
Range is $136 billion deficit in 1997 and $64 billion surplus in 2007
Source: A. Gary Shilling & Co., Inc.

fense outlays, should remain subdued with the Cold War over and no major military action in sight.

Nevertheless, as discussed earlier, wars are not extinct and at least a brief one is likely in the next decade, if history is any guide. It will push up government spending and create inflation, but for only a year or so before deflation returns. Not knowing the timing or extent of any war, we haven't built it into our forecast numbers.

We also assume slower growth in non-defense spending at the federal or state and local levels, given the ongoing anti-government mood of the electorate. At the same time, with slower overall expansion and the resulting excess capacity, outsourcing abroad, subdued consumers, and more telecommuting and teleconferencing, spending growth on hotels, shopping centers, factories, office buildings, and other business structures will be about zero.

On the plus side, producers' durable equipment will grow faster than the overall economy, driven by new tech and other productivity-enhancing spending. Net exports should move from a deficit to a surplus in the next decade, due to considerably slower growth in imports as consumers retrench. Export growth will also slow as Asia, Latin America, and other developing economies remain subdued—reflecting their stretched-out financial recoveries and the effect of a slowdown in U.S. consumer spending.

Table 26–4, the forecast table we consider the most revealing, shows how GDP shares of consumption and government spending recede while producers' durable equipment and net exports gain. Table 26–5 quantifies many of our other forecasts—price declines of 1 to 2 percent per year; a consumer saving spree; 2 percent productivity gains with little growth in compensation per man-hour; slower advances in profits; excess capacity; higher unemployment rates as a result from slower economic growth and faster productivity advances; and relative weakness in housing starts and vehicle sales (old tech areas that suffer in deflation as consumers wait for lower prices and postpone big ticket discretionary items to increase saving.)

Bear in mind that all these forecast numbers are guaranteed not to be accurate. They are only attempts to quantify our conceptual forecast. We start with ideas and then structure the numbers to match them, not the other way around.

For a recap and additional investment ideas for the deflationary years ahead, either to own or to avoid or sell short, study the business winners and losers listed in Chapters 29 and 30.

T A B L E 26–4

U.S. Long-Term Forecast of Real GDP Shares

	1987	1997	2007
Gross Domestic Product (BN$92)	100.0%	100.0%	100.0%
Personal Consumption Expenditures	67.7%	67.7%	64.6%
Durable goods	8.1%	9.2%	8.5%
Non-durable goods	21.9%	20.4%	19.4%
Services	37.6%	38.0%	36.7%
Non-residential Fixed Investment	9.6%	11.8%	15.1%
Structures	3.5%	2.8%	2.3%
Producers' durable equipment	6.1%	9.1%	12.8%
Residential Fixed Investment	4.6%	3.9%	3.4%
Change in Inventories	0.5%	0.9%	0.1%
Government Purchases	20.6%	17.7%	16.0%
Federal	9.5%	6.3%	4.9%
National defense	7.2%	4.2%	3.2%
Non-defense	2.2%	2.0%	1.7%
State & Local	11.2%	11.4%	11.1%
Net Exports	−2.8%	−1.9%	0.7%
Exports	7.1%	13.3%	18.1%
Imports	−9.9%	−15.2%	−17.4%

Source: A. Gary Shilling & Co., Inc.

T A B L E   26–5

Long-Term Forecast of Select Economic Variables
(Average Annual Percent Growth)

	1987–1997	1996–2007
Real GDP (1992)	2.6%	1.8%
GDP (current $)	5.6%	0.3%
Implicit Price Deflator	3.0%	−1.5%
Consumer Price Index	3.5%	−1.0%
Producer Price Index	2.3%	−1.5%
Personal Saving Rate*	4.4%	5.0%
Real Disposable Income	2.2%	1.9%
Output per Man-hour	1.1%	2.0%
Compensation per Man-hour	3.6%	0.5%
Unit Labor Cost	2.5%	−1.5%
Economic Operating Profits	9.4%	3.0%
Industrial Production	3.1%	2.0%
Capacity Utilization*	82.2%	85.0%
Civilian Employment	1.4%	1.0%
Unemployment Rate*	6.0%	8.0%
Housing Starts (mil units)*	1.4%	1.5%
Auto & Light Truck Sales (mil units)*	14.3%	15.0%

* Period average

Source: A. Gary Shilling & Co., Inc.

27 CHAPTER

How to Invest in Deflation

I've given you a number of suggestions for *where* to invest in deflation. But *how* should you invest—in mutual funds, index funds, individual stocks, or hedge funds?

ON YOUR OWN

In recent years, many have been managing their own portfolios, picking their own stocks and maybe a few bonds and doing very well in the process. In fact, some have been so successful that they have abandoned mutual funds or other professionally managed approaches, figuring there is no reason to pay fees for what, in most cases, have been inferior results. Some have even left their regular jobs to become full-time investors, especially those who have Internet stocks and invest through Internet brokers. Quite a few individual investors have had better investment results than many of us pros, who've been burdened with concerns over stratospheric P/E ratios, the narrowness of stock focus, similarities with previous speculative markets, and other old-fashioned ideas that show the burdens of age and battle scars of past bear markets.

Perhaps picking your own investments is the way to success for you in deflation and the difficult transition to it that I foresee. And, as you'll learn later, I don't think there is any other single approach that is clearly superior. But please realize, as we legally must say in all of our investment advisory literature, that past performance is no guarantee of further success. It is said that a rising stock market makes geniuses out of idiots, but a falling market makes idiots out of geniuses. I know I'm no genius, but maybe I'll look like one, at least briefly, if my bear market forecast comes true. The bull market that started in August 1982 is without precedent in this country, perhaps the world, and has lulled many into believing that stocks go only one way, up, and with double-digit gains in each and every year. Maybe we are in a brave new world where that is true, but I wouldn't count on it. Still, whether you're running your own portfolio or relying on others, the various strategies I suggest in earlier chapters should be useful.

MUTUAL FUNDS AND CONSUMER TRUST FUNDS

As I'm sure you're well aware, mutual funds come in every conceivable size and shape—actively managed and indexed; growth and value oriented; small and large capitalization; sector funds that concentrate on everything from high tech to energy to gold; funds oriented to the United States, the rest of the world (foreign), the whole world (global), or to Asia, Europe, or emerging markets; funds containing stocks only or stocks and bonds (balanced); and contrarian funds that sell stocks short, hoping for price declines. Consumer trust funds handled by banks and trust companies also can vary widely in investment orientation.

Few actively managed funds consistently beat the indexes they regard as their benchmarks. In the last three years, less than 4 percent of actively managed diversified funds bested the S&P 500 index. In the last five years, 273 of 294 failed to do so, as noted in Chapter 13. Why? One reason is fees and commission costs. If management and other fees for a stock fund run 1½ percent of a fund's assets, and commissions consume another 1 percent or so, the fund's investments must perform 2 to 3 percent better than its benchmark just to keep even. For front-end load funds, the manager must do even better because less than 100 percent of your money is invested after paying the initial fee.

Note, however, that benchmarks like the S&P 500 index really cannot be used when gauging the performance of actively managed money. For most investors, duplicating a benchmark is impractical and involves sizable commission costs in buying the many component stocks. Indexed mutual funds are a practical alternative, so I'd use them as benchmarks against your self-managed portfolio or those handled by others.

Investors may not care about these costs if their assets are rising at 20 percent or more year after year, but they will make a big difference in deflation, when stock gains are more in the 5½ to 6½ percent area, as noted in Chapter 25. This is already an issue with bond funds, where the average expense ratio for actively managed funds is about 1 percent. This takes a major chunk out of the return when long-term Treasury bonds are yielding 5 percent, unless interest rates are falling and generating considerable capital gains. At the same time, you also pay commissions if you manage your own money. They may be as low as mutual funds pay if you use discount or online brokers, but they are much higher if you use a full-service brokerage house.

It's also difficult for mutual funds to beat market averages unless they happen to hold the limited number of hot stocks of the day. Studies show that without the 50 top performers, which in recent years have been large stocks, the S&P 500 gains would have been cut in half over the last 12 years. Furthermore, the benchmark indices only include the survivors. Companies that went bankrupt or were sold before they failed don't appear in today's indices, but they did earlier and were owned in portfolios even after being deleted from equity indices. Try to find Packard Motor or Studebaker or Zenith in the current S&P 500.

Another problem is that investor money tends to rush into the hands of hot managers and desert the cold ones. But staying consistently hot is very difficult. A study by Leah Modigliani at Morgan Stanley Dean Witter & Co. found that a fund with a total return ranking in the top 25 percent over five years only had a 28 percent chance of repeating that success in the next five years, and a mere 51 percent likelihood of being in the top half in terms of performance over the next half decade. In effect, the managers who have had great success but who have run out of stellar ideas and luck get flooded with money, while those who have been in the dog house but who are loaded with wonderful ideas have less and less to work with. Vanguard Health Care Fund gained 40.8 percent in 1998 and was flooded with money in early 1999, while poorly performing small capitalization value funds continued to suffer outflows.

Actively managed mutual funds also can present tax issues over which the investor has no control. When stocks are sold at profits, the gains and tax liability are passed through to the shareholder, but usually only once a year. Consequently, an investor who bought a fund close to the tax declaration date could lose money in a bear market and still pay capital gains taxes on the manager's earlier winners.

INDIVIDUAL ACCOUNTS

Individually managed securities accounts may avoid those tax problems and can be tailored to the investor's tastes for investment risks, income requirements, etc. To make it worthwhile for a talented manager to devote attention to a separate account, however, requires that it be sizable, often $1 million or more. Otherwise, the fees and trading commissions, as a percentage of assets under management, would be so high that superior performance would be very difficult.

If a manager proposes a low fee for a smaller individually managed account, watch out unless he's in a start-up operation that is crying for new business. If not, he's probably a lousy performer or he's handling your account the same as many others in order to get economies of scale, simply picking one stock from Column A and one from Column B.

The Loser's Game

Years ago, Charles Ellis adapted a concept from a book on tennis by Simon Ramo and applied it to investing. Ramo pointed out that when amateurs play tennis, they make many mistakes. So, the winner of a match doesn't do so by winning many points—the ace serve or the unreachable return—but by losing fewer points than his opponent. As an amateur tennis player myself, I heartily agree with this observation. The pros, in contrast, play an entirely different game. They win points.

Ellis observed that when pension and endowment funds and other institutions first started buying stocks in the 1950s (after previously only holding bonds), they could win easily because they were competing with individual investors who dominated stock holding and trading at that time. Obviously, the amateur individual investor was no match for the pros, armed with reams of Wall Street research, superior knowledge of market trends, and free of the amateur's mistakes.

In recent years, however, the pros have come to dominate the stock market, so the pros compete with other pros. In the process, many of the trends they were able to take advantage of earlier have been eliminated. Consider this example. If a stock price normally declines by the amount of its dividend just before the ex-dividend date but then rebounds, an astute investor can buy the stock at that point, collect the dividend, and be money ahead when the equity revives. But if everybody knows this and acts, the stock will never sell off enough to make the exercise worthwhile. In effect, the pros themselves are now playing a loser's game, too—but being paid to play a winner's game. Obviously, this makes it difficult for them to beat the market. And where does it leave the amateur?

In a similar vein, keep this in mind. If a professional money manager really did know how to consistently deliver superior results without taking undue risks, why wouldn't he simply trade for his own account and forego the responsibility and problems that go with managing other people's money? Even if he didn't have a lot of his own money to start, big percentage gains compound rapidly, as you learned in Chapter 21, so he'd soon be fabulously wealthy without sharing his talents with all those stupid slobs out there. He could get there even faster using futures options or other leveraged vehicles.

INDEXED FUNDS

Many conclude that the only route to investment salvation is indexed mutual funds. They allow you to buy, in effect, the whole stock or bond market, or numerous sectors of them. Management fees are low. Vanguard charges 0.18 percent of assets for its S&P 500 index fund. Also, you avoid playing the loser's game, and taxes are low because the only purchases and sales in the funds are those needed to reflect changes in the index benchmarks.

But, and this is the big "but," the recent zeal for index funds has been heavily influenced by the 16-year bull market, especially the last four years, a time when cash was trash and when it was hard to beat the overall U.S. stock market. Indexed stock funds have grown to 8 percent of all stock-fund assets, and bond-indexed funds contain 2 percent of total bond fund assets. A more volatile market, with down as well as up years, to say nothing of the major bear market I see ahead, is an entirely different matter. A fund indexed to the S&P 500 will go down, penny for penny, with that index.

In contrast, actively managed funds at least have the potential of beating the averages in bear markets because they can reduce their stock holdings and retreat to the safe haven of bonds or cash. That's when cash goes from trash to king. Furthermore, many active managers have the right to hedge their long stock portfolios with stock index futures and other instruments.

But, you may be saying, I'll use index stock funds at times I want to be in the market. If I don't like stocks, I'll sell them and hold cash or bonds. Fair enough, but if you're actively managing your portfolio in that sense, you can do it even more cheaply. Buy futures on the S&P 500 index, the NASDAQ 100, the Value Line index, the Russell 2000, and others, for the face amount that you want to invest in stocks. Then, after putting up the small margin requirements, invest the rest in Treasury bills. The commission on the futures contracts is small and you'll earn interest on the Treasury bills over and above the appreciation in the stock index.

INVESTMENT CLUBS

Many—especially green investors—like the safety of numbers. In other words, if you go wrong, do it in the good company of your friends and investment peers. In any event, investment clubs fit the bill for many, and there are 37,000 in the United States, double the count in 1995—another product of the long bull market. Some think that the clubs provide superior performance, especially after learning of the fabulous results of the Beardstown Ladies, who boasted an average return of 23.4 percent for the 1983–1993 decade and wrote a bestseller that dispensed stock tips along with recipes. An independent audit found, however, that they actually made 9.15 percent, well below the S&P 500 14.9 percent return for those years.

Furthermore, a study by Terrance Odean and Brad M. Barber of the Graduate School of Management at the University of California, Davis, found that 60 percent of investment clubs underperformed the market from February 1991 to January 1997. Their average annual return was 14.1 percent, compared with 16.4 percent for individual investors and 17.8 percent for the Vanguard 500 Index Fund. The trouble, the professors found, is that investment clubs often trade in small lots and pay oversized commissions of 7 percent for the round trip purchase and sale of a stock. Also, bad investment ideas are often accepted because club members don't want to shoot down their friends' suggestions.

401(k)s

Obviously, you want to take advantage of any investment tax dodges, be they IRAs, Keoghs, or 401(k)s, especially if your employer is matching your contributions. In IRAs and Keoghs, you usually manage the funds yourself, and I hope the strategy elements discussed earlier are helpful. The tax-free nature of those funds make them ideal for investments with big tax liabilities, such as the zero coupon bonds I discussed in Chapter 21. Just because these funds are retirement-oriented doesn't mean they should be the most conservative part of your portfolio. After all, you should consider your personal accounts, IRAs, and company pension accounts and stock options as one portfolio and manage it accordingly.

Many 401(k) accounts and ESOPs are heavily invested in the employer's stock. It may be a great winner, but bear in mind that big exposure in the firm's equity doubles your risk. If your company is in trouble and its stock is collapsing, your job is probably in jeopardy as well. It's a triple risk if you have valuable stock options as well. I trust you're not one of those who sees no difference between your company's stock in a 401(k) and a guaranteed investment. Surveys show that such people exist. Some 401(k)s allow you complete investment freedom while others provide a menu of stock and bond funds from which you can choose. Here again, the investment strategy spelled out in Chapters 21 through 26 may help you set up your portfolio for deflation and the volatility transition to it.

HEDGE FUNDS

Hedge fund is a double misnomer because they often don't hedge their positions and they aren't funds, but limited partnerships. The original concept of A. W. Jones was to hedge by buying the best companies' stocks in a given industry and selling short the worst. Hence the net position would be isolated from the stock movements of the overall sector. There are similar sorts of hedge funds today, like *market neutral* funds, but hedge funds come in many other flavors—aggressive growth, leveraged funds, risk arbitrage, technology, distressed securities, emerging markets, short-selling, and opportunistic funds to name a few of those followed by my friends at Hennessee Group, a firm of hedge fund advisors. There are also funds of funds that invest in other hedge funds. Managed futures funds, available through major brokers, are related investment vehicles that are available to investors with much less than the minimum of $1 million in assets that hedge funds generally require.

Our own hedge fund management style comes under the heading of "macro management," although others in this category don't necessarily share our investment approach. We start with our global view of economic, financial, and political forces and develop from it our investment themes. We then use the most direct vehicles for implementing them, be they long or short stocks and bonds, futures, or options. Often, futures provide the purest play. With our deflationary outlook, for example, we have been negative on crude oil prices for over a year (Chapter 26). Prices have declined, but if we had shorted Exxon or Mobil earlier, we would have lost money when they announced a merger and both stocks jumped. A Pyrrhic victory. In contrast, our sales of crude oil futures have worked splendidly. Other themes such as our productivity enhancers and manufactured housing and rental apartments (Chapter 25) can only be implemented with stock positions.

The Common Thread—Leverage

The common thread among hedge funds is that they almost always use financial leverage. So, if they're right, they're very, very right, and if they're wrong, they're awful. This volatility has a lot to do with their bad reputation. Furthermore, because of the immense quantities of money they control, their actions spread that volatility to many markets around the world. Recall that Malaysian President Mahathir blasted hedge funds and other speculators for causing the Asian financial woes.

Hedge fund fees tend to be high, often a 1 percent or 2 percent management fee, and an additional performance fee of 20 percent of the gains over a benchmark return such as the 90-day Treasury bill rate. Mitigating these fees, in some cases, is a high watermark, meaning that the manager cannot collect performance fees unless the fund value is above its previous peak. This avoids the manager being paid in the good years with no recognition for any intervening years of bad performance.

The size of these fees should be put in perspective, and may not seem unreasonable if a hedge fund manager can do well when most investors do poorly, *e.g.*, bear markets in U.S. stocks. Also, note that the average no load mutual fund charges 1½ percent for the average index fund and has worse performance, more commission costs and more tax liabilities for the shareholder.

Back in the early 1990s, when we and apparently virtually all other hedge-fund managers were making money hand-over-fist in U.S. and foreign bonds and many other vehicles, I often wondered: If we were all gaining, who was losing? After all, in futures and related derivatives, winnings are exactly matched by losses. It's a zero sum game, unlike long positions in stocks, bonds, or real estate where all investors can gain, on balance, as markets rise.

I was told by old hands in futures trading that the losers were genuine hedgers who didn't really mind because their losses were in effect insurance premiums. For example, a hedge fund might profit from being in long wheat futures in a rising market, but the grain processor who sold short would regard his losses as the cost of locking in a price and protecting against even greater potential losses on his wheat inventories.

A Changed Atmosphere

I don't know if that explanation was valid, but in 1994 the atmosphere changed dramatically. Either the genuine hedgers retrenched, hedge-fund activity exploded, or some combination of the two occurred, because it became apparent that hedge funds were no longer competing against genuine hedgers or some other group, but against themselves. They all tend to see the world and the various markets pretty much in the same way, whether from a fundamentals viewpoint as we do or from the market timing or technical perspectives that others favor. This means that what I call the "3S" problem has dominated since then. All of the major players in many markets are on the *same* side of the *same* trades at the *same* time, and with huge financially leveraged positions to boot.

For example, the default on Russian government bonds and nose-dive in the ruble when the Russians stopped supporting it in August 1998 instantly revealed to the world the complete list of the positions of Long-Term Capital Management and similar hedge funds. These backed up violently. Junk bonds were junked as Treasuries spurted. U.S. stocks tanked and the yen, which everyone was short, skyrocketed, while Japanese stocks leaped. Those players who couldn't sell their illiquid Russian securities to raise capital to meet margin requirements dumped whatever they could sell, so liquid markets got clobbered as well.

These violent moves dragged in Tiger Management, which lost $2.1 billion, or 10 percent of its capital, in September 1998 with its short positions on the yen and Japanese financial stocks. Then Tiger lost $3.4 billion more in October. Ditto for Travelers Group's Salomon Smith Barney's bet that with the approach of the euro common currency, government-bond yields of the various European countries would converge. Furthermore, it soon became evident that not only were Merrill Lynch, Goldman Sachs, and other Wall Street firms financing these highly leveraged positions, but they were investing in them as well. Apparently they were only too happy to lend large sums to Long-Term Capital, with its Nobel-prize-winning, exotic-model-building economists on staff, because they figured that the relationships would give them a peek at the hedge fund's positions and let them duplicate them in their own shops.

The hedge funds, then, tend to all be in the same boat. When one position goes against them, they bail out of all the rest to preserve their profits or limit losses. These actions not only tend to increase the correlations among stock, bond, and other markets around the globe, but also jack up their volatilities. This only augments the increased volatility spawned by global diversification, as discussed in Chapter 23.

SHOULD YOU INVEST IN HEDGE FUNDS OR MANAGED FUTURES?

With all this volatility, do hedge funds or managed futures have a place in your portfolio? Maybe they do, but recognize the possible bias of one who manages them. To be sure, no normal investor should have more than a small portion of his investable funds in these vehicles, perhaps one-quarter or one-third, maximum. Nevertheless, they can provide balance to the rest, especially in a major bear market in stocks, assuming that the investor's long-term portfolio is basically equity-oriented. I'll cite two reasons.

First, most hedge fund managers don't hesitate to sell stocks short. That's certainly true with us. Unlike most investors and others—investment radio and TV shows and investment newsletters who have a vested interest in ever-rising stocks—we're just as willing to be short as long. Stocks fall faster in bear than bull markets, so the short seller can make money faster. In addition, the shorter position has little competition because most managers think that selling short is unpatriotic. As a result, a hedge fund can be your anchor to windward in a bear market and offset the losses you'll take on the bulk of your portfolio if it remains invested in stocks. It's important to avoid losses, as you'll see vividly described in Chapter 28. This offset to equity declines also eases the mental strain of losing big money and helps you keep things in perspective, especially in the volatile markets we foresee.

Second, hedge funds are involved in many markets besides stocks and bonds—foreign securities, currencies, commodities, etc.—and can make money even if U.S. stocks and bonds are deadly dull. When someone asks me, "How did the market do today?" I know they're referring to U.S. stocks. I'm tempted, however, to ask in return, "Which market?" because we follow dozens and tend to be invested in six to ten at any given time. This diversity of market involvement also means that a hedge fund investment doesn't necessarily mimic your core stock holdings on the up and down sides, but can instead have a low or negative correlation with them. This, at least, has been the case with our hedge funds, which have negative correlations with the S&P 500 index over time. Their involvement in many different markets, then, can also make hedge funds an important offset to losses you may suffer during a major bear market in U.S. stocks.

28
CHAPTER

Market Timing, Stock Exposure, and Leverage

"Buy and hold" is the battle cry of investors today, and why not, given that the record-breaking bull market in U.S. stocks is apparently still healthy and snorting. The proponents of this strategy also note that trying to time the ups and downs of the stock market, even a more normal one in which there are downs as well as ups, is difficult. It can kill your performance. Charlie Ellis points out, for example, that from 1926 through 1996, almost all of the total gain on stocks occurred in only 60 months, or a mere 7 percent of the total. Conclusion: if you weren't aboard that 7 percent of the time, you blew it, and because you don't know in advance when those luscious months will occur, you better be fully invested all the time. Forget trying to time the market.

MARKET TIMING

We looked at this issue some years ago, and I wrote an article for the March/April 1992 *Financial Analysts Journal* entitled, "Market Timing: Better Than a Buy and Hold Strategy." Well, you already know my conclusion, but let me tell you exactly how I reached it.

> In the postwar era, common stocks have been uncommonly good investments. From January 1946 through December 1991, the Dow Jones Industrial Average (DJIA) rose at an 11.2 percent annual rate, compounding quarterly and including the reinvestment of divi-

dends but with no deductions for taxes. In other words, $1 invested soon after World War II was worth $116.20 at the end of last year . . .

Why Mess With Mother Nature?

Performance this good might suggest that the best investment policy is simply to increase their assets by purchasing high-quality stocks and then either sit back and relax or leave for a long trip to Hongo Bongo, where communications with the outside world are nonexistent. It seems to imply that investors should keep their cotton-pickin' hands off their portfolios, that trying to time the market by moving into and out of stocks merely risks ruining a good thing. . . .

Another, and perhaps most important, reason for the buy-and-hold strategy is that stocks haven't appreciated in a smooth fashion, but in spurts, and the investor who is in and out of the market risks being out at times of great appreciation... In fact, if the investor missed the 50 strongest months in the postwar period, his total return would have shrunk from the 11.2 percent annual growth shown in the first line of (Table 28–1) to a shocking pittance of 3.7 percent annual gain and only fourfold appreciation (line 2) . . .

Bye-Bye to Bad Times

Before we conclude that, like honesty, being fully invested is the best policy, let's consider several alternatives. Suppose, just sup-

T A B L E 28–1

Dow Jones Industrial Average Simulation (January 1946–December 1991)

	50 Strongest Months	50 Weakest Months	All Other Months	Appreciation	Average Annual Return
1	Long	Long	Long	116.2	11.2%
2	0	Long	Long	4.0	3.7%
3	Long	0	Long	2540.8	19.0%
4	0	0	Long	97.2	10.8%
5	0	Short	Long	1820.3	18.2%
6	Short	Short	Long	76.6	10.2%
7	Long	Short	Long	44967.3	26.9%

Source: A. Gary Shilling & Co., Inc.

pose, that an investor had the clairvoyance to be fully invested in the DJIA except for the 50 weakest months in the postwar era, and was in Treasury bills during those 50 months. I'm using the 50 weakest simply for symmetry with the 50 strongest. Line 3 of Table 28–1 indicates that this vastly improves investment results. Thus $1 invested in January 1946 would have grown at a 19.0 percent annual rate to $2,541—70 percent more than the compound return of the fully-invested-at-all-times approach.

Why this vast improvement in return? It has a lot to do with the simple yet crucial fact that, after a given percentage loss in a stock's price, a bigger percentage gain is necessary to return to the original price. If, for example, a stock drops 50 percent in price, it must then double to get even again. Despite its simplicity, this reality is not well understood. . . By avoiding the 50 weakest months, the investor would have had much more money to invest the rest of the time . . .

The benefit of being out of stocks during the periods of big market decline is even more powerfully shown in line 4. There we assume that the portfolio was out of stocks and in Treasury bills in both the 50 strongest and 50 weakest months of the postwar era. As shown, the average return of 10.8 percent almost equals the 11.2 percent return in a portfolio that was fully invested all the time.

This is extraordinary—almost the same performance even though the 50 months of greatest market advance are excluded . . . The 50 strongest months witnessed more gain than the decline experienced during the 50 weakest months. In fact, $1 invested and compounded only in the 50 strongest months, in chronological order, would have been worth $24.48 in the 50th of those months, while $1 sold short in the 50 weakest months would have been worth less—$21.27—in the 50th of the weak months. . .

As noted above, however, when a stock falls 50 percent, it must then double to get back to its original price, and by being absent during that decline, the shareholder has twice as much money to invest later. Being out of the market in the weakest months is very beneficial, even if the investor also misses the strongest months.

This fact is extremely comforting to anyone trying to time the market, since he can hardly expect to be in cash in the biggest down months of bear markets without also being absent during some of the frequent final blow-off months of the bull markets that precede them. A shining example of the benefit of sitting out a bear market, even if the exit is early, can be found in 1987. In the spring of that year, some astute investors recognized the frothy, speculative nature of the U.S. stock market and liquidated their portfolios, only to see the DJIA spurt another 500 points. Nevertheless, at year-end they were well ahead of those who had held stocks throughout the year and seen much more than that final 500 points removed by the Crash and the aftermath. And those bears weren't sacred by devastating losses and therefore in much better psychological shape to assess analytically the 1988 investment outlook.

Shorts and Longs

Of course, an investor could choose not only to own no stocks in the months of greatest stock market decline, but to sell them short . . . Line 5 (Table 28–1) shows the results when the portfolio was out of the market during the 50 strongest months of the postwar era and short the DJIA during the 50 weakest. Even if the 50 most robust months are missed entirely, the investor had far better performance by being short the 50 weakest months than if he were fully invested at all times. Line 5 indicates that $1 turned into $1820-and 18.2 percent compound annual gain, compared with the 11.2 percent annual gain from the buy-and-hold strategy (line 1).

The difference between an 11.2 percent compound annual gain and 18.2 percent doesn't seem great, but it makes for a difference in portfolio value of 15.7 times in the course of 46 years (1,820 compared with 116.2). Compounding is potent! This difference is huge, but it makes sense. If the investor sells short and the stock falls 50 percent, he has gained one-half on the value of the stock. If he had been long instead, he would have lost 50 percent. Consequently, the bear, with 150 percent of his starting portfolio, is three times better off than the bull, whose portfolio has dropped to 50 percent of its original value. Repeating and compounding this sort of gap over time results in a huge difference.

Take it one step further and suppose the investor is a perennial bear and shorted the DJIA not only in the 50 weakest months, but also in the 50 strongest months. Despite his error in taking exactly the wrong action in the strongest months, his short position in the 50 weakest proves to be so beneficial that he winds up with a 10.2 percent annual gain (line 6), almost as rewarding as the perpetual bull (line 1). This, to me, makes a very powerful statement. Being negative on stocks in the weakest times pays well even for the investor who is negative during the strongest months as well! He could make a lot of mistakes in being bearish and still have an excellent performance.

The best results would obviously be achieved by the portfolio that was long in the 50 strongest months and short in the 50 weakest. As usual, we assume the portfolio was long in all other months, whether the DJIA rose or fell. Any investor clairvoyant enough or lucky enough to own that portfolio would have seen each dollar invested in the DJIA in January 1946 turn into $44,967 by the end of 1991—a 26.9 percent annualized gain. Wow! The combined, compounded effect of being long the bull months and short the big bear months is spectacular.

The moral of this exercise is clear. It's profitable to be in stocks during bull markets, but it's even more profitable to be short stocks, or at least out of the market, during bear markets—even if many of the major bull market months are missed completely.

I'm convinced that this analysis and my conclusion for market timing is just as valid in 1999 as when I wrote that article in 1992, maybe even more so. It may be meaningful for you. Unless you're that unusual investor with a cast-iron stomach and nerves of steel who will not panic at the bottom of a major bear market but ride it out without hesitation, some reduction of stock exposure makes sense. As shown by our analysis, you can forego the last exuberant months of a bull market and still be ahead, financially and psychologically, if you're on the sidelines and even more so if you're short when the big bear emerges from hibernation.

WATCH YOUR STOCK EXPOSURE AND LEVERAGE

You may also think that you don't need to worry about the stocks in your 401(k), IRA, or Keogh plan in a major bear market because you won't need those funds for years and the market will revive, eventually. All true, but will you keep your cool? Maybe you will, but many others probably won't.

When stocks dropped the summer of 1998, 401(k) savers switched from stocks to fixed-income vehicles with gay abandon. A study by Hewitt Associates examined the activity in accounts totaling $62 billion that were invested in mutual funds and found that between July 27 and 31, on days the Dow fell more than 100 points, switching from stocks to bonds and money market funds caused trading activity to double or even triple. In early October, the market nose-dive saw trading in 401(k) accounts jump to four times the norm. In August, stock mutual funds experienced their first outflow since the early 1990s.

It's not really surprising that 401(k) participants reacted to falling stock prices so quickly and violently. The tax-free nature of these funds means they can switch investments without any tax consequences. More important, most employees today need to worry much more about stock performance in terms of their retirement funds than they did earlier. As indicated by Figure 28–1, in the mid-1970s, the vast majority of pension plans were the defined-benefit type. Whether the employee contributed or not—and many were funded entirely by company contributions—these plans provided regular payments upon retirement that were entirely the company's responsibility. If the company invested the plan assets in stocks and did well, it didn't have to contribute as much in future years or could even withdraw surplus funds. If its portfolio value fell, it had to contribute enough to fund future pension com-

FIGURE 28–1

Percentage of pension-plan contributions by type of plan, 1975–1994

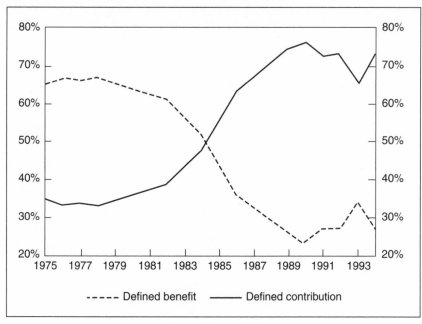

Source: U.S. Department of Labor, Pension and Welfare Benefits Administration

mitments. But either way, the employee had no concern. Even if the company went bankrupt, the federally sponsored insurance pool took over and funded the pension plan.

Now, however, defined-contribution plans dominate. (The latest available data is from 1994, but the trends shown in Figure 28–1 have undoubtedly continued.) The employer and employee usually both contribute, but the amount of money available to the employee upon retirement depends entirely on the success in investing those contributions with no further employer liability. Obviously, this makes employees, you included, much more sensitive to stock market performance for those funds with heavy stock market exposure. Even more so when you can direct the investments yourself, as is generally the case with 401(k)s, Keoghs, and other similar plans. The fact that most postwar babies have saved little beyond their pension plan contributions, noted in Chapter 12, further adds to the sweat they will exude when stocks tumble.

Surveys show—and it's hard to believe—that the average postwar baby has less than $14,000 in other forms of financial savings. And, according to a recent *Wall Street Journal* survey, 74 percent of adults are not confident that Social Security will still be providing retirement benefits when they reach retirement age. They obviously are depending on stock appreciation to do the job.

MORE MARGIN THAN YOU MAY BELIEVE

You also need to be equally aware of your financial leverage, especially if you are among the majority who save little or nothing out of your current income and rely on stock appreciation instead. If you are saving essentially nothing (and that's what American consumers as a whole are doing as shown in Figure 12–2), then the only way you can increase your assets is by increasing your liabilities. And indeed, that's exactly what many are doing as they contribute to 401(k)s and otherwise increase their assets by purchasing stocks or mutual funds and finance them with ever-increasing borrowing (Figure 12–1).

Of course, you may not see yourself as taking a leveraged play on stocks by incurring debt to buy them. You may think you're borrowing to buy a car or refinancing your home and then, as a separate action, contributing to your 401(k)s out of current income, perhaps even through payroll deductions. But you may learn otherwise if your 401(k)s and other stock and mutual fund assets become very soft in the next bear market while your debts remain rock hard. I suggest that you take a hard look at all of your assets and liabilities now, and reduce any leverage you aren't prepared to live with under the worst of conditions. Otherwise, your response to the bear market could well be to dump stocks before additional losses further impair your overly leveraged balance sheet.

The problems of over-leverage may persist beyond the bear market and into deflation. Stocks will revive, but real estate will probably fall in price and, with high real borrowing costs, the losses on heavily mortgaged property may be devastating, as shown by example in Element 3 of my Personal Strategy in Chapter 30.

WINNERS AND LOSERS

Tables 28–2 and 28–3 are checklists for investment winners and losers in deflation. Be aware that these lists refer to a steady state of deflation, after a rough transition that may produce quite different interim results. For example, as noted in Chapter 25, a major bear market in U.S. stocks in the transition will be devastating for Wall Street firms, but during deflation they should profit as they help individuals invest their rapidly rising savings.

As noted earlier, investment winners in an era of falling prices are likely to be those that enact my business strategy for deflation while the losers don't. Please turn to Chapter 29 to learn about this strategy's 25 elements.

T A B L E 28–2

Investment Winners in Deflation

Treasury coupon and zero-coupon bonds

Utilities with competitive-minded managements and reasonable regulatory climate

U.S. stocks in general

New technologies such as:
- Semiconductors
- Computers
- Telecommunications
- Biotechnology
- Internet related

Imports of consumer essentials and their distributors

Strong brands and popular products that are consumer essentials and their distributors

Goods and services with effective patent protection

Goods and services appealing to affluent consumers:
- Foreign and high-end domestic travel
- Upscale recreation
- Luxury goods and services

Small luxuries

Financial services for savers and investors:
- Stock brokers
- Financial planners
- Asset managers
- Trust companies
- Banks oriented toward high net worth customers
- Mutual funds
- Life insurance companies

Manufactured housing

Productivity enhancers:
- Productivity-oriented plant, equipment, and software
- Temporary help agencies
- Consultants, especially economic

Commodity users

The dollar
- Domestic-oriented companies

Source: A. Gary Shilling & Co., Inc.

T A B L E 28–3

Investment Losers in Deflation

Bonds of weak currency countries

Junk bonds

Stocks of weak currency countries

Old technologies, especially consumer discretionary goods and services:
- Autos
- Appliances
- Site-built housing
- Airlines
- Aircraft manufacturers
- Middle-brow cruise ships
- Many retailers
- Mid-priced restaurants

Industrial commodities:
- OPEC
- Commodity industry suppliers

Agricultural commodities:
- Suppliers

Real estate and tangibles (except some oriented toward productivity enhancement and affluent consumers):
- Builders and contractors
- Developers
- Lenders
- Shopping malls
- Hotels and motels
- Site-built single-family housing

Plant and equipment that increases capacity rather than productivity

Most government contractors

Multinationals

Firms with heavy exposure to developing countries

Producers of farm equipment and supplies

Internet victims:
- Travel agents
- Small car dealers
- Real estate brokers

Credit card issuers and sub-prime lenders

Financial institutions that:
- Rely on hard assets or collateral:
  - Residential
  - Commercial real estate, especially older buildings
  - Inventories
- Borrow short and lend long
- Are spread lenders

Commercial real estate insurers

Source: A. Gary Shilling & Co., Inc.

PART FOUR

BUSINESS AND PERSONAL STRATEGIES FOR DEFLATION

29

CHAPTER

Twenty-Five Business Strategies for Deflation

The disinflation that's been going on for nearly two decades has drastically altered business strategy. Disinflation requires businesses to develop new approaches to management, productivity, and cash flow. What worked well in inflationary times is no longer appropriate. Deflation will intensify many of these new approaches and add still more. If you own or manage a business, the following 25 elements of my business strategy for deflation may prove useful to you during the coming deflationary period.

1. CONTINUE TO CUT COSTS AND PUSH PRODUCTIVITY

The need for ruthless cost-cutting and aggressive productivity enhancement is obvious in the transition to deflation, considering the troubled economies and financial markets in developing countries, gyrating foreign exchange rates, surging imports at substantially lower prices, weak American exports, and a major bear market in U.S. stocks followed by consumer retrenchment and a recession. Enough said?

Continued restructuring will also be necessary in the steady-state deflation that lies beyond that transition. Automation and the relentless drive for more efficiency at lower costs will be the key to success. Note that cutting base employee wages is extremely difficult, so if your selling prices are falling, you need productivity growth to bridge the gap. Otherwise, it's bye-bye profits. Any one who believes in quick fixes or plans to simply postpone some advertising and travel is hopelessly behind the times, much less prepared for the future. The coming deflation will be driven by excess supply rather than collapsed demand, but it still means excess capacity and wrenching competition in most businesses.

2. ANTICIPATE DEFLATION

Prepare for deflation by avoiding unnecessary investments in plant and equipment that may burden you with excess capacity. Wait for lower prices before investing, if at all possible. Keep the pressure on suppliers for lower prices. Continually search for lower-cost sources and production sites abroad as cost savings and currency devaluations against the dollar present opportunities. And, oh yes, be prepared for pressure from your customers to reduce your prices.

GM, for one, obviously, doesn't expect deflation. The auto maker recently signed contracts with 40 steel companies worldwide to supply its needs for four years. GM figures that it can lock in current low prices for that time period. I think steel will be even cheaper later.

At the same time, anticipate declining real estate costs. Don't buy land ahead of need. Its declining value will be brutal, given high real financing costs. Lease it if you can and include de-escalator clauses to reduce your rent as land value falls. Similarly, rent offices, warehouses, and factory buildings with short leases and de-escalator clauses. If utility and building maintenance costs (and maybe even taxes) fall, you should benefit. As in so many other areas, try to reverse the approach needed to deal with inflation.

3. AVOID EXCESS CAPACITY

There is a tremendous urge to increase capacity in anticipation of fondly hoped-for market expansions. No one wants to lose customers to competitors because he doesn't have the capacity. But there also seems to be innate business zeal to expand, to increase sales and market share regardless of the consequences. The Japanese have been notorious for this trait, and it worked as long as their targeted markets grew rapidly.

American CEOs have contracted a milder but still virulent strain of the excess-capacity bug. Most are aware of increasing global glut, but each plans to be one of the shake-out's survivors. It may work for a few, but it can't work for all. CEOs are accustomed to winning, and the battle for market share is one more fight to test their mettle. In addition, they hope to get big enough to scare competitors away. Some hope that the mere announcement of new capacity plans will do the job.

Good luck in a deflationary world, guys! Be fully aware that building and equipment costs will fall like almost everything else in deflation, while the real interest costs of financing them will be high. So, excess capacity will be a double disaster.

4. KEEP INVENTORIES SLIMMER THAN BARE BONES

If you can remember the 1970s' days of high inflation, you'll recall that holding inventories wasn't all it was cracked up to be. Sure, if inflation drove the value of your stocks up 20 percent, that was pure inventory profits. But if you paid a 40-percent tax rate on that profit and, say, 10 percent interest to finance your stocks, your net after-tax gain was slashed to 6 percent. And after the goods were sold, you had to replace your inventories at the new higher price, kick in more net cash, and pay more interest to finance the higher dollar value of your inventories.

In deflation, holding inventories is worse, much worse. Even if you aren't among those with a warehouse full of PCs, which are now falling in value by 1 percent per week as obsolescence rages, your inventories will be very expensive. If your inventory value dips by 10 percent per year, you start with a pretax 10 percent loss. Of course, a 40 percent tax rate cuts that to 6 percent after tax, but if your borrowing rate is 5 percent, you have a net after-tax loss of 9 percent. You can replace your inventories after they've sold at the lower prices, and your cash flow increases a bit, but you still lost money.

The moral of this exercise is simple. Inventories are assets, which generally decline in value in deflation, while high real interest rates make them expensive to carry. The fewer you have, the better.

5. EMPHASIZE NEW TECHNOLOGIES, NOT OLD

New technologies like semiconductors and computers are well acquainted with deflation, create rapid obsolescence for their products, help their customers promote productivity, and open vast new markets as prices fall, as you saw in Chapters 5 and 24. But buyers will wait for lower prices before purchasing the output of old technology industries, especially if they produce postponable discretionary consumer goods and services, like autos, appliances, and airline travel. Some will be eliminated by new tech substitutes.

Interestingly, even automakers sense this. They have innovated in the past, but often superficially, as part of their planned obsolescence strategy, as noted in Chapter 24. Now, however, with 1999 likely to be the third straight year of declines in the real prices of vehicles, they are turning to radically different models—designed and built quickly by use of computers and common subassemblies—to stimulate sales.

6. GO FOR VOLUME

If your selling prices are falling, you need significant volume growth to achieve decent earnings. Ongoing restructuring alone won't do the job, as discussed in Chapter 25. Chapters 22, 24, and 25 give clues to where volume growth may be found in deflation—financial services that help zealous savers and investors, productivity-enhancing capital equipment, new technology industries, deregulated and expanding utilities, manufactured housing and, of course, new tech. Consumer luxury items, both big and small, may offer exciting volume growth opportunities, as well as other upscale consumer goods and services, once setbacks in Asia and Latin America are absorbed.

7. DEVELOP PROPRIETARY PRODUCTS

Volume growth is easier in products with patent protection or brand identification, which will be better sheltered from domestic and foreign competition—and from price erosion. As the Internet increasingly provides consumers with voluminous information on products and services, however, brand loyalty may be increasingly difficult to maintain.

8. EXPLORE NICHE BUSINESSES

Niche businesses can be safe havens from the nonstop onslaught of foreign competition in basic commodity-producing industries and from domestic competition as well. They may involve the production of special sizes and shapes, businesses where high service content or fast delivery time is important, or areas where fad or fashion changes so fast that it would be impossible to get the items made in Asia and shipped to the United States before demand for them disappears. Domestically oriented businesses with limited import competition also fit this category.

After-market sales is another attractive niche. For some, service contracts are more profitable than the original equipment. After-market activity also provides the opportunity to establish closer ties with customers. Training customer technicians to service your equipment—and that of your obviously inferior competitors as well—is a case in point.

9. USE THE INTERNET

The Internet can be a cheap way to market your products and improve your reputation. Don't put your head in the sand because selling online will antagonize your existing sales force. As noted in Chapter 6, your competition will probably use the Internet, and you may be stuck with an unprofitable and obsolete marketing system. It may be worse if you're a travel agent, real estate broker, car dealer, investment banker, or in another business where fees may be reduced by Internet competition.

Obviously, you don't want to junk your existing structure until a new one proves itself, and the Internet won't sell everything. Complicated life insurance policies may never be purchased with the click of a mouse. Nevertheless, most businesses will need to take advantage of the Internet or lose their cutting edge. If you're near my age, the Internet may seem like a passing fad, just like the CB radios that we all used to have in our cars. But to our kids and even more so, our grandchildren, it will be their way of life.

Tupperware is an interesting case study. The firm, founded in 1942, initially succeeded by selling its plastic food storage boxes at parties held in agents' homes. Then women left home to work, but Tupperware refused to sell in retail stores for fear of alienating its dwindling but still essential sales force. As a result, the firm has had to rely on sales abroad; in 1998, U.S. sales were only 15 percent of the total, with a mere 3 percent of its operating profits earned here.

Now the company is making a U-turn and is planning to sell through Web sites as well as mall kiosks and TV "infomercials." Will they still give party favors if you visit their Web sites, but don't buy? And whatever happened to the Fuller Brush man?

10. IN COMMODITY BUSINESSES, BE THE LOW-COST PRODUCER OR GET OUT

Businesses in which the technologies are universally available and the products are indistinguishable are difficult at best in deflation. In a world of surpluses and strong competition, the key to success is being the low-cost producer. These cost differences often boil down to labor and transportation, because raw materials, capital, and other costs are similar for all producers.

To achieve this status, it may be necessary to move production to cheaper areas in the United States or abroad, merge to cut overhead, and innovate lower-cost production techniques. If a firm can't become the low-cost producer, it should seriously consider exiting the business, unless other considerations, such as the need to produce a complete product line, prevail.

11. GET INTO THE PRODUCTIVITY-ENHANCING BUSINESSES

Productivity-enhancing businesses are my all-time favorites. It doesn't matter whether it's high tech, low tech, or no tech, any good or service that can measurably and significantly enhance others' productivity or help cut their costs is a sure winner. We all tend to think of high tech in terms of productivity enhancement, but it can be as simple as a scheduling system that ensures an adequate, but not excessive number of checkout clerks in a supermarket throughout the day. As mentioned in Chapter 25, economic consulting is a superb example, and it's hardly high tech. In fact, huge computer models of the economy have proved lousy forecasters and take so much time to maintain that they get in the way of the fundamental thinking that leads to insightful prognostications.

12. WATCH OUT FOR PROTECTIONISM

Buchanan, Perot, Gephardt, and Detroit are now being joined in their protectionist harangues by the steel industry, and many more will join them when the U.S. economy cools and unemployment rises. (See Chapter 17.) U.S. protectionism may impede imports that compete with your products, but exports and the foreign operations of U.S. firms will suffer as other countries retaliate. Don't automatically assume that you can avoid the effects of protectionism. If you aren't directly in its cross-hairs, your customers or suppliers may well be.

13. BE PREPARED FOR MORE COMPETITIVE DEVALUATIONS

Russia, Brazil, and other Latin American nations have joined Asia in big competitive devaluations. As noted in Chapter 10, China may well join the crowd and touch off another round in the Asian currency-cutting race for the bottom. Hedging is nearly impossible in most developing countries and expensive everywhere, as discussed in Chapters 12 and 23—even prohibitively expensive if it's a complete hedge. Perhaps the best defense against losses from foreign currencies is to develop big enough profit margins to absorb a lot of decline. In any event, if you have foreign operations, anticipate currency translation losses and treat them like depreciation, a continuing deduction from revenues in deriving earnings. Your stockholders may well applaud your realism and the reduced risk of nasty surprises.

If falling foreign currencies help you, I wouldn't worry about hedging against their revival. Most foreign currencies are unlikely to rise appreciably against the dollar beyond dead-cat bounces.

14. EXAMINE FOREIGN OPPORTUNITIES CAREFULLY

I'd be reluctant to rush back into beaten-up foreign economies, even if they look like opportunities to get in on the ground floor. Nevertheless, some already are doing so. With all of her financial woes, Japan has been forced to open up her financial sector to foreign ownership and many are stampeding in. Among well-known

American firms are GE Capital, Merrill Lynch, T. Rowe Price, Goldman Sachs, Marsh & McLennan, Morgan Stanley Dean Witter, Citigroup, and Fidelity Investments. American and European auto companies are working out deals with their Japanese counterparts. Although portfolio money continues to flood out of the Asian Tigers, some direct investment is returning to the better performing countries like South Korea.

Still, I think it's early. Asia isn't a permanent disaster, but as discussed in Chapter 11, revival there may take at least a decade— as it did for Latin America to come back after the 1980s debt crisis. At a minimum, I'd go slowly until the next recession in the West comes and goes. As noted in Chapter 13, it will have further depressing effects on Asian and other export-led economies.

15. STICK TO BUSINESSES YOU KNOW

Business strategies come and go, but the current trend is clearly toward divesting non-essential activities of secondary importance in order to devote full management attention to the firm's principal business. This certainly makes sense in the deflationary era we see ahead and the tough transition to it.

Outsourcing is an important part of this approach. Many successful firms are turning to outsiders to supply maintenance, food services, auto fleet management, computer management, and even economic forecasting. Shouldn't you join the crowd if you haven't already?

Unless you're a real estate professional, selling and leasing back your offices and production facilities is another way of avoiding headaches and focusing on your main business. Selling real estate also gets rid of excess capacity that may become more excessive as restructuring and mergers lead to more layoffs. The cash proceeds can be used to bolster your core business or to improve your balance sheet (see Element 22). Your stockholders will be glad you're out of illiquid property, and they and your bankers will applaud a stronger financial statement. In either case, there are bound to be better investments than real estate which, in general, will decline in value in deflation.

16. PURSUE MERGERS AND STRATEGIC ALLIANCES INTELLIGENTLY

The urge to merge has been strong recently, but not always for the right reasons (see Chapter 4). Many merger partners talk about great strategic fits, but are really only using the mergers to do what they should have done earlier—cut costs, dump unprofitable operations, and increase productivity. That still has to be done, merger or no merger, and is often difficult while trying to combine two corporate cultures. Furthermore, a merger is never a one-shot quick fix. The need for constant restructuring remains.

Still, mergers and strategic alliances should be pursued in preparation for and during deflation. They can expand product lines and geographic reach; cut overhead costs and duplicative marketing, research, and other functions; achieve a better geographic distribution of facilities; and improve market penetration and customer service. Be sure, however, that your actions do what your public relations people tell the outside world they will do.

17. EMPHASIZE SERVICE TO CUSTOMERS

Everyone agrees that the customer comes first, but not all businesses act that way. In any event, deflation and the intensified competition it brings to many industries will increase the necessity of attending to customers' needs and wants. Furthermore, customer-driven businesses are much quicker to understand important and even critical changes in the marketplace than those who simply wait to fill the orders that filter back to them and concentrate on production.

Without question, an all-out customer orientation can turn a mundane commodity business into a proprietary niche. A friend of mine sells stationery and envelops, a highly price-sensitive commodity business. Yet he thrives by having a thorough understanding of his customers, even their personal activities. Before calling on a prospect, his salesman gathers information on that person to the point that at their first powwow he can discuss specific areas of mutual interest, be they sports, colleges attended, or charitable activities. When they meet for the first time, it's old home week.

My late father-in-law, Ed Bloete, sold business forms, another highly competitive commodity. Yet for years, he prospered and was the principal supplier for all of Avon representatives' order forms because of his service orientation. Among other things, he was willing to get up at 3:00 A.M. to deliver a needed shipment personally, while his much larger competitors stayed in bed until regular business hours.

Alliances with customers in the design of new products, training of their sales people, and joint advertising programs are easy examples of the many ways your firm can build more solid and lasting links to customers.

Customers are hard to get and easy to lose. The easiest sale is to your existing customer, is how I like to put it. That statement has two important meanings. First, your existing customer, if properly treated, knows and trusts you and is receptive to additional business. Second, you have to keep him sold, and it's a lot easier to do that than to start from scratch with a new prospect.

18. UNDERSTAND YOUR END CUSTOMER

Years ago, we were hired by an original equipment manufacturer in the auto industry to help make the firm's key people more sensitive to the economic environment and how it affected their business. We discovered that all that the division managers cared about was meeting the release dates, dictated by the firm's customers, for parts shipped to Detroit's auto assembly plants. The automakers were perennially too optimistic in their sales forecasts, but our client accepted them and often got stuck with excessive inventories and costly plant close-downs. We tried to introduce them to their ultimate customer, the buyer, and help them forecast his spending patterns to supplement what they heard from Detroit.

Another client manufactured appliance motors and could suffer huge swings in business activity because neither they nor the appliance manufacturers had a good idea of the inventory levels in the wholesale and retail distribution system. Here again, we encouraged them to learn more about the spending patterns of the final buyer. Regardless of how many steps there are between you and him, he ultimately calls the shots. Get to know him.

19. SHARE COMPANY RISK WITH EMPLOYEES AND PAY MORE FROM THE BOTTOM LINE

In times of inflation, it's relatively easy to correct a mistake in paying an employee too much or to handle one whose productivity has slipped. As noted in Chapter 3, you just don't give him any more pay increases and let inflation erode his real compensation back to the proper level. That can't be done in deflation. In fact, real salary and benefit costs go up even if nominal pay remains flat. Consequently, firms need to be much more careful in hiring and promoting—and more aggressive in terminating overpaid people who can't be made cost-effective.

You should also pay as much of total compensation as possible in bonuses and other incentives linked to your firm's success. This can take the form of productivity sharing, pay for knowledge, profit sharing, or stock options, among others. That not only inspires diligence and productivity, but also permits pay to be more closely linked to changing internal and external conditions, including deflation.

Sure, nobody likes to take pay cuts, and reducing ongoing wages and salaries is extremely difficult. Nevertheless, in a deflationary world, whenever business turns down without the cushion of inflation, compensation cuts may well be necessary, and at other times as well. Paying people substantial amounts from the bottom line means that those reductions are effective immediately, with the arguing done later and not while the company is still paying oversized amounts. And it's certainly easier than cutting salaries or laying off people.

More compensation linked to company results is also needed for middle- as well as upper-management. As the need for cost control and restructuring continues to bring terminations on all levels, in big and small companies alike, job security in large corporations no longer exists. Earlier, many top-flight employees balanced their shot at higher rewards and higher risks at smaller companies, against the less likely crack at the brass ring but greater job security at large corporations. Because career risk is now prevalent throughout the spectrum, incentives for valued managers at all levels are needed, in large firms as well as smaller ones.

It's often easier to share the risks with employees through fringe benefits than with cash compensation. Meaningful employee co-payments and medical savings accounts not only reduce costs, but also cut out what I call "recreational medicine"—an afternoon off work to see a physician when an employee feels any ache or pain and isn't paying much of the cost. Shifting from defined-benefit pension plans, in which the company is responsible for pension payments irrespective of the investment success of the funds set aside, to 401(k) and other defined-contribution plans, with employees responsible for the investment results, also shares more risks with them, as noted in Chapters 3 and 28.

You'll also want to pursue all the techniques, discussed in Chapters 3 and 19, for cutting labor compensation without embarking on the nearly hopeless task of reducing basic salaries and wages, unless your business is new tech or something else that has rapid growth. The techniques are well-developed: outsourcing to non-union shops and to lower-labor cost areas in the United States or abroad; buying out older, over-paid employees and replacing them with younger, cheaper ones; using part-time and temporary people; increasing employee participation in medical costs; and so on.

20. BE REALISTIC ABOUT YOUR PROFITS

Earnings are the lifeblood of any company, especially if it's public and shareholders are peering over the shoulders of management. Profits will be under pressure in deflation and even more so in the rough transition to it, as discussed in Chapter 20. That chapter also noted that earnings for many firms are not as good as they seem because of declines in interest costs, tax rates, and depreciation as well as overly aggressive write-offs and the favorable effects on pension fund contributions from the stock market boom.

I suggest you examine carefully the effects of these five factors on your bottom line, because none are likely to be sustainable. And while you're at it, I'd set up a line item for currency translation losses if you have any foreign sales, as suggested earlier in Element 13. With a strengthening dollar, they're likely to continue.

21. PREPARE FOR VIGILANT STOCKHOLDERS

Shareholders, especially state pension funds and other institutional investors, have become much more active in recent years, but you haven't seen anything yet. Wait until the long bull market ends and shareholders who have enjoyed the longest period of market gains in U.S. history look for scapegoats in corporate management. This will mean more pressure for short-term profits even at the expense of long-term results—pressure you should usually try to deflect.

As is already the case, some of those beating up on corporate management will be the same corporate management, at least indirectly. More than once I've witnessed a CEO complaining bitterly about pressure by pension funds and other institutional holders for better quarterly results, then leave our meeting to attend a pow-wow with the firm's pension fund managers to demand better portfolio performance, quarter by quarter!

22. BUILD FINANCIAL STRENGTH

Fortress-like balance sheets are certainly appropriate in the uncertain transition to deflation, and on into the era of generally declining prices. Financial strength protects against squeezes on earnings and also provides the wherewithal to buy some of the attractive but distressed companies that will be served up by deflation.

This means establishing and maintaining good relations with investment bankers, commercial bankers, and other lenders. The more they understand your business, the more helpful they can be, especially in stressful times.

In this regard, if you run a small business, resist the temptation to use your personal credit cards for financing. Many have succumbed to this because of the ease of borrowing, but they are paying very high interest costs that will only get higher in relation to selling prices as deflation unfolds. Furthermore, they are not developing relations with sympathetic lenders. Do you think that the credit card clerk who is dunning you for missed payments will offer the same forbearance that you just might get from an experienced loan officer?

23. ADAPT TO HIGHER REAL INTEREST RATES

Nominal interest rates may be lower, but both short- and long-term real rates are likely to be higher in deflation than they were in the earlier postwar era, as discussed in Chapter 20. In other words, stated rates may seem low, but if your selling prices are falling, borrowing is expensive.

This also means that falling selling prices must be taken into account in calculating the returns needed to justify capital investment, especially if it is financed by borrowing, as noted in Element 3.

24. BE PREPARED FOR A FLAT YIELD CURVE

As discussed in Chapter 20, the "normal" or "positive" yield curve, with long-term interest rates exceeding short-term rates the vast majority of the time, is confined to the inflationary post-World War II era. Historically, it's been flat, on average, with short rates exceeding long rates half the time, not just 14 percent as has been true since World War II. Higher short rates, especially in real terms, is another reason for keeping inventories slim (see Element 4).

The flat yield curve, on average, will also make spread lending difficult. It's one thing to borrow short and lend long when the yield curve is steeply positive—assuming that temporary spikes in short-term interest rates don't kill you as they did the S&Ls of yesteryear. It's quite another when the yield curve is inverted half of the time. Banks and other lenders will learn the easy way or the hard way that matching the maturities of their assets and liabilities is essential in deflation. The profit opportunities of many financial intermediaries will be squeezed.

Here's something else that those involved in spread lending should keep in mind. In the postwar era, short and long rates moved up and down together 90 percent of the time. But, in the earlier history of the nation, when deflation reigned except during brief shooting wars, the correlation between the two was only 40 percent. Furthermore, the volatility of all interest rates was much higher back then and that high volatility may return. If it does, you'll need greater prospective returns to offset greater uncertainty.

25. WAIT TO ISSUE BONDS, BUT FLOAT STOCKS YESTERDAY

History shows that in periods of declining interest rates, most corporate bonds are issued well before the bottom in yields. This probably reflects human nature. Corporate treasurers who sweated out the preceding jump in rates want to grab the money before rates return to their old highs and cost them their jobs. Also, most underestimate the extremes in rate swings, both up and down. The recent rash of corporate bond issues indicates that this historical pattern continues. But if deflation is in the cards, it's still far too early to rush new bonds to market, about two and a half percentage points too early.

Stocks, on the other hand, are selling at record-high P/Es and record anything else you can imagine, as discussed in Chapter 13. Those levels may prove justified by lower interest rates once deflation is firmly established, but in the recessionary transition to deflation, declining earnings will do a lot of damage to stock prices. Don't count on declining interest rates to push up P/Es from current levels. In fact, they will probably fall as speculation evaporates, and individual investors are punished by losses and lose faith in stocks. In my judgment, any firm contemplating equity financing—and not just those with '.com' in their name—should do so immediately or be prepared to delay financing plans for some years. Recent heavy insider selling in a number of companies suggests that many corporate officers and directors agree.

SUMMARY

Just as deflation has significant ramifications for investors and business people, so too does it impact people in their personal lives, as you'll learn in Chapter 30. But first, have a gander at my lists of business winners and losers in deflation, listed in Tables 29–1 and 29–2.

T A B L E   29–1

Business Winners in Deflation

Winners will be firms that:
Cut costs and promote productivity ruthlessly
Have competition-oriented managements in deregulating industries
Anticipate deflation
Are involved in new technologies
Avoid excess capacity
Profitably expand volume
Hold low inventories
Produce proprietary, patented, and branded products
Are niche-oriented
Don't expect mergers to solve all problems
Build realistic strategic alliances
Are the low-cost producer especially in commodity businesses
Produce small and upscale luxuries
Concentrate on goods and services preferred by upscale consumers
Use the Internet prudently
Are involved with imported consumer essentials
Help others enhance productivity
Are concentrated in industries they know
Are customer-service–driven
Understand their end customers
Share risks with employees
Have good relations with investment and commercial bankers
Build fortress-like balance sheets
Don't use credit cards for business financing
Adapt to high real interest rates
Are prepared for a flat yield curve
Are domestically oriented in industries with limited import competition
Are relatively immune from protectionism
Invest abroad carefully
Can benefit from a strong dollar and cheap imports
Are realistic about their profits
Anticipate shareholders' vigilance and build credibility among them

Source: A. Gary Shilling & Co., Inc.

T A B L E 29–2

Business Losers in Deflation

Losers will be firms that:
Fail to adapt to deflation
Rely on regulation that is fading
Believe that inflation, even low inflation, will return
Don't cut costs and pursue productivity aggressively
Remain in old technologies
Believe that restructuring and all else can be handled by mergers
Aren't realistic about strategic fits
Don't control capacity
Are in commodity business unless they are the low-cost producer
Have slow volume growth and falling selling prices
Are high-cost producers
Are widely diversified
Ingore the Internet
Are production-driven, not customer-service–driven
Don't care about their end customers
Have inflexible compensation structures
Expect the yield curve to be positive
Have weak balance sheets
Have high inventories
Don't know any investment or commercial bankers
Have high financial leverage
Use credit cards for business financing
Have high exposure to foreign currencies and developing-country markets
Compete directly with imports, especially from developing countries
Rush into investments abroad
Are exposed to protectionism
Are involved in real estate and tangibles, with some exceptions
Are oriented toward agriculture outside of biotech
Don't examine their stated profits critically
Believe shareholders will be friendly and sympathetic regardless

Source: A. Gary Shilling & Co., Inc.

30
CHAPTER

Six Personal Strategies for Deflation

The last 18 years of disinflation have drastically altered the personal economic climate for Americans, and most have adapted to it, at least in part. Few still view real estate and other tangibles, the darlings of the inflationary 1970s, as great investments. The vast majority now admires financial assets, especially stocks. Not many expect automatic pay increases that are designed to offset inflation and then some. Many know, first hand, what restructuring can do to disrupt employment.

As disinflation turns into deflation, much of this climate will remain, but much will change and some new storm clouds will gather. If you adopt the following six elements as your personal strategy, you will probably avoid getting soaked.

1. WAIT FOR LOWER PRICES BEFORE BUYING

Deflationary expectations are an important part of my forecast of widespread and chronic price declines, so join the happy throng. Hold off on buying nonessentials, especially imported items and their domestically produced competitors. On big-ticket items like cars, you may save a bundle. And don't forget deflation in service prices. With full seats in recent years, airline fares have leaped in some markets, but remember the fare wars a short while back when they were empty? Those days will be back in spades. I don't recommend, however, postponing purchases of aspirin unless you expect deflation to be worry-free.

Delaying purchases until prices fall in deflation isn't just for the thrill of saving money. It will also be a necessity for many as their income rises little if at all in current dollar terms. The only way for them to enjoy rising living standards will be to take advantage of falling prices.

2. SAVE MORE

A switch by American consumers from their decades-long borrowing and spending binge to a saving spree is also part of our deflation forecast. I suggest you lead this parade, especially if you've saved little out of your ongoing income in recent years and you are relying on your stock portfolio to support today's heavy spending, to put the kids through college, and finance your retirement. Look back at the table in Table 13–1 to see what I mean. The stock market gains on your saving over the years could largely evaporate in the next big bad bear market, whenever it comes—and it will, sooner or later. In fact, you might consider a more conservative investment stance now, like more cash and bonds and fewer stocks.

Once stock and bond markets have adjusted to deflation, you'll want to return to stocks as well as continue to hold some bonds, as observed in Chapters 21 and 22, but that could be some time off.

Increased saving also makes sense now because there will be rainy days, no doubt lots of them, as restructuring-related layoffs intensify and the impending recession takes its toll. Be assured that the current economic atmosphere for Americans is about as good as it can get—close to zero inflation, strong economic growth, multiple job offers for anyone with any skills, a soaring stock market.

Saving is also important because of the tremendous power of compound interest, touched on in Chapter 21. Albert Einstein said that one of the world's great miracles is the power of compound interest. He's right. If you invest with a steady interest return and reinvest the interest payments for 30 years, 86 percent of your total return comes from compounding, or from the interest on interest. This means that, if you spend all the interest your receive year-by-year, your return will only be 14 percent as much.

Table 30–1 shows an example of compounding power that my good friend Richard Russell put in his well-known "Dow Theory Letters" newsletter. It is so spectacular that I sent copies to each of

T A B L E   30–1

The Power of Compound Interest Rates

Age	Investor A Contribution	Investor A Year-end Value	Investor B Contribution	Investor B Year-end Value
1–18	0	0	0	0
19	0	0	2,000	2,000
20	0	0	2,000	4,620
21	0	0	2,000	7,282
22	0	0	2,000	10,210
23	0	0	2,000	13,431
24	0	0	2,000	16,974
25	0	0	2,000	20,872
26	2,000	2,200	0	22,959
27	2,000	4,620	0	25,255
28	2,000	7,282	0	27,780
29	2,000	10,210	0	30,558
30	2,000	13,431	0	33,614
31	2,000	16,974	0	36,976
32	2,000	20,872	0	40,673
33	2,000	25,159	0	44,741
34	2,000	29,875	0	49,215
35	2,000	35,062	0	54,136
36	2,000	40,769	0	59,550
37	2,000	47,045	0	65,505
38	2,000	53,950	0	72,055
39	2,000	61,545	0	79,261
40	2,000	69,899	0	87,187
41	2,000	79,089	0	95,905
42	2,000	89,198	0	105,496
43	2,000	100,318	0	116,045
44	2,000	112,550	0	127,650
45	2,000	126,005	0	140,415
46	2,000	140,805	0	154,456
47	2,000	157,086	0	169,902
48	2,000	174,995	0	186,892
49	2,000	157,086	0	169,902
50	2,000	216,364	0	226,140
51	2,000	240,200	0	248,754
52	2,000	266,420	0	273,629
53	2,000	295,262	0	300,992
54	2,000	326,988	0	331,091
55	2,000	361,887	0	364,200
56	2,000	400,276	0	400,620
57	2,000	442,503	0	440,682

TABLE 30–1

The Power of Compound Interest Rates (Continued)

Age	Investor A Contribution	Investor A Year-end Value	Investor B Contribution	Investor B Year-end Value
58	2,000	488,953	0	484,750
59	2,000	540,049	0	533,225
60	2,000	596,254	0	586,548
61	2,000	658,079	0	645,203
62	2,000	726,087	0	709,723
63	2,000	800,896	0	780,695
64	2,000	883,185	0	858,765
65	2,000	973,704	0	944,641
Less Total Invested		**(80,000)**		**(14,000)**
Equals Net Earnings		**893,704**		**930,641**
Money Grew		**11-fold**		**66-fold**

Source: A. Gary Shilling & Co., Inc.

our four kids. I hope it convinced them to put off some spending in their early adult years and save, and I think they all have.

In this example, investor B opens an IRA at age 19 and puts in $2,000 per year for seven consecutive years with a return of 10 percent annually. After seven years, he makes no further contributions. Investor A lives it up until age 26—the year after investor B finished his contributions—but then catches the saving bug and puts in $2,000 per year until he reaches age 65. He makes 40 contributions and earns the same 10 percent annually. When both investors reach 65, who has more money? Investor B, impossible as it seems. He put in $14,000 while the late saver contributed $80,000, but his contributions grew 66-fold, while investor A only got an 11-fold increase. Investor B did so much better because his money compounded for seven more years, and that early and extra compounding was worth more than investor A's 33 additional contributions. Amazing! Save!

3. REDUCE YOUR FINANCIAL LEVERAGE

Deflation generally pushes up the real value of financial assets, so you want more of them. It also increases the real burden of debts, so you want less. And don't be misled by the siren call of lower nominal borrowing rates to finance either assets or liabilities. As noted in Chapter 20, real interest rates are likely to remain high even as nominal rates fall. In other words, even if mortgage rates drop to 4 percent, it doesn't do you much good if the market price of your house is falling 2 percent or more each year.

Financial leverage works both ways, as many homeowners (*i.e.*, former real estate speculators) in California, Texas, and elsewhere learned painfully in the 1980s. If you put down 20 percent on a house with a 10 percent mortgage and the price rises 15 percent a year, you make a cool 35 percent on your investment per year. But with the same down payment and a 4 percent mortgage, you lose 26 percent each year if the market value of the house falls only 2 percent per annum.

By the way, once deflation is established, a flat yield curve, on average, is likely with long- and short-term interest rates about equal, as discussed in Chapter 20. Then there will be no advantage in adjustable-rate mortgages, tied to short rates, compared to fixed-rate mortgages. In the transition to deflation when long rates will still be declining, however, I'd stick to adjustables.

Chapter 25 noted that with the prices of houses no longer appreciating, and in all likelihood falling in deflation, older people who don't enjoy doing home repairs may sell their single-family houses earlier than when they were great investments during inflation, and move into rental apartments. Similarly, younger families will probably rent longer before buying their own homes. If you're in either of these categories, consider renting, but on short leases. With weak real estate and cheaper new apartments, rents will fall (see Chapter 26), so you don't want to lock yourself into a long lease in an old building. You will need to follow the exact opposite of the winning behavior during inflation, when long leases were preferable and new apartments cost more than old.

Not all interest rates adjust with inflation. Credit card rates are notoriously stable and have declined little in recent years as inflation and market interest rates have plummeted. Deflation provides a further incentive to pay off your debts on the plastic. It's a lot more onerous to pay 20 percent rates when your pay hardly rises year after year than if your compensation is climbing 6 or 8 percent per annum.

Finally, unless you've got great incentive to finance with borrowing, it's always better to a lender than a debtor. And that will be the case in the world I foresee, especially after deflation gets established. Sure, I see a continuation of "the bond rally of a lifetime," as we first dubbed it in the early 1980s when long-term Treasuries yielded almost 15 percent. But after they rally to a 3 percent yield in the transition to deflation, they'll probably remain there as long as deflation remains in the 1 to 2 percent area. Stocks will probably take a header in the transition and then provide total returns of 5½ to 6½ percent. Both bonds and stocks will be attractive investments, especially in inflation-adjusted terms, but risk adjusted, not worth mortgaging your house at 4 percent in order to buy more. Real estate and other tangibles don't do well in deflation. What's left to make you want to borrow big time?

As discussed in Chapter 28, many Americans are now more leveraged than they think, because they've borrowed one way or another to finance their stock purchases and even 401(k) investments. I suggest a thorough review of your finances to make sure you understand exactly where you stand. In the process, calculate the distribution of your entire portfolio among stocks, bonds, houses and other real estate, and other investments. Your 401(k) and other retirement accounts differ from your personal holdings, but stocks are still stocks. Make sure you're not so heavily weighted that a bear market would not only slash your total net worth to uncomfortable levels but also scare you into bailing out just at the wrong time.

And talk about borrowing, I'm amazed and concerned that lenders are now offering and borrowers are accepting refinanced mortgages at over 100 percent of their values. What will happen when property prices fall in deflation? Furthermore, many low-income families, whose meager incomes may be in jeopardy in deflation and the recessionary transition to it, are now buying houses with tiny down payments. In 1998, about a third of new mortgages involved 10 percent or lower down payments. Mortgage loans to encourage low-income family home ownership are supported by the federal government, community groups, and Fannie Mae and Freddie Mac, but will this support persist and increase if these people become financially pressed? And keep in mind that the value of their houses, like all real estate, won't appreciate but depreciate in deflation.

My dad tells a great story about a trip by car that he, my mom, and his parents took many, many years ago to visit one of my uncles in Wheeling, West Virginia, some 200 miles away. With the condition of the roads back then, 200 miles was a full day's drive. All the way down and all the way back, Grandpa Shilling delivered a nonstop lecture to my dad that had one and only one point. If you're borrowing money, you pay 5 percent interest. If you're lending money, you get paid 5 percent interest. The difference between paying 5 percent and receiving 5 percent is 10 percent, a huge net gain back then—and in the deflation years ahead. That's more clearly true now that income tax rates are much lower than in the earlier postwar era; for the first time in decades, a saver in the top tax bracket gets a positive after-tax, after-inflation return, even on Treasury bills.

4. ADD VALUE TO YOUR EMPLOYER

An old friend, Don Bein, then at A. O. Smith, used to tell me that, in any business, value-added *must* exceed cost. And that applies not only to capital investments and software, but also to employees. Restructuring has driven this point home to many people. They're aware that layers of paper-shuffling middle management are gone. They've seen the exit, with varying degrees of employer encouragement, of older employees whose pay was raised beyond their economic value by managements that wanted to buy employee peace with excessive annual raises. They also realize that their own jobs may be next on the block.

Deflation adds another dimension to the necessity of being worth at least as much to the boss as he's paying you. As you saw in Chapters 3 and 29, in deflation, when few pay increases are justifiable, employers have to be very careful about over-paying people. If they do, there's no inflation that can be used to erode their real cost back to realistic levels. In fact, as the firm's selling prices fall, the real cost of even a steady wage rises, unless the employee's productivity rises at least as much as the gap between the two.

There's not much point in my giving you a definitive list of ways to increase your value to your firm, or more importantly, to your firm's customers. It's all the usual suspects: harder work, smarter work, more education and training, more attention to the needs of customers, etc. But you also might want to avoid jobs in firms that think your value-added exceeds their costs, but the market for the company's goods and services doesn't agree, or soon won't.

5. WORK FOR THE WINNERS, AVOID THE LOSERS

It's certainly easier to get a better position with more advancement potential, higher pay, more job security, and more psychological satisfaction in a growing company than in a failing one. Similarly, entrepreneurs look for expanding industries unless they see workout or consolidation profits in the weak sisters.

I suggest computers, semiconductors, the Internet, biotechnology, telecommunications, and other new tech industries as the areas of greatest employment opportunities. They are dynamic and not for 9-to-5 clock watchers, but their rapid growth can have marvelous career effects. Microsoft, where our oldest son, Geoff, has risen rapidly to become a product manager, has many others in their thirties with high-level positions. They work unbelievably hard—that's the Microsoft culture—and are smart, but it's also true that the firm has expanded so fast that people with only a few year's experience are seasoned veterans. It's like in World War II when the Army Air Corp mushroomed so rapidly that men in their twenties were squadron commanders.

Other attractive industries in deflation include financial services, productivity enhancers, and others that I cite as successful areas for investment (see Chapters 22, 24, and 25 and Table 28–2). You should also zero in on companies that have the winning characteristics that I explored in Chapter 29 and listed in Table 29–1.

At the same time, I'd steer clear of most jobs in the old tech industries that will suffer in deflation as buyers wait for lower prices and compress sales and earnings. In Chapters 3 and 4, I wrote at length about layoffs, with or without mergers, in many industries. Future layoffs can be expected in any industry with excess capacity and weak pricing power, even if restructuring has been going on for years, and almost irrespective of international competition. My candidates (Table 30–2) include motor vehicles; paper, chemicals, petroleum and other commodity producers; steel and non-ferrous metals; farm and construction equipment; aircraft and defense con-

TABLE 30–2

Industries with Big Layoff Potential

Motor vehicles
Aircraft
Household appliances
Industrial & electrical machinery
Medical equipment producers & suppliers
Farm & construction equipment
Petroleum
Food processing
Textiles & apparel
Food stores
Many other retailers
Banks
Hotels & motels
Restaurants
Drugs
Steel
Non-Ferrous metals
Paper & chemicals
Aircraft & defense contractors

Source: A. Gary Shilling & Co., Inc.

tractors; drugs; many retailers as consumers switch from borrowing and spending to saving; overbuilt hotels and motels; medical
equipment; household appliances; textiles and apparel; and industrial and electrical equipment. In the transition to deflation but
probably not thereafter, banks and insurers are especially vulnerable. Brokers and the business news media will see more and bigger
layoffs when the 16-year bull market ends.

Other less favored industries for employment include the investment losers discussed in Chapters 24, 25, and 26 and listed in
Table 28–3. If you don't want to invest in them, why would you
want to work for them? Also avoid those that aren't likely to follow
the business strategy for deflation (found in Chapter 29) as well as
the losers list (Table 29–2). I'd also be wary of industries that will no

longer be protected as deregulation introduces them to the blowing winds of competition; the same goes for union jobs in an era of accelerating outsourcing to non-union shops here and abroad.

6. AIM FOR INCOME GUARANTEES—MAYBE

In Chapter 29, I advised employers to keep compensation as flexible as possible and pay more from the bottom line. As an employee, however, you should think—but maybe only think—about doing the opposite. I'm simply reflecting the fact that deflation raises the purchasing power of any fixed payment, including a salary. If nominal pay isn't likely to rise, except for those who add more value and are therefore worth more, the greater the portion of compensation in fixed form, the better for the employee. People on fixed pensions and social security obviously make out like bandits in deflation.

Note, however, that I said you should "maybe only think" about getting more of your pay in fixed form. In an uncertain era of intensifying restructuring, employers want more, not less flexibility. Because cutting wages and salaries remains taboo in most companies, fixed compensation arrangements encourage layoffs when costs need to be pared. On the other hand, if a lot of pay is linked to performance and profits, employees may suffer with their firm's misfortune, but still keep their jobs.

Furthermore, the greater the portion of compensation that is fixed in wage and salary form, the lower the total amount will be, or at least should be. When I'm negotiating compensation with a prospective employee in our firm, I point out that the total has three components—the salary, the benefits, and the bonus. The total is the firm's cost of the employee's services, and there is absolutely no distinction between a dollar paid in salary and a dollar contributed to our 401(k) plan and a dollar of bonus. They're all fungible, except for the element of uncertainty. The more of the total paid in salary, the more the risk is on the firm's shoulders. The more that goes into bonus, the more the employee assumes the uncertainty over its size. Higher risks must be compensated with higher rewards. Our employees who are less demanding on salaries not only get bigger bonuses, they get bigger total compensation.

You should also be prepared for your boss's plans to cut payroll compensation without cutting basic wages and salaries, unless

T A B L E 30–3

Personal Winners in Deflation

Personal winners in deflation will be:

Those who wait for lower prices before buying
Savers and lenders
Avoiders of credit card borrowing
Those with low financial leverage
Well educated and trained people
Employees in new tech and other rapid growth industries
Customer-oriented employees
Employees whose value to employers vastly exceeds their cost
People on social security/fixed private pensions
Renters
Those not looking for free lunch
Entrepreneurs
U.S. tourists abroad
Those who take the advice of A. Gary Shilling & Co. and subscribe to *Insight*

Source: A. Gary Shilling & Co., Inc.

you're in a new tech or other rapidly growing industry. He'll no doubt enact or continue to pursue the measures outlined in Chapters 3 and 19, such as using more temps and part-timers, outsourcing more activities, buying out older highly paid employees, and encouraging greater employee participation in health care and other fringe benefit costs.

Check out Tables 30–3 and 30–4 for my lists of personal winners and losers as you prepare your own life for deflation.

SUMMARY

Finally, finally, finally, thanks for reading this book to its conclusion—and I hope you did so. I also hope it was a good investment of your time and thinking, and will help as you face the challenges and opportunities in deflation. We'd love to hear your comments, so please fill out the enclosed business reply card if you find this book useful—and even if you don't.

T A B L E   30–4

Personal Losers in Deflation

Personal losers in deflation will be:

Impulsive buyers

Big spenders with huge credit card debts

Those with high financial leverage

Heavy credit card borrowers

Net debtors

Poorly trained and uneducated people

Employees of old tech and other slow growth industries

Overpaid employees

Union members

Government employees

Those with less value to employers than their pay

Those who believe the customer be damned

Free lunch advocates

Source: A. Gary Shilling & Co., Inc.

Index

Abelson, Reed, xxiv
Acme Metals, 27
Advanced Micro Devices, 41
Aetna, 32
Aging population, 15-18, 103
Airline Deregulation Act of 1978, 59
Airline industry, 31
Alex Brown, 58
Alumax, 265
Aluminum Co. of America, 265
Amazon.com, 48, 216, 245
America Online, 114, 118
American Federation of Labor, 145
Amoco, 31
Antiques and collectibles, 274-275
Apple Computer, 63
Argentina,
    economy in, 82
    prices in, xxi
Asia,
    currency collapse in, 79, 97
    economic growth in, 78, 84
    economy in, 108
    exports in, 84, 96, 276
    financial crisis in, xix, xxi, 111, 158-159,
        162, 173, 174
    trade, 98
Astra, 32
AT&T, 28, 33, 44
Atlantic Richfield Co., 27
Australia, 9
    deregulation in, 57
    restructuring in, 34
Automobile industry, 26-27, 31, 64, 67
    Eastern Europe, 67
    use of Internet by, 52, 55-56

Baby boom, 16, 103
Bank of England, 14, 173, 175
Bank of Japan, 14
Banking industry,
    Asian, 172
    deregulation of, 58-59
    Internet and the, 50
    Japanese, 89, 174
    U.S., 81, 159, 160, 217
Barber, Brad M., 284

Barnes & Noble, 54, 245
Beardstown Ladies, 284
Bed, Bath & Beyond, 54
Bein, Don, 326
Belarus,
    automobile industry in, 67
Bell Atlantic, 33, 44
Berkshire Hathaway, 114
Bessemer Trust Company, 270
Bianco, Jim, 192, 214
Bianco Research, 192, 214
Blair, Tony, 9, 166
BMW, 27, 31
Boeing Co., 27
Bonds, 215, 230, 231
    interest rates on, 209-213
    investing in, 209-213, 228-229, 325
    issuing, 317
    Treasury, 209-213, 214, 216-217
    yields on, 209-213, 231-232
    zero-coupon, 213-215
Borders Group, 54, 113, 245
Brazil, xix, 164, 232, 265
    currency devaluation in, 107, 112, 174, 234
    economy in, 80-81
    prices in, xxi
    steel industry in, 27
    U.S. banks' exposure to, 81
Bridge/Commodity Research Bureau
    index, xix
British Aerospace, 31
British Petroleum, 31
Buchanan, Pat, 163
Buffett, Warren, 114
Bundesbank, 14
Bureau of Labor Statistics, 26
Business Council, xx

Canada, 9, 67
    Asian financial crisis' impact on, 162
    commodity prices in, 162
    copper production in, 264
    population in, 16
    restructuring in, 34
CarMax Group, 55
Carnegie, Andrew, 247
Case Corp., 28

Caterpillar Corp., 28
Central banks, 11-15, 172-176
Charles Schwab, 53
Chevron Corp., 27
Chicago Board Options Exchange, 45, 170
Chicago Mercantile Exchange, 45
Chile, 232
    economy in, 82
    retirement in, 113
    saving in, 18
China, 66, 72, 86
    copper production in, 264
    currency devaluation in, 83, 85
    economic conditions in, 84-86, 189
    prices in, xxi
    special economic zones in, 86
Chrysler Corp., 52
Cigna, 32
Cisco Systems, 48, 114
Citicorp Group, 58, 65, 310
Citicorp-Travelers Group, 30
Citizens for a Sound Economy, 61
Clinton, Bill, 8, 114
Coca-Cola Co., 107, 226
Colombia,
    economy in, 82
Commodities,
    cartels' control of, 265-267, 269-270
    deflation's effects on, 262-263
    developing countries' reliance on, 81
    prices of, xx, xix, 139, 162, 267-269
Compaq Computer, 48
Computer industry, 40-43, 51
    effects of Y2K on, 171-172, 260-261
Conoco, 27
Consumer Price Index, xxii, 131, 134
Consumer trust funds, 280-281
Costco, 245
Credit Suisee, 255
CVS, 54
Czech Republic,
    automobile industry in, 67
    industrial production in, 83
    prices in, xxi

DaimlerChrysler, 26, 31
Deflation (Lakeview Publishing, 1998), xix,
    xxi, 48, 77, 111, 219, 220
Dell Computers, 48, 114
Denmark,
    prices in, xxi
Deregulation,
    airline industry in Europe, 60
    airline industry in Japan, 60
    airline industry in U.S., 59

banking industry in U.S., 58
electrical power industry in
    Australia, 57
electrical power industry in U.S., 60
financial services industry in Japan, 61
financial services industry in U.S., 57
ocean shipping in U.S., 97
telecommunications industry in
    Germany, 61-62
trucking industry in U.S., 59
utilities in U.S., 221
Derivatives, 169-170
    dangers of, xix
Deutsche Post, 62
Deutsche Telekom, 62
Disney Co., 115
Dolan, Ken and Daria, 246-247
Dow Theory Letters, 321
Dresser Industries, 27
Duisenberg, Wim, 14

Earthweb, 116
Eastern Europe,
    automobile industry in 67
Economist Intelligence Unit, 67
Ecuador,
    economy in, 82
Electrical power industry,
    deregulation of, 57, 60-61
Electronic Data Systems, 22
Ellis, Charles, 282, 290
Employee compensation, 21-23, 188-189,
    313-314, 329
    bonuses, 21
    employee stock ownership plans,
        285
    medical insurance, 21
    pay for performance, 21
    stock options, 21
Employment,
    compensation and, 313
    layoffs and, 103
    restructuring and, 33, 63
Enron Corp., 222
Europe, 67
    commodity prices in, xix
    economy in, 107
    effects of Asian crisis on, 159, 162
    government spending in, 9
    population in, 16
    protectionist sentiments in, 164-165, 166
    trade, 98
    unemployment in, 9
European Central Bank, 14, 76, 262
European Union, 16

Exports,
  Asian, 95, 97, 98
  Latin America, 97
*Extraordinary Popular Delusions and the
  Madness of Crowds,* 115
Exxon Corp., 31

Farmer, John, 146
Farrell, Robert, 117
Federal Reserve Board, xxiii, 11-14, 72,
  124-125, 158, 173, 174-175, 177, 198, 261
Fiat, 31
Fidelity Investments, 310
Fidelity Magellan Fund, 117
Financial Analysts Journal, 290
Financial institutions,
  deflation's effects on, 254
Financial services industry, 306
  deregulation of, 57, 61
Fleet Bank, 58
Ford, Henry, 148, 155
Ford Motor Corp., 31, 56
Foreign currencies, 78
  Asian, 79
  Brazilian real, 80
  Canadian dollar, xix, 34
  Chinese yuan, 72, 85, 86
  devaluation of, 309
  eurocurrency, 9, 35, 75-76
  Hong Kong dollar, 166
  Indonesian rupiah, 158
  Japanese yen, 217
  Russian ruble, 166
  U.S. dollar and, 69-72, 259-260
France, 166
  unfunded pension liabilities in, 17
Free-PC.com, 42

Gallup Organization, 112
Gartman, Dennis, 120, 270
Gartman Letter, The, 270
GE Capital, 310
General Motors Corp., 31, 52, 226
General Re, 114
General Signal, 33
Gephardt, Richard, 163
Germany, 9
  deregulation in, 61-62
  labor unions in, 35
  market economy in, 167
  prices in, xxi
  restructuring in, 35
  unfunded pension liabilities in, 17
Gillette Corp., 28
Glass-Steagall Act, 58

Gold, 141, 180, 263
Goldman Sachs, 288, 310
Government spending, 6, 9
  British, 8
  defense and, 4
  deficits and, 4
  deflation and, 131
  Japanese, 9
  New Zealand, 9
  non-defense, 5
  U.S., 3, 4, 6, 7, 8, 216, 275-276
GPU Corp., 33
Graduate School of Management at the
  University of California, Davis, 284
Great Britain, 148
  government spending in, 8
  labor unions in, 8
  market economy in, 166, 167
Great Depression, 140, 142, 144, 163
Great Society, 7
Greenspan, Alan, 14
GTE, 33
Guangdong International Trust and
  Investment Corp., 86

Halliburton, 27, 34
Hastings, Charles W., 270
Haute Etudes Commerciales, 234, 235
Hedge funds, 285-289
Heritage Foundation/Wall Street Journal
  Annual Index of Economic Freedom, 166
Hewitt Associates, 294
Hewlett-Packard, 48
Hillenbrand Industries, 51
Hoescht, 32
Home Depot, 54, 186, 245
Honda Motor Corp., 56
Hong Kong, 92, 112, 184, 232, 236
  economy in, 79, 80
  interest rates in, 95
  prices in, xxi
  real estate in, 72
  stock market in, 233
Hungary,
  automobile industry in, 67
Hussey, Obed, 151

IBM, 33, 63
India, 65
  U.S. companies in, 63
Indonesia, xxi, 77, 78, 79
Inespal, 265
Inflation,
  effects of budget deficits on, 4
  effects of government spending on, 5

Inflation (*cont.*)
    effects of money supply on, 12
Insurance industry,
    deregulation of, 58
Intel Corp., 41, 48, 114
Interest rates, 12, 80, 166, 316
    bonds and, 209-213
    deflation's effect on, 192-198
    high tech and, 242-243
    money supply and, 178
    real estate and, 272-273
    U.S. long-term, 196, 197
    U.S. short-term, 193, 194
Internal Revenue Service, 131
International Institute for Management
    Development, 73
International Monetary Fund, 77, 92
International Paper Co., 27
International Securities Exchange, 45
International Telecommuting Association, 40
Internet, 174, 307-308, 327
    automobile industry's use of the, 55-56
    banking on the, 50-51
    distribution through the, 54-55
    real estate and the, 49
    selling on the, 48-56
    shopping on the, 49-50, 52
    stock performance of companies
        involved in the, 115-118, 244
    stock trading on the, 49
Inventory, 304-305
Investment clubs, 284-285
Investment trusts, 258
Isuzu Motors, 31
Italy,
    prices in, xxi
    restructuring in, 35

Japan, xxi, 67, 73, 164, 167, 309, 310
    banking industry in, 89-90, 173
    bankruptcies in, 90
    deflationary depression in, 9, 14-15, 31,
        89, 174, 175-176, 223
    deregulation in, 60-61, 262
    economy in, xix, 88, 91, 158, 162
    excess capacity in, 31, 36
    government spending in, 9
    Nikkei stock index in, 90, 91
    population in, 16
    prices in, xxi
    protectionist sentiments in, 164
    restructuring in, 91-92
    saving rate in, 88, 89
    steel industry in, 27
    stock market in, 224
    unfunded pension liabilities in, 17
    U.S. investment by, 217

John Deere, 63, 151
Jospin, Lionel, 166
J.P. Morgan, 28
Junk bonds, xix, 219

Keynes, John Maynard, 167
Kodak Co., 27, 226
Kondratieff, Nikolai, 137
Kondratieff Wave, xxiv, 137-143, 144, 147,
    148, 154, 181
    gold production in, 141
    prices in, 138, 139
    protectionism in, 140
    U.S. economy in, 138
    wars in, 138, 139, 142
KPMG Peat Marwick, 102

Laclede Steel, 27
Lafontaine, Oskar, 167
Latin America, 276
    economic growth in, 82
    economy in, 107, 158, 162
    privatization in, 67
    trade, 98
Leuthold, Steve, 121
Leuthold Group, 121
Levitz Furniture, 29
Long-Term Capital Management, xix, 112,
    170, 173, 234, 288
Los Angeles Times, 28
Lowe's, 54, 245
Lucas-Varity, 32
Lucent Technologies, 205

Maastricht Agreement, 9
Mackay, Charles, 115
Malaysia,
    currency controls in, 96
    economy in, 79, 80
    interest rates in, 95
Marsh & McLennan, 310
MCI WorldCom, 22, 32
McKinsey & Co., 32
Mercury Asset management, 255
Merrill Lynch, 28, 53, 117, 255, 288, 310
Mexico,
    economy in, 82
    U.S. companies in, 64
Microsoft Corp., 38, 63, 114, 327
Mobil Corp., 31
Modigliani, Leah, 281
Money supply, 11-13
    growth of, 174-179
Monsanto Co., 43
Moos, Ed, 220
Morgan Stanley Dean Witter, 53, 255,
    281, 310

Morningstar Inc., 113, 234
Mortgage Bankers Association of
   America, 50
Mutual funds, 280-282, 283-284

NASDAQ 100 index, 284
National Association of Purchasing
   Managers, xix
National Association of Realtors, 49
National Automobile Dealers Association, 56
National Bureau of Economic Research,
   153
National Federation of Independent
   Business, xx
Netherlands, The,
   stock market in, 233
New Deal, 6
New York Stock Exchange, 119
New York Times, The, xxiv
New Zealand, 34
   prices in, xxi
Nissan Corp., 31, 56
Nordstrom, 51
Nucor Co., 27

Odean, Terrance, 284
Office Depot, 54
Oil industry, 27, 31, 265-267
   exports of, 268
   imports of, 268
Oliver, John, 151
OnSale.com, 245
Organization for Economic Cooperation
   and Development, 53
Organization of Petroleum Exporting
   Countries, 265, 266, 267, 269, 270

PacifiCorp, 33
Paine Webber Inc., 112, 119
Pegasus Fund Managers Ltd., 92
Perot, Ross, 163
Petrobras, 31
Petrofina, 31
Petroleos de Venezuela, 31
Petroleos Mexicano, 31
Pharmaceutical industry, 32
   R&D spending in, 38
Phelps Dodge, 27, 270
Philippines,
   economy in, 80
   exports, 98
Phillips Petroleum, 27
Poland,
   automobile industry in, 67
   retirement in, 113
Population,
   world, 15

Prices, xix, xxi
   aluminum, 265
   commodity, xix
   copper, xix, 265
   crude oil, xix, 266
   deflation and, 128-129, 133-136
   European pork, xix
   Japanese wholesale, 91
   oil, 135
   raw sugar, xix
   soybean futures, xix
   U.S. consumer, xxii
   U.S. gasoline, xix
   U.S. lean hogs, xix
   U.S. manufacturing, xix
   U.S. wholesale, 145, 152
Privatization, 67
Procter & Gamble, 52
Productivity, 26, 74, 75, 185-188, 303, 308
   deflation and growth in, 187-188
   enhancing, 258-259
   manufacturing, 36
   U.S. non-farm sector, 185
   U.S. service sector, 23
Proposition 13, 7
Prudential Insurance Co., 32

Quick & Reilly, 58

Raytheon Co., 33
Reagan, Ronald, 7
Real estate investment trusts, 258
Recession,
   1920-21, 139
   1973-75, 7, 115, 139, 250
Renault, 31
Republic Industries, 55
Retirement and retirement plans, 21, 103, 295
   defined benefit plans, 103, 296
   401(k), 21, 103, 285, 294-297, 329
   individual retirement accounts, 103,
      285, 294
   Keoghs, 285, 294, 296
   saving for, 121-122
   Social Security, 103
Revco, 54
Rhone-Poulenc, 32
Riegle-Neal Interstate Banking and
   Branching Efficiency Act of 1994, 58
Right Management Consultants, 32
Rolls Royce, 31
Romania,
   automobile industry in, 67
Russell, Richard, 321
Russell 2000 index, 116, 284
Russia, xix, 164
   automobile industry in, 67

Russia (*cont.*)
exports, 67
financial crisis in, 28, 80, 112, 158, 166, 170, 173
industrial production in, 67
oil production in, 267
steel industry in, 27

Safeway, 56
Salomon Brothers, 65
Salomon Smith Barney, 58, 288
Sanford Bernstein & Co., 235
Sanofi, 32
Saudi Aramco, 31
Saving rate,
Japanese, 88, 89
U.S., 101, 102, 122-123, 321
Schroeder, Gerhard, 35, 166
Scottish Power, 33
Semiconductor industry,
R&D spending in, 38
Semiconductor Industry Association, 43
Shell Oil Co., 27
Singapore, 92
economy in, 80
interest rates in, 95
prices in, xxi
retirement in, 114
saving in, 18
Slovakia,
automobile industry in, 67
Slovenia,
automobile industry in, 67
Smith, Adam, 269
Social Security System, 16-18, 103
Soros, George, 213
Sotheby's, 117
South Africa,
gems market in, xxi
South Korea, 92, 310
automobile industry in, 26
computer industry in, 183
economy in, 79-80
farm population in, 79
prices in, xxi
restructuring in, 94
stock market in, 237
SPX Corp., 33
Standard & Poor's 500 index, 105, 110, 111, 112, 113, 114, 225, 226, 227, 229, 280, 281, 283, 284
Standard Industrial Classification (SIC), 26
Suzuki Motors, 31
Sweden,
prices in, xxi

Switzerland,
deflation in, 174, 223
prices in, xxi
stock market in, 224
Synthelabo, 32

Taiwan,
computer industry in, 183
economy in, 79
prices in, xxi
Tele-Communications Inc., 33
Telecommunications industry, 28, 32-33, 44, 130
R&D spending in, 38
Teligent, 44
Templeton, Sir John, 120
Texaco Corp., 27
Texas Instruments, 63
Thailand, 77, 92, 99
currency devaluation in, 78
economy in, 79-80
interest rates in, 95
prices in, xxi
Thatcher, Margaret, 8
Theglobe.com, 116
3M, 28
Tiger Management, 288
Total, 31
Toyota, 31
Travelers Group, The, 58
T. Rowe Price, 310
Trucking industry,
deregulation of, 59
TRW, 32

Ukraine,
automobile industry in, 67
Unemployment,
changing attitude toward, 7
Unisys Corp., 51
United States,
agricultural equipment industry in, 27, 28, 150-153
airline industry in, 27, 59-60
automobile industry in, 55
balanced budget in, 216
banking industry in, 50, 58-59, 217
bear market in stocks in, 119, 120-121, 133, 169
borrowing in, 161
competitiveness, 73
computer industry in, 38, 48
consumer debt in, 101, 325
consumer spending in, 100, 123-124, 128-129, 133-136, 248-249, 250-251, 320-321

United States (*cont.*)
  corporate debt in, 101,160
  corporate earnings in, 107, 109, 199-206, 314
  corporate financing in, 315
  deficits in, 5
  deflationary forces in, xxiii
  deregulation in, 57-61, 97
  economic growth in, 38, 154, 275, 277, 278
  economy in, 3, 106, 138
  electrical power industry in, 60
  employment in, 108, 145
  exports, 26, 71
  farmland prices in, 28
  Federal Reserve's role in precipitating deflation in, 172-179
  financial services industry in, 57
  foreign exposure by banks in, 81
  global sourcing by companies based in, 63-65
  grain industry in, 27
  high tech's impact on economy in, 38, 39
  housing market in, 256-258
  imports, 20, 70, 71, 107
  incentives to save in, 101
  industrial production in, 148-149
  industrial revolution in, 182
  inflation in, 5, 12, 19-20, 130
  insurance industry in, 32, 58
  interest rates in, 193
  labor markets in, 130
  labor unions in, 21, 22, 63
  layoffs in, 25-26, 103, 328
  manufacturing in, 20, 106
  manufacturing employment in, 66
  manufacturing productivity in, 36
  metals industry in, 27
  monetary policy in, 11-14
  money supply in, 12, 13, 15, 175, 176, 178
  new technologies in, 239-252, 306, 327
  outsourcing in, 21
  paper industry in, 27
  population in, 15-16
  pressed-glass industry in, 149, 152
  prices in, xix, xxii, 145, 152
  productivity in, 75, 185
  productivity growth in service sector in, 186-187
  protectionist sentiments in, 162-164, 309
  railroad industry in, 149-150

United States (*cont.*)
  real estate market in, 130, 271-274, 304, 324
  restructuring in, 63
  retirement in, 103
  saving rate in, 101, 102, 321
  service sector in, 23
  steel industry in, 27, 164
  stock market in, 104, 110-125, 161, 169-171, 222-228, 290-294, 317
  trade, 98
  two-tier economy in, 106
  unemployment in, 7, 33-34, 145, 146, 164
  utility stocks in, 221-222
  wholesale prices in, 3
U.S. Department of Commerce, 38, 50
U.S. Department of Transportation, 59
U.S. General Accounting Office, 59

Value Line index, 284
Vanguard 500 index fund, 285
Vanguard Health Care Fund, 281
Van Kampen American Capital, 355
Vearley, Douglas C., 270
Venezuela,
  economy in, 82
Victoria's Secret, 49
Vietnam War, 7, 138
Volkswagen, 31, 64
Volvo, 27, 31

Wall Street Journal, The, 14, 35, 66, 77, 118, 268, 296
Wal-Mart, 54, 186
Warburg Pincus Asset Management, 255
Wars, 3, 4, 6, 138, 142, 174, 189, 190, 192, 193, 195
  government spending and, 3
  inflationary periods and, 190
Wealth of Nations, The, 269
White, Harry Dexter, 167
Winnebago, 115
World War I, 138
World War II, 6, 19, 142
WorldCom, 32
W.R. Hambrecht & Co., 50

Yugoslavia,
  automobile industry in, 67

Zeneca Group, 32

ABOUT THE AUTHOR

Dr. A. Gary Shilling is president of A. Gary Shilling & Company, Inc., economic consultants and investment advisors, and publisher of *INSIGHT*, a monthly report of economic forecasts and investment strategy. Dr. Shilling advises Thematic Investment Partners and Thematic Futures Fund, investment partnerships oriented toward economic, financial, and political themes.

A regular columnist for *Forbes* magazine since 1983, he is also a columnist for Standard & Poor's *CreditWeek*, a member of *The Nihun Keizui Shimbun (Japan Economic Journal)* Board of Economists, and appears frequently on business radio and television shows. He was twice ranked as Wall Street's top economist by *Institutional Investor* magazine's poll of financial institutions. *Futures* magazine ranked him the country's number one Commodity Trading Advisor in 1993. Well known for his forecasting record, in 1973 he alone among major forecasters predicted the world was entering a massive inventory building spree to be followed by the first major global recession since the 1930s.

His first book, *Is Inflation Ending? Are You Ready?* (McGraw-Hill, 1983), co-authored with Kiril Sokoloff, correctly forecast the unwinding of inflation and the shift in investment winners from real estate and other tangibles to stocks and bonds. *The World Has Definitely Changed: New Economic Forces and Their Implications for the Next Decade* (Lakeside Press, 1986) foresaw the global transition from shortages to surpluses, and *After the Crash, Recession or Depression? Investment and Business Strategies for a Deflationary World* (Lakeview Economic Services, 1988) raised the possibility of deflation. *Deflation: Why It's Coming, Whether It's Good or Bad, and How It Will Affect Your Investments, Business, and Personal Affairs* (Lakeview Publishing Co. 1988) explicitly forecasted deflation.

Dr. Shilling received his A.B. degree in physics, magna cum laude, from Amherst College, where he was also elected to Phi Beta Kappa and Sigma Xi. He earned his M.A. and Ph.D. in economics at Stanford University. Before establishing his own firm in 1978, Dr. Shilling was Chief Economist of White, Weld & Co., Inc. Earlier he was Merrill Lynch's first Chief Economist at age 29 after a stint with Standard Oil Co. (N.J.).

He is a Director of National Life of Vermont, the Heartland Group of mutual funds, the American Productivity and Quality Center, Palm Harbor Homes, and the Episcopal Preaching Foundation (Chairman); an Advisory Director of Austin Trust Company; a Trustee and the Treasurer of the General Theological Seminary (Episcopal); and Chairman of the New Jersey State Revenue Forecasting Advisory Commission. He is also an avid beekeeper.

For more information about economic consulting and investment advisory services of A. Gary Shilling & Co. and Dr. Shilling's monthly newsletter, *INSIGHT*, contact the firm at 500 Morris Avenue, Springfield, New Jersey 07081-1020, telephone: 973-467-0070, fax: 973-467-4073, e-mail shil@ix.netcom.com, Web site: www.agaryshilling.com.